Notes on Footnotes

Notes on Footnotes

Annotating Eighteenth-Century Literature

EDITED BY MELVYN NEW AND ANTHONY W. LEE

The Pennsylvania State University Press
University Park, Pennsylvania

Library of Congress Cataloging-in-Publication Data

Names: New, Melvyn, editor. | Lee, Anthony W., editor.
Title: Notes on footnotes : annotating eighteenth-century
    literature / edited by Melvyn New and Anthony W. Lee.
Other titles: Penn State series in the history of the book.
Description: University Park, Pennsylvania : The Pennsylvania
    State University Press, [2023] | Series: The Penn State series
    in the history of the book | Includes bibliographical
    references and index.
Summary: "A collection of essays by scholars of eighteenth-
    century literature, sharing their experiences as both
    producers and users of explanatory annotations"—Provided
    by publisher.
Identifiers: LCCN 2022037230 | ISBN 9780271093970
    (hardback) | ISBN 9780271093987 (paper)
Subjects: LCSH: English literature—18th century—History
    and criticism. | Bibliographical citations. | LCGFT: Essays.
Classification: LCC PR443 .N68 2022 | DDC 820.9/005—
    dc23/eng/20220915
LC record available at https://lccn.loc.gov/2022037230

Copyright © 2023 The Pennsylvania State University
All rights reserved
Printed in the United States of America
Published by The Pennsylvania State University Press,
University Park, PA 16802–1003

The Pennsylvania State University Press is a member of the
Association of University Presses.

It is the policy of The Pennsylvania State University Press to use
acid-free paper. Publications on uncoated stock satisfy the
minimum requirements of American National Standard for
Information Sciences—Permanence of Paper for Printed
Library Material, ANSI Z39.48–1992.

This collection is dedicated to Patrick Hume (fl. 1695), whose annotations to *Paradise Lost* (1695) are considered the first for any English writer; to Pierre Bayle (1647–1706), who taught us that no informative annotation can be too lengthy; and to Edmond Malone (1741–1812), whose eighteenth-century work on Shakespeare, Dryden, and Boswell paved the way for the rest of us.

CONTENTS

Preface | ix
Anthony W. Lee

Introduction | 1
Melvyn New

1 "Many Excellent Good Notes": Annotating
John Aubrey's *Brief Lives* | 10
Kate Bennett

2 Annotating Dryden, Southerne, and Defoe | 26
Maximillian E. Novak

3 Annotation in Scholarly Editions of Plays:
Problems, Options, and Principles | 41
Robert D. Hume

4 Annotating Topical Satire: The Case of Swift | 61
Stephen Karian

5 A Picture Is Worth a Thousand Words:
Annotated Facsimiles as Ideal Editions | 73
Shef Rogers

6 Annotating Pope | 95
Marcus Walsh

7 Uninformed Readers and the Crisis of Annotation | 112
Michael Edson

8 Footnote Failure | 130
Thomas Lockwood

9 The Angry Annotator Annotated | 144
Melvyn New

viii | Contents

10 Annotating the Yale Edition of the Works
of Samuel Johnson | 160
Robert DeMaria Jr.

11 Annotating *The Rambler / The Annotated Rambler* | 171
Anthony W. Lee

12 Annotation and Scholarly Conversation: The Musings
of a Non-Editor Annotator | 185
Robert G. Walker

13 Annotation and Editorial Practice: Twenty-Five Years
(and Counting) | 203
Elizabeth Kraft

14 The Rhetoric, Ethics, and Aesthetics of Annotation:
Some Reflections | 219
William McCarthy

List of Contributors | 235
Index | 239

PREFACE

Anthony W. Lee

Samuel Johnson once famously remarked that notes "are necessary evils."[1] Anthony Grafton echoes Johnson's language while discussing the great nineteenth-century historian Leopold von Ranke's attitude toward citation: "At best he saw the presence of annotation in his work as a necessary evil."[2] Noel Coward offers a more humorous metaphor: "having to read a footnote resembles having to go downstairs to answer the door while in the midst of making love."[3] In 2018, the *New Yorker* poked fun at the potential unwieldy pretentiousness of notes in mocking the nonexistent *Oxford Book of Footnotes*.[4] Despite negative and satiric jabs such as these, scholarly annotation has a rich and significant history that deserves our serious attention.

The long eighteenth century (1660–1815) witnessed the burgeoning of professional editions devoted to British writers. While scholarly editions of classical authors were undertaken almost two millennia earlier, when the Alexandrian Aristarchus of Samothrace produced his groundbreaking edition of Homer, and continued through the early modern era, it was not until the late seventeenth and early eighteenth centuries that critical editions of major modern authors began to appear on the British literary scene. See, for example, the editions of two of the greatest English authors since Chaucer: Patrick Hume's redaction of *Paradise Lost* (1695) and Nicholas Rowe's Shakespeare (1709).[5] These rapidly proliferated into a trend, as the century witnessed the production of Richard Bentley's edition of *Paradise Lost* (1732), the still valuable Grey edition of Samuel Butler's *Hudibras* (1744),[6] William Warburton's rebarbative edition of Pope (1751), and that scholar's scholar Edmond Malone's crowning achievement, *Critical and Miscellaneous Prose Works of John Dryden*—a work that fittingly appeared in 1800, precisely one hundred years after Dryden's death. Furthermore, some authors, such as Pope, Johnson, and

Thomas Gray, provided their own notes to assist their readers.[7] The long eighteenth century thus may with full confidence be described as an "age of annotation." How fitting, then, that a volume should be dedicated—as is the present one—to exploring and analyzing the phenomenon of modern editorial annotation of eighteenth-century texts.[8]

The intent governing *Notes on Footnotes* is to explore modern editorial engagements from both practical and theoretical perspectives. Contributors participating in recently completed projects (for example, the Florida Edition of the Works of Laurence Sterne and the Yale Edition of the Works of Samuel Johnson) as well as presently ongoing ones (for example, the Oxford Edition of the Writings of Alexander Pope and the Cambridge Edition of the Works of Jonathan Swift) meditate on issues modern editors face when annotating and commenting on authors centuries removed.

When, more than two years ago, we suggested to scholars connected to major editing projects (and others whose interest in and practice of annotation came to our attention), we were uncertain, as those proposing collections typically are, of the response. Now, with the chapters in hand, we agree, having separately edited a dozen or more collections of essays on eighteenth-century subjects, that this has been the easiest and most efficient gathering we have ever experienced, even amid a "plague year" worthy of Daniel Defoe's authorial attention. We believe this speaks to our contributors' eagerness to reflect on and share the vocation to which many of them have devoted a lifetime. Moreover, this collection invites and allows them to explain and justify to colleagues and future editors some of their personal dilemmas and decisions when confronting Johnson's "necessary evil." What emerges in chapter after chapter of this collection is that the contributors all began (and will end) their careers as annotators with an abiding admiration, indeed love, for the eighteenth-century author or authors being annotated, and a desire to preserve for the future a greater understanding of these prized writers: as Maximillian Novak observes, the primary charge of our vocation is "what annotators are supposed to be doing—passing on knowledge to future scholars" (*NoF*, 39).

The personal tone struck by many of the editor/annotators here provides valuable background into the conception and execution of some particularly well-known editions. Thus, we learn that Novak's work on Dryden's *All for Love* (a redaction of Shakespeare's *Antony and Cleopatra*) allowed him to accumulate enough material on the history of the doomed lovers to compile a book (one, unfortunately, never written). For him, the greatest joy of annotation lies in the primary research preceding composition of the note. After quoting a footnote from the Victorian editor of Johnson's *Lives of the Poets*, G. B. Hill, Robert DeMaria Jr. comments: "I love this bibliographical information" (*NoF*, 165) but goes on to demonstrate the many flaws found in it. Elizabeth Kraft admits at the head of her chapter, "Had I been an expert, I could have wielded my expertise at will. However, I undertook my first editorial enterprise as a complete novice" (*NoF*, 203). (This is something that Elizabeth and I have in common.) Kate Bennett exercises "a little playfulness" (*NoF*, 23) in discreetly denominating John Aubrey's "An Account of the Conversion of William Twisse (1574–1646)" as a "tale of a haunted latrine" (24). Contributor Thomas Lockwood likewise spices his essay with play and a pinch of intrigue. Closing his chapter with "but *ars longa*, etc.," his final typographical flourish is, with decisive relevance, a note.[9]

In addition, the contributors' accounts of their work provide invaluable insight into the art and craft of annotative theory and, above all, practice. For example, we learn from Bennett that "Editing is not merely a scholarly exercise of compiling information. It is a rhetorical art which presents a consistent argument through coherently related strategies of overt and subtle communication" (*NoF*, 19). William McCarthy echoes this point when he observes, "annotators *imagine* an audience and aim to provide what they believe that audience needs. To satisfy the audience they must convince it that their annotations are credible. Thus, annotators engage in rhetorical acts, according to the Aristotelian idea of rhetoric" (*NoF*, 219). These reflections concisely put paid to the notion of the annotative editor as aloof and austerely objective, as one who dismisses lower beings and projects with cold indifference. Lockwood goes further:

> Even when you think you have got the right handle on a crux of meaning or reference beyond pure fact, it is rare to feel quite certain, or it ought to be rare. I am assuming here, by the way, that there is an evidence-informed meaning to be found, and that its recovery and explanation, however difficult or liable to failure, is the goal of annotation. That assumption might be challenged as a matter of theory, where editorial intervention itself is seen to make any objective determination impossible, but at the workaday level of annotation most editors, certainly including me, proceed as if there is an answer out there and their job is to find it. (*NoF*, 130–31)

On the other hand, Robert D. Hume, more systematically, breaks annotative theory/practice down into this anatomy: (1) named persons, (2) literary and xii | Preface

historical allusions, (3) concepts in the history of ideas, (4) social customs and dress, (5) the value of money compared to modern currency (*NoF*, 42–44).[10] He concludes with "If I were asked for a fundamental principle which an editor of long-eighteenth-century plays should abide by, it would be very simple: adopt a modus operandi which recognizes the enormous diversity of these plays, and apply 'logic,' not 'rules'" (*NoF*, 54). Like Hume, Stephen Karian focuses on a specific genre, in this case, satire: "Annotators must therefore immerse themselves in contemporaneous accounts to try to recapture a reading experience as close as possible to the time when the satire was written and circulated" (*NoF*, 61–62). Others focus on specific authors (as Marcus Walsh on Pope) or specific texts (Lee on the *Rambler*), while DeMaria devotes his efforts to an entire series, the Yale Edition of the Works of Samuel Johnson.

Shef Rogers offers an innovative perspective on "editions in a facing-page format [arguing] that literature of the eighteenth century is ideally suited to such a format, [one that] enables an editor to offer a clearer and richer set of annotations, and that such editions offer a practical solution to some of the key challenges of editorial theory" (*NoF*, 73–74). Michael Edson, on the other hand, situates himself in a space apart: "unlike most of the authors in this volume, I am a user rather than a maker of explanatory notes" (*NoF*, 112), ultimately settling on four recommendations for future annotators (126–27). Robert G. Walker, a self-described "annotator without portfolio," places himself in a similar position and uses his scrutiny of some important critical editions to offer "what it is we [editorial annotators] do or should be doing" (*NoF*, 185).

The long eighteenth century was an age of narrative, wit (in many senses of the word), elegant stylistic precision, and probing philosophic inquiry into the ethical dimensions of humanity and society. Yet it was also a period of satiric lambast, vituperation, and vigorous—often personal—polemic. The scholars collected here share their personal stories of a lengthy engagement with their own particular subjects, while also revealing less subjective and importantly conveyable advice on the annotative and editorial processes. That is to say, they practice the Horatian dictum valued by most eighteenth-century writers, *utile et dulce*: they at once inform and entertain; they follow the traces left by their eighteenth-century forebears while striking new paths forward. Few collections of scholarly essays will evince a more convincing aura of genuine enjoyment, indeed relish, of scholarship than that displayed in this volume. We are confident that the following pages exhibit the modus operandi practiced by some of today's best editors and annotators, as they successfully exhume, dust off and polish, and present with clarity the authorial and cultural secrets of our collective past. For those interested in annotation, editing, and critical editions, as well as reading the authors who profit from these attentions, here indeed "is God's Plenty."[11]

NOTES

1. Samuel Johnson, "Preface to *Shakespeare*," in *Johnson on Shakespeare*, The Yale Edition of the Works of Samuel Johnson 7–8 (New Haven: Yale University Press, 1968), 7:111. I discuss Johnson's more complex attitude toward notes in my chapter below.

2. Anthony Grafton, *The Footnote: A Curious History* (Cambridge, MA: Harvard University Press, 1997), 64.

3. Ibid., 70.

4. Bruce McCall, Shouts and Murmurs, *New Yorker*, October 15, 2018, 27.

5. For a discussion of glosses and annotations—but not of critical editions—see Grafton, *Footnote*, 26–33.

6. See Mark A. Pedreira, "Zachary Grey's Annotations on Samuel Butler's *Hudibras*," in *Annotation in Eighteenth-Century Poetry*, ed. Michael Edson (Bethlehem: Lehigh University Press, 2017), 169–88.

7. It should be noted that these eighteenth-century authors had predecessors in the Renaissance, most notably Spenser's E.K. in *The Shepheardes Calendar*, who apparently collaborated in some way with the author (or was in fact a pseudonym of the author), as well as Ben Jonson's self-annotation of his *Masques* in his 1616 *Workes*, and Abraham Cowley's copious commentary on *Davideis*.

8. For an absorbing study of eighteenth-century writers and editors, see Michael Edson, *Annotation in Eighteenth-Century Poetry* (Bethlehem: Lehigh University Press, 2017). The present volume may be seen as complementary to Edson's project, which focuses on contemporary annotation of eighteenth-century authors, while we focus on modern annotation of eighteenth-century texts.

9. "Look it up yourself" (*NoF*, 143).

10. Hume is specifically addressing the annotation of plays, but his précis can be valuably applied to other genres. For a different schematic of the salient elements of annotative practice—this one drawn from the practice of Samuel Johnson—see my chapter (*NoF*, 179–82).

11. John Dryden, "Preface to *Fables*," in *The Works of John Dryden*, vol. 7, ed. Vinton A. Dearing (Berkeley: University of California Press, 2002), 37; see also *The Poems of John Dryden*, vol. 5, ed. Paul Hammond and David Hopkins (Harlow, UK: Pearson, 1995–2005), 76. Dryden alludes to / translates "Goddes foison," from "The Miller's Prologue and Tale," l.3165, in Geoffrey Chaucer's *The Canterbury Tales*, ed. Jill Mann (New York: Penguin, 2005), 116. For possible sources/analogues, see Dryden, *Works*, 7:624n492–93, and Dryden, *Poems*, 76n522.

৫৶ Introduction

Melvyn New

In our invitation to potential contributors for this collection, we offered Simon Leys's final sentence in his review of a book on Chinese calligraphy as a particularly laudatory celebration of the annotator's medium: "Which one of us would not dream that it might be said of his work of a lifetime: 'He wrote a few good footnotes.'"[1] It would be, we hoped, a recognizable sentiment, the aspiration of all those who have spent much of their academic careers annotating the work of others. Would that some of our notes, deemed of especial value to future readers, did indeed "swim down the gutter of time"[2] with the works of the literary geniuses we have annotated.

The mind of an annotator is revealed by what might be a typical reaction to what I have just written. Obviously, my accompanying endnotes are factual: they provide the source of the quotation, but also, in the first, a bit of information about its author, who is not a name familiar to eighteenth-century scholars, and a source for more information. In the second note, I failed to add my own involvement with a sentence central to everything I have written about Sterne over the last half century. For many readers this brevity will be sufficient; for the annotator, however, it immediately raises one of the most difficult of issues, discussed by several contributors herein: we all know where to start, but when to stop is the agonizing question we regularly confront. For example, at this point I was tempted to add to my brief first footnote some dressing that might have included my admiration for Leys, my regret that his literary criticism of Western literature is not more widely read, and most of all my enjoyment of his political attitudes, which echo what I often think but rarely have the courage to express. Thus tempted, I might even have included in my footnote a comment Leys made in response to a late suggestion in Edward Said's *Orientalism* ("We should question the advisability of too close a relationship between the scholar and the state"), namely, "You bet we should! . . . It is nice to see that Said is now rediscovering such a basic notion; I only deplore that it took him 300 pages of twisted, obscure, incoherent, ill-informed and badly written diatribe to reach at last one sound and fundamental truism."[3]

Clearly, I was able to resist the temptation of including Leys's critical voice in my first annotation because I knew I could find a place for it in my text (or a subsequent note); like other human beings, annotators are able to resist everything except temptation.[4] Scholarly annotators will vary greatly in their liberties and restraints, but it is important to acknowledge that every footnote confronts the annotator with a temptation further to elaborate. At the most basic level, an echo of another author in the text will be provided with a citation of that author, title, and date of the source. Is this sufficient or should the note contain the sentence or passage being quoted as well, and most particularly if there are differences between the original and the passage as it now reappears or if the source will be difficult for the reader to consult? If we quote one sentence, should surrounding sentences also be quoted, and should we provide any additional context for both the author and the work being cited? Elaboration seems almost always possible and too often desirable as well.

In a contrary direction, the annotator is often confronted with decisions concerning economy rather than elaboration. Does "blessed are the meek" require annotation? Always we have to remind ourselves of our audience; annotators of an eighteenth-century text in the twenty-first century must take into account that today's scholars are not as familiar with Scripture as they were a mere fifty years ago. Still, citing the source of "blessed are the meek" will certainly seem superfluous to most. And when we narrow our audience to the eighteenth-century scholarly community, if Alexander Pope is mentioned, do we need a footnote telling us he was "a major poet of the period"? Obviously not, but if our author has, without attribution, opined that "a little learning is a dangerous thing," should we cite its source? And if we do, should we quote the second line of the couplet, which effectively undoes the celebration of ignorance that some have read into the first line?

In a letter Richardson wrote to Edward Cave (August 9, 1750) he praises the *Rambler* (after reading the first thirteen issues) and mentions the *Spectator*. One never can tell what the expected audience is for a volume of the Cambridge edition of Richardson's correspondence, but one suspects its only readers will already be familiar with those periodicals and their authors. Still, having identified Cave, it might seem remiss not to identify the other names and titles in the passage, and perhaps even to write something about Richardson's familiarity (or lack thereof) with Johnson at the time.[5] I agree with the decision to do so but then also wonder if being told that Johnson was an "author and lexicographer" is superfluous information for any conceivable reader of this volume. And returning to augmenting one's annotation, could the note have been valuably enriched by suggesting the essays that might have especially appealed to Richardson among the first thirteen, most obviously *Rambler* 4, where Fielding's *Tom Jones* is roundly criticized.[6] One can probably second guess almost every annotation ever written, which again returns us to Leys's "few good footnotes"—observe, no hope for a few *perfect* ones.

These seemingly trifling issues are, perhaps unfortunately, at the heart of the annotator's enterprise, and especially in an era in which publishers covet scholarly editions that have wide general appeal to an increasingly illiterate population.[7] As for economic considerations, whether they apply to the need to collate multiple texts at multiple locations, the contract calling for completion within two years, or the requirement that annotations fit an allotted number of pages, every annotator will, as a professional responsibility, consider the life of a scholarly editor a "warfare on earth"—or at least warfare with one's publisher. The source of that sentiment need not be annotated for my present readers.

Was it academic condescension to assume Simon Leys was unknown to most English literature scholars, or that Oscar Wilde needed to be cited? So much of our knowledge is haphazard that, setting aside what we might hope eighteenth-century scholars are already familiar with, gauging the information being brought to one's annotations by individual readers is impossible. I first heard of Leys just ten years ago, having lived to age seventy without him; the Wilde quote is familiar enough, but I thought it was from *Dorian Gray* and was saved by the annotator's latest best friend, the internet. Indeed, the last editorial project for the Florida edition of Sterne's works was an annotator's dream: identifying his two thousand subscribers. When I started this effort in the late 1970s, every name was written on a 3 × 5 index card and information slowly accumulated as I (and student assistants over some thirty years) scoured genealogies, newspapers, periodicals, and the like.

4 | NOTES ON FOOTNOTES

For example, for the "Mrs. Ord" who subscribed in 1769, I eventually decided (with a suitable question mark) on Anna Dillingham (1726–1808), who married William Ord (*d.* 1768), an eminent Newcastle surgeon; she was well known in bluestocking circles, and I connected her to Sterne's known acquaintance with Elizabeth Montagu and Elizabeth Vesey. Recently, however, I discovered a 1752 subscription list with quite a few names in common with Sterne's list, including William Ord, but also Robert Ord, two John Ords, Joseph Ord, and George Ord. If all or even some of them were married, Mrs. Ord is back among the unidentified. And that is just one list, tied to Sterne by geographical proximity, but of course his subscribers were located throughout Britain (and some beyond).[8]

Good annotators will have at least one abiding certainty: whatever we annotate will be too little for some, too much for others, and in either case, boundaries defining our content will change over time. The questions we ask, the audience we address, the answers we find, are all time-bound. As I wrote at the very end of my introduction to the final volume of the Florida edition, which began with volumes 1 and 2, published in 1978, and ended with volume 9 in 2014: "what a scholarly editor learns . . . is that after the final volume . . . nothing remains but to start over again" (9:xxxiii). Apropos this present collection of essays on annotative practices, I also suggest that our "annotations are only responses to questions [our] contemporaries ask" (9:xxxiv). Yet, as strongly as annotators feel the limitations of their work, bound as it is by time and chance, I suspect that we all hope our work, richly dependent as it is on the annotators who have gone before us, will in turn be of help to others, including those annotators who will follow us with a scholarly edition for their own generation.[9] It was no accident that at this point in the introduction to the last volume of my forty-year engagement with Sterne's works I invoked the clichéd "shoulders of giants"; what I had specifically in mind, however, was not the adage but Robert K. Merton's brilliant *On the Shoulders of Giants: A Shandean Postscript*, the annotator's bible. Merton began with the idea of annotating "we are like dwarves standing on the shoulders of giants," supposedly originating with Newton; he ended, digressing and progressing at the same time, with a book of 350 pages, my own vision of the annotator's paradise.[10]

With this expansiveness now in mind, I realize that I failed to annotate my first paragraph sufficiently. Surely some additional context for the quotation from Leys is required, and perhaps a check, as well, on the appropriateness of the sentence to this collection. Quoted sentences always exist in a context worth exploring, and a good annotator would feel it necessary to inform readers just how and why Leys reached his conclusion about footnotes. Thus, my scant footnote could be elaborated with new information, namely, that Leys had criticized the book under review[11] for its critical obfuscations and suggested that Thoreau's "famous warning 'Beware of all enterprises that require new clothes'" be applied to "discursive essays: 'Beware of all thoughts that require new concepts'" (311). Having voiced that criticism, however, Leys then concludes his review by indicating that there was much of interest in "the abundant and remarkable footnotes of Billeter's book," and assuring us that such praise was not "veiled irony" but sincere and weighty: "Which one of us would not dream that it might be said of his work of a lifetime: 'He wrote a few good footnotes.'"

This context, unfortunately, leads to the question of accuracy—or at least, of pertinence: when Leys praises footnotes, he is obviously referring to the notes we add to our own scholarly writings, rather than the notes by which we document and explore the writings of others. While these two modes of annotation have many similarities, their differences also matter. Setting aside, for example, the documentary aspects of annotating our own texts, when we use our footnotes to amplify, modify, or contradict ourselves, we are usually guided, as Robert Walker notes in his essay below, by the longstanding advice that if the contents are not important enough for the text, a discursive note is unnecessary. This urge toward brevity is reinforced by journals with arbitrary word limitations and by book publishers with their eyes always on their financial spreadsheet, even those invested in scholarly editions. The alternative, especially when writing a monograph, is to heed the advice not to argue with oneself in annotations but instead pad the text with sentences that should have been in the notes—many an essay has been turned into a book using this strategy.

Other authors will just refuse to limit their self-annotation, and their footnotes (or, more frequently, backnotes) will be so rich with substance that we may well reach the same conclusion with Leys, that the notes are more informative than the text, but lament that they are in such minute print, and crowding the bottom of text pages or lost in a sea of ink in back pages.

Still, both literary critics and editor/annotators are alike in that both will relish (and, I hope, understand) Leys's praise of good footnotes. Indeed, it is no accident that the contributors to this volume have all published literary criticism as well and would be hard-pressed to indicate whether they view themselves as of one discipline rather than the other. Setting aside the essential biographical and bibliographical aspects of annotation, most critical commentary shares with annotative editing the desire to explicate the text under study.

The primary difference is that the literary critic will explicate within a committed exposition (with notes subordinated to it), while the editor is restricted to separate and distinct notes. An editor's space for exposition will usually take its form as a supposedly noncommittal introduction.

Many years ago, the issue of annotation versus interpretation was raised concerning Martin Battestin's introduction (and annotation) to his fine Wesleyan edition of *Joseph Andrews*.[12] With that debate in mind, the text of the Florida edition of *Tristram Shandy* appeared in two volumes, without any prefatory matter, in 1978. The first overt appearance of the editor was on page 814 of the second volume, in a textual introduction. On the other hand, in the third volume of the Florida edition, *The Notes* (1984) to *Tristram Shandy*, a discursive introduction preceded the notes, although its main thrust was purportedly documentary, alongside an argument distinguishing between explication and interpretation. Of course, accompanying a so-called novel with five hundred pages of annotations was itself an interpretative strategy, an argument that *Tristram Shandy* required the annotative intensity of eighteenth-century satirists like Pope or Swift or what Charles Kerby-Miller did so splendidly in his annotations of *Memoirs of Martinus Scriblerus*—and not the relatively thinner annotation required of novels. Given my bias toward a satiric reading of *Tristram Shandy*, no one was fooled by the "neutral" introduction, but the actual result was not a limited set of notes but the opposite, what the general editors of the Cambridge Richardson, Thomas Keymer and Peter Sabor, have, in private communication, labeled the "Florida style"—by which I hope they mean, though I suspect they do not, a richness of commentary that refuses to skip over moments in the text that do not support a particular discursive reading of the text.

Put simply, the critic is at liberty to select passages for commentary, eliding those that seem unnecessary for the interpretive argument being offered, while the annotator must not do that—each moment in the text that requires annotation makes its separate and equal demand. Both endeavors practice what is, despite other claims, the world's oldest profession: a responsiveness to an imaginative text that moves us toward further explanation. In the beginning, we are told, was the Word, but before that, there was an ineffable, unknowable Mystery, without name, without character, without gender, indeed without language: "I am that I am." So amorphous a Being (or, more philosophically, Non-Being) needed definition and explication—the evolved human mind seems unable to think, even to imagine, without explanation.

Thus, annotation arises—without too much exaggeration we might even suggest that all Western cultural discourse, certainly at its highest imaginative

Introduction | 7

reaches, can be read as one continuous stream of annotators explaining the writings of earlier annotators, back to the very first attempts to know the unknown, to give meaning to the ineffable. To separate those who comment on an original text, singled out as inspired rather than imagined, from those who comment on the many generations of commentators who have followed, down to the present time, is futile: both early and late, commentary merely gropes toward an understanding of the nonutterance of the mystery of Being (or not Being) "I am that I am"—five words that are already a commentary on an unknown and unknowable (hence nonverbal) mystery.

Literary scholars in the modern era consider themselves part of the dominant secular enlightenment that is today's academic institution, but surely we remain steeped in a tradition as old as the rabbinical scholars and church fathers, laboring away year after year, century after century, on texts, the imaginative essence of which is that they can never be satisfactorily explicated or interpreted, our tools for doing so being always finite and explanation always infinite.

This is a large claim to make for the lowly annotator of an eighteenth-century text, but if we think of, say, *Tom Jones* as a commentary on *Paradise Lost*, and *Paradise Lost* a commentary on both Scripture and *The Iliad* (to make a simplifying leap), we might suggest that those who offer interpretations of Fielding are within a tradition of commentary that stretches back to the unknown Word. And all along that route, alongside the brilliant—and even less than brilliant—bursts of insight and artistic merit, each text deemed worthy has been accompanied by annotations that underwrite interpretation; the two would seem to be inextricably linked, even at times indistinguishable. Odd as it may sound, no work of imaginative genius has ever survived very long without annotation because none can survive without being read, and being read means being commented on, and commentary, informed and continual over time, depends on annotation. Little did I think when I started this introduction that I would discover the annotator to be the operative cog in the great chain of literary being, but so it turns out. Q.E.D.

The essays in this collection make a united effort to reestablish the legitimacy of the relationship between the annotations one finds in critical (interpretative) essays and monographs and those in scholarly editions, a relationship that seems to have grown wider in recent years, so that the more elaborate the scholarly texts and annotations being made available, the less likely they seem to be consulted by those writing about the same authors and the same texts. To be sure, economics plays its part: many scholarly editions are priced out

8 | Notes on Footnotes

of the reach of all but major research libraries, and even when they are made available online (e.g., Oxford Scholarly Editions Online) the cost is prohibitive.[13] Does using the best text available make any difference? Have the scholarly readings of Fielding or Smollett improved with the availability of scholarly editions? Did Pope criticism leap forward after the Twickenham edition, and will it again leap forward once the new Oxford edition is available? Will Behn scholarship move beyond its excessive quantity today to some higher quality tomorrow when a scholarly edition is available? These are questions that should concern everyone writing about literature today—and tomorrow. It is to be hoped that some answers will be found in the essays gathered in this volume on annotating eighteenth-century texts.

NOTES

1. Simon Leys, *The Hall of Uselessness: Collected Essays* (2011; New York: New York Review Books, 2013), 313. Simon Leys is the pen name of Pierre Ryckmans (1935–2014). Born in Belgium, Leys migrated to Australia, where he taught Chinese literature for many years at the Australian National University and then the University of Sydney. He also wrote extensively on contemporary literary and political subjects across both Eastern and Western culture. A biography by Philippe Paquet, translated by Julie Rose, *Simon Leys: Navigator Between Worlds* (Melbourne: La Trobe University Press, 2019), is worth reading.

2. I quote Laurence Sterne, *Tristram Shandy*, vol. 9, chap. 8, Tristram's hope for his book's posterity, "for what has this book done more than the Legation of Moses, or the Tale of a Tub that it may not swim down the gutter of Time along with them?" Why Sterne linked himself to William Warburton, who comes down to posterity as the epitome of a bad annotator, and to a work that needs more annotation than perhaps any other eighteenth-century work (as Marcus Walsh, a contributor to this volume can attest) must be left to annotators to explicate and critics to interpret.

3. Leys, *Hall of Uselessness*, 363. Since my annotative spirit rebels at this lonely quotation, I will continue to define Leys's political sensibilities by noting his dismissal of Roland Barthes on Maoist China by means of a sentence from George Orwell: "One has to belong to the intelligentsia to believe things like that: no ordinary man could be such a fool" (178). Leys's essay on Orwell in *Halls of Uselessness* (174–89) is splendid. As for my second footnote, I could have gone on with references to my own writings, but I listened to Sterne after his description of the dying Le Fever: "Shall I go on?—No" (*Tristram Shandy*, VI.10).

4. Oscar Wilde, *Lady Windermere's Fan*, act I.

5. I refer to vol. 10, *Correspondence Primary on Sir Charles Grandison*, ed. Betty A. Schellenberg (Cambridge: Cambridge University Press, 2015), 10:29–30.

6. Less obvious but certainly an essay that might have touched Richardson, the printer-author, is *Rambler* 9 (April 17, 1750), in which Johnson celebrates both the artisan and the professional as of usefulness to the world. And here one might mention Richardson's later contribution to the *Rambler* (February 19, 1751), because of its relationship to *Sir Charles Grandison*; but perhaps we are meant to recall that it was discussed in the introduction.

7. The great experiment of our era in this regard is the Yale Johnson; Robert DeMaria and Anthony W. Lee engage that project in their essays below, so here I will only opine that a "general audience" for eighteenth-century figures is a chimera of academic publishers and growing more fanciful every year.

8. See *Statutes, rules, and orders for the government of the Infirmary for the Sick and Lame Poor of the Counties of Durham, Newcastle upon Tyne and Northumberland* (1752), available on ECCO. I assume it was available online before the publication of my findings in 2014, but I failed to find it. The amount of material already online and being added every day does suggest how quickly any printed set of annotations may be rendered obsolete by new documents being scanned and posted. The internet is both the annotator's dream and nightmare—infinitely fecund and infinitely random. Issues of reliability and accuracy are, of course, still to be dealt with.

9. Lest I be accused of false modesty by suggesting editorial replacement of the Florida Sterne within a generation, I will exempt Sterne's *Sermons* from this expectation since I doubt anyone before the end of the twenty-first century will want to reedit them once they realize the number of sermons to be read in preparation. On the other hand, given the many borrowings uncovered prior to online resources, the internet will surely allow us to uncover many more; eventually, every sentence of every sermon can be searched for similar wording in the plethora of sermon literature. As with nuclear fission in the twentieth century, the twenty-first century will have to separate the constructive and destructive uses of this new source of energy—the World Wide Web is too much with us and Googling or tweeting we lay waste our powers.

10. The eighteenth century has its own models of annotative richness (or excess, depending on one's taste), my own favorite being Matthew Poole's two-volume folio *Annotations upon the Holy Bible* (1683), the source text for all Protestant scriptural annotators for the next hundred years—perhaps to the present day. I would also want modern annotators to think about Pierre Bayle, whose *Dictionnaire historique et critique* (1697) is a wonderful trickle of text in a sea of annotation—even his annotations have annotations. If only there were contemporary book publishers willing to let annotators go on and on, but indeed, only one comes to mind: Liberty Fund does seem to have deep pockets; thus, its edition of Pierre Bayle's *A Philosophical Commentary on These Words of the Gospel, Luke 14:23, "Compel Them to Come In, That My House May be Full"* (Indianapolis: Liberty Fund, 2005)—his commentary (annotation) runs to six hundred pages in this reprint of the 1708 translation.

11. Jean François Billeter, *The Chinese Art of Writing* (New York: Skira Rizzoli, 1990); the review was published in 1996.

12. See Melvyn New, "The Sterne Edition: The Text of *Tristram Shandy*," in *Editing Eighteenth-Century Novels*, ed. G. E. Bentley Jr. (Toronto: Hakkert, 1975), 67–89.

13. The need to visit a research library to secure a scholarly edition is not an onerous task (except, obviously, in a time of plague), and certainly not a valid reason for citing in one's scholarship a textbook edition, although it is so frequent a practice today that "best edition available" no longer seems standard practice. Despite present online resources, working with the collections in major libraries must still be among the most rewarding experiences of the literary scholar—Max Novak's essay below speaks eloquently to this.

CHAPTER I

ᐺ "Many Excellent Good Notes"
Annotating John Aubrey's *Brief Lives*

Kate Bennett

Biography, in one seventeenth-century tradition, is a form of ethical argument, providing exemplars for virtuous emulation. But for John Aubrey, liveliest of seventeenth-century life-writers, it was a mixed dish the ingredients of which included a form of annotation.[1] The "Life of Erasmus" in *Brief Lives* is partly based on Aubrey's notes in his copies of the humanist's books, and on a Cambridge anecdote about one who "long since wrote in the margent" of a copy of Erasmus's *Epistolæ* (*BL* 1:16–17, 2:770–2). Aubrey's *An Apparatus to the Lives of Our English Mathematical Writers* incorporates biographical notes intended to supplement John Selden's annotations on the Lives of medieval mathematicians and scientists published in Arthur Hopton's *A Concordancy of Yeares* (*BL* 1:724). One of the aims of the 2015 Oxford edition of *Brief Lives* was to address a culture of annotation that was essential to the period's intellectual life. It is the first complete critical text of any Aubrey work, but with 963 pages of commentary, it is also the first to have systematic explanatory notes. In what follows, I recount my efforts to make annotation conform to the specific needs of Aubrey and his *Brief Lives* rather than to any generalized theory.

A central function for the Oxford commentary is to support the editorial policy of what material should properly constitute the text of *Brief Lives*. This is not obvious. There is a considerable overlap between the three-volume manuscript that Aubrey called *Brief Lives* (1680–81) and the fruits of a forty-year period of life-writing. Aubrey began to make biographical collections from a very early date. Some of these early notes were later copied into his topographical works (but were not all published by the editors of those works) and transcribed in variant forms in *Brief Lives*. Between 1667 and 1695 Aubrey wrote letters and sent papers to Anthony Wood, which the Oxford antiquary used for his *Historia et Antiquitates Uniuersitatis Oxoniensis* (1674) and then for his *Athenae Oxonienses* (1691), a history of Oxford writers.[2] In 1679, Aubrey wrote a collaborative *Life of Thomas Hobbes of Malmesbury*, and then in 1680–81 he wrote *Brief Lives*, which was in Wood's custody for a considerable period of its composition, while Aubrey continued to work on it, adding many papers, additions, and corrections on occasional brief visits to Oxford. Wood destroyed a large part of *Brief Lives*, so the second volume is a fragment reconstructed by Edmond Malone in 1792. Aubrey's other works all contain biographical information or references to the people or subjects treated in *Brief Lives*, and frequently the same passages occur in more than one work and in a different context in each. All these sources remain in manuscript or in unsatisfactory and incomplete editions.

It can be a little confusing. For his 1898 Clarendon Press edition, *"Brief Lives," chiefly of Contemporaries, set down by John Aubrey, between the Years 1669 & 1696*, Andrew Clark's workmanlike approach was to transcribe a selection of biographical passages from all these texts, including most of the material in *The Life of Thomas Hobbes* and *Brief Lives*, expurgate the worst of the bawdy, and organize the resulting corpus by biographical subject, alphabetically ordered. As "regards notes and explanations," Clark had not attempted very much. The *Brief Lives* "supply an inviting field for comment, correction, and addition," he conceded; but "even so treated," he considered that the value of *Brief Lives* lay not in "facts," but rather in Aubrey's "remarkably vivid personal touches."[3] Editing and annotating Aubrey meant dealing with an editorial heritage which had profoundly shaped the way Aubrey was received in the academy and among general readers. There were other problems, too. His credit was damaged by the fact that the only work he printed was his *Miscellanies* (1696), a collection of "divine dreams," apparitions, and narratives of "fantastical Freeks" like a barrel of salt that marched around the house of a Devon man whose shoelaces were enchanted by "some discontented Dæmon."[4] Readers of his work were often unsure what they were dealing with, and how much credit to give to it.

Aubrey had hoped to "preserve" and "propagate Trueth" in his biographical work, but in the event, an overwhelming sense of suspicion and anxiety hovered over his fidelity.[5] I found myself with the classic concern of my editorial predecessors who had edited Lives and letters: that of defending (or at least considering critically) the author's personal *bona fides* and respectability. This meant that, in addition to treating *Brief Lives* for the first time as a literary text, considering composition, readerships, sources, language, and idiom, I judged it not merely helpful to the reader but essential to the whole project to consider, case by case and in detail, its vexed status as historical record, a process which then shaped both the more discursive introduction and also the index. As I worked on the text, and as I uncovered Aubrey's books, papers, letters, sources, and unpublished manuscripts, it became clear that by the normal standards of seventeenth-century biography his concern for fact was extraordinary and his zeal for obtaining reliable sources both tenacious and resourceful. Yet so ingrained was his reputation as a hasty and frivolous gossip that scholars were wary of giving his statements serious attention.

Most of Aubrey's other manuscripts, and the collections of those with whom he collaborated, such as Anthony Wood's vast collections in the Bodleian Library, are unpublished. Because none of them has received the attention of textual critics, their own textual history, such as their highly complicated sequence of composition, or the identity of annotators who had read the manuscripts, was unclarified. This made the task of annotation far more onerous. Scholars who had used some of Aubrey's statements in their work had frequently contented themselves with a quotation and a phrase like "if Aubrey is to be credited," so where Aubrey's own materials were concerned there was a lack of secondary material on which I could draw. As it was also widely assumed that Aubrey, like Lucifer, was the father of lies, even documents with unequivocal information relating to him were sometimes assumed to be misleading. For example, in an edited catalogue of the surviving early collections of the Ashmolean Museum, one scholar ignored Aubrey's donations to the Museum, listed in the manuscript catalogue, and another overlooked a letter in which Edward Lhuyd discussed with Aubrey how his gifts to the Museum would be identified by the abbreviation "Au" in the catalogue. These had instead been transcribed as "aurum," gold.[6] This meant that the commentary required research and explanation necessarily exceeding the specific text under consideration. As to edit a work is to pay it a great compliment, editions advocate for the status, reputation, and influence of their text and its authors, an argument most persuasively made in Aubrey's case through the richness of the annotation.

In addition, Aubrey's intentions are not always possible to discern or easy to carry out while maintaining scholarly distance. A collaborative author in life, Aubrey expected to continue this collaboration "50 yeares hence," through the assistance of someone whom he liked to call an "Aristarchus," some bright young fellow with antiquarian tastes and good Latin who would "methodise" his chaotic work.[7] Aubrey's first posthumous edition, Richard Rawlinson's edition of *A Perambulation of Surrey*, published by Edmund Curll in 1719, is duly presented as an antiquarian continuum: *The Natural History and Antiquities of the County of Surrey. Begun in the Year 1673, By John Aubrey, Esq; F.R.S. and continued to the present Time.* Rawlinson had to rewrite, supplement, and fill the lacunae in Aubrey's incomplete manuscript to make it publishable, a task which required him to perambulate Surrey on his own behalf in the summer of 1717.[8] This tradition continued. The formula "Wiltshire Collections. Aubrey & Jackson" on the cover and half-title page of Canon John Jackson's edition of Aubrey's *An Essay Towards the Description of the North Division of Wiltshire* (1862) presents Jackson, not as Aubrey's editor, but as his coauthor. The title page describes the work, in a phrase which originated in sixteenth-century didactic publications, as "corrected and enlarged" by Jackson, who used Aubrey's text as a basis for his own mountainous antiquarian annotations. Jackson was the vicar of Aubrey's parish, and rather than seeking an editorial distance, his personal sense of identification with Aubrey was so great that he forged letters between Hobbes and Aubrey and even persuaded himself that his own "hand-writing is not unlike his."[9] Poor Jackson was subjected to much *de haut en bas* scorn in the *Saturday Review*. "This large quarto," the reviewer proclaimed, is

> a thorough mistake. It is too bad for Mr. Jackson to talk of "correcting and enlarging" Aubrey. It is too bad to stick his own name outside like the member of a firm—"Aubrey and Jackson," as if they had worked together like Tate and Brady. It is too bad to put a view of Mr. Jackson's parish-church as the frontispiece to the volume, and to thrust Aubrey, in his wig and laced bands, into quite a second place. It is still worse to smother Aubrey altogether with Mr. Jackson's notes, and even to venture on innovations in his text. What was wanted was Aubrey's own jottings, with a few notes, correcting any distinct errors, answering Aubrey's numerous "Quæres," and filling up his numerous blanks.

"Mr. Jackson gives instead long notes" of a "dull and ponderous" kind which, the reviewer argues, are often incorrect.[10]

So, the 2015 edition required delicacy. Like my fellow editors in this collection, I had to find a way of approaching the Aubrey texts from the perspective of a rigorous critical editor, while still producing a book that anyone would want to read. I also had to write some very long notes without smothering Aubrey or being dull and ponderous. The policies for the 2015 text, introduction, notes, and index were deeply interdependent. While readers were accustomed to finding all the separate material relating to a biographical subject in the same place, alphabetically ordered, I found that this made it impossible to explain what was actually happening. Nonbiographical material got relegated, contexts disappeared, sequences of composition, including the places where Aubrey recorded the results of further enquiries that disproved earlier statements, became impossible to address, and the editor's voice drowned everything out. I decided that the new edition must focus for the first time on the three manuscript volumes of *Brief Lives*, exploring their genesis and bringing out their antiquarian materiality. The text would be presented as it is found in the manuscripts, with reordering in only very limited cases, and the material which was either not at all biographical (notes on agates) or only tangentially biographical (notes on mummified bishops) would not be excluded. Such a distinction was not made by Aubrey himself, and there is some very miscellaneous material in *Brief Lives*: for example, there are two parts to the account of a brewer who believed himself to have purchased the petrified kidney of a Jesuit priest who had been executed for his alleged part in the Popish Plot (*BL* 1:32, 672).

I represented not only the textual content of the manuscript but its material characteristics, such as coats of arms, examples of the biographical subject's handwriting, and so on. The text includes all the marks of revision, composition, and collaborative authorship, and almost nothing has been removed from the text to the *apparatus criticus*, even fragments of an excised page or the commentary of Wood, Malone, or Philip Bliss, and the papers they had added to the manuscripts. That establishes the edition on a clear empirical basis that I hope will enable subsequent editions to take their place beside it, without compromising them by confusing the relationships between the texts.

This decision gives a starring role to the commentary, without stepping in front of the star. Crucially, it stands apart from the edited text, with a structure of its own, thus allowing the textual cake to be cut any number of ways. As well as organizing the work by biographical subjects, with headnotes and annotation, it explores other matters. Readers can find textual information: that some of the text was found in a scrap of notes from Aubrey's miscellaneous pocketbook, that pages were missing from the manuscript but that evidence for their possible content was found in other sources, or that several Lives of English poets were grouped together in the manuscript. These matters are

"Many Excellent Good Notes" | 15

discussed in a headnote, with further annotation, and in some cases more discursive treatment in the introduction. Such organization also makes it possible to consider items from two or more viewpoints. Each biographical subject had a headnote, with a long discussion pulling together the different parts of each Life and its offshoots and diverse notes and additions within the manuscript, and the additions themselves also have a headnote where that makes matters clearer. This procedure also makes it possible to consider the evidence for whether a section of rough notes might represent notes from an interview, preparatory notes for an unwritten Life, additions or corrections for a lost Life, or something else entirely.

There is plenty to talk about: we are still arguing about whether one memorandum relates to Shakespeare or to William Beeston, and every so often Aubrey supplies a title that is clearly a mistake. The annotation also offers a commentary to the manuscripts at various stages of their existence (before pages were removed from them, before Edmond Malone reordered them, before they went to the Bodleian, and as they now are), as well as to the edited volume of text. Absences from the text (such as the fragments of the Lives of Richard Boyle and of Sir Christopher Wren, cut out of the manuscript) are addressed in the commentary by a detailed consideration of the surviving biographical evidence in other sources, that is, treated in the same way as an extant Life, as well as considered in the textual introduction as a feature of the work as a whole. The commentary offers the opportunity to pursue any number of strategies of investigation, primarily biographical. For example, Robert Hooke was a major source of statements in *Brief Lives* as well as an influence on several of Aubrey's other projects. The headnote to Hooke's Life, which runs to seven pages, considers all aspects of this relationship, including Hooke's nature as a biographical source. The headnote for the "Life of Ben Jonson" traces Aubrey's attempts to provide sources and glosses for Jonson's poems and plays, a thread running through several of the *Brief Lives*.

The only way to achieve this was to have two volumes, one of text and the other of commentary, with sequential pagination and running heads and a combined index to the two volumes of text, introduction, and commentary. An alphabetically ordered list of Lives at the front of the first volume functions as an internal index, which pulls together diverse parts of *Brief Lives*. This list was intended to compensate for abandoning the alphabetical order readers were used to, and for not reordering the text; another strategy was to cross-reference the commentary. The second volume has a matching "List of Biographical Commentaries," also arranged alphabetically. Within the commentary are a series of interrelated stories of the *Brief Lives* and their evolution, through Aubrey's researches, writings, and collaborations, and his engagement with an extraordinary range of people and things, from William Penn and Andrew Marvell to a Gloucestershire conjuror named Bub who sold magic bracelets. These were unreliable, and one purchaser came to a sorry end (*BL* 2:1657).

Although the annotation dealt to the fullest degree with Aubrey's legacy of manuscripts, books, and objects, there is no separate section on the books. They are numerous and some contain heavy annotation, so his library would be a more fitting subject for a separate publication. Some were already known, but a good number were identified during the work on the project. Many annotations in his books were the earliest versions of memoranda which became part of *Brief Lives*, and they furnished sources for headnotes or general annotation. Where Aubrey had a collection of his biographical subject's publications, or had secured copies for other people, a full account was added to the headnote of their Life. Readers expecting to find the content of Aubrey's letters and other material, which Clark had published as part of his 1898 text, can find them, in fact many more of them, in the commentary, properly introduced and contextualized and subject to a consistent policy of inclusion. All quotations were taken afresh from manuscripts or printed books written or used or owned by Aubrey, even where some of the content was available in nineteenth-century editions. This is because he is himself a reader and annotator, discussing, supplementing, and emending these works: these are never subsidiary "sources" for his own creations.

Annotation in the critical edition must cohere as a sustained form of investigation and interpretation of the text. All commentary needs to be approached with disciplined consistency, with an underlying coherence of intellectual purpose, presenting the reader with a precise but dispersed argument. It must strictly serve the explanatory purpose, although, as I have indicated, the fact that Aubrey's texts overlap means that the editor needs to show some relaxation of too strict a policy in his particular case. As this is a biographical text, every person Aubrey mentioned was identified, apart from a few obscure figures who defeated me. I combed through all of Aubrey's manuscripts seeking every mention of a name, place, or subject in the *Lives*. This revealed to my fascinated gaze a wholly unexpected and vast network of relationships for which there was no other possible form of publication than the commentary, which developed into an introduction and finding aid to Aubrey's whole biographical and social project where that affects the sources and subject matter of *Brief Lives*.

"Many Excellent Good Notes" | 17

I never considered using a biographical appendix. This is because each Life required a headnote with a biographical element, so biographical annotations fell more naturally within the text, one of which took the role of master annotation, with an equivalent level of comprehensiveness as the headnotes, with the others providing such annotation as the local circumstances required. The index provided readers with a full survey of the information. This led to some minor duplication, unavoidable in so large a commentary. Aubrey's biographical references often require some form of discussion, particularly when suggesting the identity of persons referred to in the text only by initials. The annotation confined itself strictly to Aubrey, his circle, and his texts and did not duplicate published material: where possible I gave the most scholarly modern biography. It was an immense labor: within the commentary as a whole, I did the same thing for every person mentioned in *Brief Lives*, with one long biographical note, usually at the point when the person is first mentioned, so that Aubrey's circle and his biographical interests all have the same degree of context.

Why do this? I felt it was one of the most valuable contributions I could make in a work intended to be the flagship for Aubrey studies. During work on *Brief Lives*, I was repeatedly asked the same questions: Had Aubrey not made all this up? Had he perhaps invented bogus informants to conceal that fact, and so on? The answer was, in all cases, no: these encounters took place in good earnest, these now obscure people had a place in their society that only Aubrey can reveal to us. His manuscripts are socially inclusive, leading us to a very wide range of people not mentioned with this degree of abundant and humane detail elsewhere in the record. For example, he preserved tantalizing details of women's interest in the arts, medicine, poetry, and antiquities, and interviewed women about their family members. Aubrey knew a great many luminaries very well indeed, but he also knew an immense number of gifted autodidacts who are easy to overlook and whose contribution should not be dismissed.

As well as offering a resource for scholars, the commentaries tell a story about early modern conversation, respecting the text's anecdotal character by showing how Aubrey spent time, not in idle gossip but in listening to people and noting down what they talked about, often over a sustained period. I used the annotation of the *Lives* to record the breadth of interests of these early modern polymaths, particularly those who had little formal education. These include the early accountant John Collins, the tailor Henry Coley, who was also an astrologer and mathematics tutor, and Absolom Leech, who kept a bowling alley at Kingston upon Thames and had a range of interests, from

18 | Notes on Footnotes

alchemy and medicine to keeping cormorants for fishing. Aubrey's insatiable curiosity and lack of interest in political and religious affiliation meant his net was spread unusually wide. He is able to reveal a very different aspect of well-known people such as Israel Tonge, informer and possible inventor of the Popish Plot. At a time when Aubrey was considering becoming a Jesuit novice to flee his debtors, he was spending Christmas with the Catholic-hating Tonge and talking about Hebrew punctuation (*BL* 2:968). Aubrey's relationship with Milton's nephew Edward Philips was not confined to their discussion of Milton and his poetry; the two men talked about the sarsen stones near Avebury and Philips's own publications, and kept in touch for several years (*BL* 2:1619).

In one of those times when Aubrey is himself an annotator, he is weaving together a Life of someone he calls Bess Broughton, who appears briefly in Jonson's poem "An Execration upon Vulcan." It is difficult to learn his precise source, as, while he believed he had seen "the first Edition in 8°," there is no octavo edition, although I suggest other possibilities. Aubrey wants to put this line in the epigram in a biographical context, and among other sources he quotes "an old song of those dayes which I have seen in a Collection. 'twas by way of Litanie. viz, 'From the Watch at Twelve a Clock / And from Bess Broughtons buttond smock / Libera nos Domine.'" In my note, I did not linger on the song, quickly suggesting that it was probably "Captain Squiers Lettany," found in *An Antidote upon Melancholy* of 1669, because I wanted to get on to Aubrey's very curious marginal annotation, which says that "Barbara Countess of Castlemaine" (or B C. C. in the margin) "had such a one: my Sempstresse helped to worke it." Aubrey asked the seamstress if she could explain to him this reference in the "old song." When Pepys saw Castlemaine's lace smocks hung out to dry in the Privy Garden at Whitehall, he was dazzled: the seamstress must have been first-rate. Aubrey seems to have sought out craftspeople patronized by the rich and famous, not only so he could appear properly equipped to take his place in the society to which he aspired, but also so that he could absorb all manner of information from them. As well as Castlemaine's seamstress, he patronized Selden's saddler, and records a bawdy quip by him in the "Life of Selden." I made enquiries about what a "buttond smock" might have been in the minds of litany-makers and Aubrey's seamstress, but found nothing conclusive. It might imply a raised embroidery stitch, or perhaps a set of gold or jeweled buttons (*BL* 1:27, 335, 406; 2:799–800, 1215).

As this example illustrates, I researched Aubrey's statements to discover their factual or other content, assuming that for many readers that was why they were reading the book. *Brief Lives* is partly a literary work, partly a work of

"Many Excellent Good Notes" | 19

reference, dipped into as much as read all the way through, and I tried to supply enough information locally in annotations to serve readers who did not have time to read pages and pages of introduction. The Lives of Milton and of Shakespeare, in particular, are handled in a more expansive and discrete fashion than the others. Aubrey and his circle were polymaths, and I wanted to do justice to this quality, rather than allowing the biographical, bibliographical, and philological concerns to dominate. Aubrey saw and owned some wonderful books, and he is adept at capturing the circumstances in which he saw them: on booksellers' stalls, in private homes, or an old torn one mending a window. To scholars, books can seem an index of Aubrey's scholarly seriousness, but I wanted to give equal priority to all of his interests, so there are notes about paintings, clocks, banking, alum mining, garden history, furniture, cookery, medicine, card games, glass manufacture, mathematics, and botany. The extracts from or references to Aubrey's other manuscripts quoted in the commentary are supported with brief explanations. In the long biographical note for Anthony Ettrick, who had a "Roman sword" found when a barrow was dug around 1665, I quote Aubrey's description that "It was of the Roman length and fashion: but it is now spoiled and lost. They used it for a Cheese-toster." I explain that this sword would in fact have not been Roman, but an Anglo-Saxon secondary burial in the prehistoric barrow (*BL* 2:1009).

Editing is not merely a scholarly exercise of compiling information. It is a rhetorical art which presents a consistent argument through coherently related strategies of overt and subtle communication. Annotation, more than any other scholarly skill, must consider the reader's attention span and present as much knowledge in as convenient and palatable a form as possible. If it is too dry, few will want to read it; if it cannot be found quickly, few will try. If it is not in a convenient place, few will even realize that they can read it. Annotation is an art of brevity and of restraint. Yet where possible, notes should be a delight, putting pressure on details to produce a critical art in miniature, attentive to the rhetorical character of the edited work. It would be too bad to spoil Aubrey's charm, wit, sense of humor, eye for the poignant detail, omnivorous interests, and intellectual curiosity. I hoped to be the sympathetic editorial "Aristarchus" of Aubrey's frequently expressed dreams and had no wish to be his Dunce. Where I could, I sought pleasure, selecting engaging detail or examples, and brightening my sober editorial tone with Aubrey's irresistibly lively voice. Glossing the story about a plump Cambridge alderman who was repeatedly "preached at" for falling asleep during the sermon, I slipped in a detail from a Jonsonian masque, which Aubrey knew well: "Aldermen were

20 | Notes on Footnotes

traditionally sleepy (two 'aldermen lobsters' are 'asleep in a dish' in Jonson's *The Gypsies Metamorphos'd*), but the 'good fatt' one here emblematizes the severe predestinarian climate of the 1590s, in which sermon-sleeping was taken as a disastrous sign of reprobation" (*BL* 1:82, 2:849).

Aubrey combed Jonson's *Works* (1640) for antiquarian and biographical detail, and Jonson remains a sympathetic source for contextual material for my current work annotating the *Life of Thomas Hobbes*, where Aubrey writes:

> At Oxford He (Mr T. H.) used in the Summertime especially to rise very early in the morning, and would tye the <u>leaden Counters</u> (which they used in those dayes at Christmas at Post and Payre) with strings, (pacthreds) which he did draw through (besmere with) birdlime and and bayte them with parings of cheese and the Jackdawes* would spye them a vast distance in the aire, as far as Osney-abbey, and strike at the bayte, and so be harled in the string which the wayte of the Counter would make cling about their wings.
> <*this story he happened to tell me discoursing of Optiques to instance such a sharpnes of sight in so little an Eie.>[11]

It is not quite clear whether in the parenthetical comment "which they used in those days at Christmas at Post and Payre" Aubrey is weaving into his account an annotation on the customs of their native Wiltshire, or whether Hobbes himself was the annotator, and told the story much as we have it in the *Life of Thomas Hobbes*. My annotation takes the hint and pursues the antiquarian thread:

> Post and pair was a card-game involving gambling with lead counters: the "post" being the stake, and the "pair" the cards each player is dealt. Charles Cotton observes that it was "very much play'd in the West of *England*" (*The Compleat Gamester* (1674), 150–1), and card games were a feature of Christmas and the New Year. In Jonson's *Christmas, His Masque* (1616), a character named Post and Paire enters, along with Caroll, Minc'd Pie, New-Years-Gift, and Wassail, with the winning hand, "a paire-Royall of Aces in his Hat, his Garment all done over with Payres, and Purrs; his Squier carrying a Box, Gards, and Counters."

I added for cheerful good measure the detail that you win post and pair with two aces.

"Many Excellent Good Notes" | 21

The policy to record the whole breadth of Aubrey's social and intellectual interactions with the people in the *Lives* resulted in long lists, which I labored over, trying to make them readable and intelligible. To take the example from the note on the Welsh alchemist Meredith Lloyd:

> Lloyd supplied JA with information about St Dunstan's and George Ripley's alchemical manuscripts (*BL*, i. 525, 585); Welsh "whispering-places" and antiquities (*BL*, i. 504, 579); blood transfusion (*BL*, i. 189); roe deer in Montgomery (*A1*, f. 130v), the German author of a work on fountains (*A1*, f. 41), and described seeing at "Dollkelly in Merionithshire" (Dolgellau in Merionethshire) a hundred or more "poor people of Eighty yeares of age at Church in a Morning; who came thither barefoot and bare-legg'd a great way," perhaps for their health (*A1*, f. 11v). Lloyd wrote a letter about silver, gold, and copper mines in Shropshire; he had an interest in turning base metals into silver, and in mining valuable minerals (*A26*, f. 3, and *passim*). He knew Old Welsh, and had considerable interest in the history of Welsh, in English etymology, and in the origin of Welsh place-names (*A4*, f. 7a; *A5*, ff. 4–5v; *BL*, i. 447; *F39*, f. 347v; T. G. c 25, ff. 53, 66ᵛ, 95eᵛ). (*BL* 2:903)

Nothing could make this list of manuscript folios lovely to the eye, but I tried to group these brief notes in a rational way and to make them sound enticing, with a balance between paraphrase, short quotation, and longer examples, using a little detail to lighten an indigestible, if rich, mixture.

I provided translations for texts in languages other than English, using where possible a contemporary text. When Aubrey used his own very free translation for a Welsh poem, I supplied a more literal version (*BL* 1:1653). Where Aubrey had made errors, I gave a corrected version in the commentary. Some readers of the work in draft were surprised that I did not correct the many errors in his Latin and Greek in the text itself. I would not have considered doing so, any more than I corrected errors of fact or of transcription or any other kind in the original text, with the exception of very small repetitions, which I pointed out in the *apparatus criticus*. In an edition based on the author's holograph, the commentary and not the text is the place to correct errors made by the author or to consider their implications. In Aubrey's case I felt this held true even when he was transcribing a published source. There seems to be an assumption that the learned languages constitute a special case, but I do not see a rationale for this. There is one phrase in Hebrew, where Aubrey's poor rendition of the script (perhaps badly executed in his source, a wall painting which is no longer extant) meant that it was impossible to transcribe without the emendation implicit in the printed character itself. I do supply a facsimile of the manuscript page, so a reader interested in wall paintings and mottoes can see the original (*BL* 1:411).

I glossed every word not in the *Shorter Oxford Dictionary* but did not provide a separate glossary. Several of Aubrey's unusual words are deployed in full awareness of their archaic or dialect character and required discussion. In the "Life of Ralph Kettell," president of Trinity College, Oxford, Aubrey says, "Dr Kettle when he scolded at the idle young boies of his colledge, he used these names. viz Turds, Tarrarags (these were the worst sort, rude Rakells) Rascal-Jacks, Blind cinques, Scobberlotchers (these did no hurt, were sober, but went idleing about the Grove with their hands in their pocketts: and telling the number of the Trees there, or so)." Aubrey's Trinity friends used these words as a nostalgic in-joke for decades after leaving the college, so the note for "Scobberlotchers" quotes a letter John Hoskins of Trinity wrote to Aubrey of the "sauntring scobberlorching life," and another Aubrey wrote to Wood saying that "I wish you had some more such impertinent, slobberlockings (Dr Kettle) agents that wish as well to carrying on such publique workes as these, as I doe." These were both from unpublished letters which illuminated the anecdotal origins of the Life and its vocabulary, and this information seemed enough for the context: the *OED* definition tentatively suggests an etymology that added nothing conclusive, and *OED* was in any case the obvious place for a reader to turn if they wanted to take matters further. *OED* occasionally has Aubrey as the only source for dialect words (such as the Wiltshire word "shale," meaning to shed a tooth), and sometimes these entries are either slightly inaccurate or there are better examples to be found in his work, which I supplied. Unusual words in the commentary, such as Aubrey's nonce word "apricate," to bask in the sun, are glossed immediately after the bibliographical reference (*BL* 2:1178).

Aubrey entwines personal memories with his reading, and I tried to be sensitive to this when annotating, as also to the nature of the interrelationships among Aubrey's manuscripts. In a section in *Brief Lives* on the history of guns, Aubrey says he remembered many "Calivers" (a light, portable musket) "before the Civill-warres in Gentlemens Halls, for then the Soldiers converted them into Carbines" (*BL* 1:34). As is often the case, there is a fuller comment in another manuscript. My note runs:

As JA puts it in the Preface to the *Wiltshire Antiquities*:

> The Halls of Justice of the Peace were dreadfull to behold; the Skreenes were garnished with corsletts, and helmetts gaping with open mouth; with coates of mail, Lances, pikes, halberts; browne bills, batterdashes, bucklers and the moderne Calivers, and petronells, (in King Charles I. time) turned into Musketts, and pistolls. (*A3*, f. 9a)

JA may be thinking of Jonson, *Epicene*, where Sir Amorous is reported to be advancing on Daw thirsting for his blood and "so hung with pikes, halberds, petronels, calivers, and muskets that he looks like a justice of peace's hall" (*CWBJ*, iii. 472). However, John Britton remembered a room "with several pieces of old armour, and other characteristics of an ancient mansion" in JA's birthplace at Easton Piercy in the late 18th c. (Britton, *Memoir*, 26). (*BL* 1:795)

The fact that there is a more comprehensive treatment of the development of the gun in the *Wiltshire Antiquities*, where Jonson's absurdly specific list of guns is extremely close to Aubrey's version, and may be influencing it, means that this note functions as an annotation on both manuscripts and indeed might almost be considered a note on the *Wiltshire Antiquities*. But in that work, the point about how the guns had been converted by the soldiers for use in the fighting is not made. The *Brief Lives* version is nearer to personal reminiscence, a tone supported in the note by the inclusion of John Britton's recollection from 1780 of his own boyhood in Aubrey's parish. If Aubrey had been edited by a team, another policy might perhaps have been adopted, with the topographical manuscripts functioning as the primary site for such commentary. But this would have been hard to have carried out consistently, as even this example shows, and most cases of such overlap are far more complicated and diverse, taking in several manuscripts. To create generic boundaries alien to Aubrey's thinking, so important to his Victorian editors, was not something my edition thought proper to do.

Most annotators allow themselves a little playfulness, a moment of participation in the world of the text. *Brief Lives* deals with confidences and anecdotes, not only of learned readers and their books but of people whose "very Pudenda were not hid," and with stories of the inadvertent, the unsuccessful, the wildly implausible, and the incomplete (*BL* 1:38). Annotation aims

24 | Notes on Footnotes

at strict objectivity or disciplined speculation; the commentary is no place for airing mere subjective opinion. But comments do comment, and a tone had to be found to describe the counterfactual matter in *Brief Lives* that would achieve a balance between making no comment or treating it with scorn. In an account of "Twisse D. D. of Newbury," Aubrey recounts how he was told by a divine called Robert Twisse a story of how his father, William Twisse, when a "wild" boy at school at Winchester College, visited the "House of office" at night. Here he met the ghost of a dead schoolfellow, who told him, "I am damn'd." Twisse, who, Aubrey notes, was "melancholique and Hypocondriaque," amended his ways at once and became very devout. I give this the title "An Account of the Conversion of William Twisse (1574–1646)" but begin it by calling it a "tale of a haunted latrine" before giving the likely date of its composition and the text of a later version in the *Miscellanies* (*BL* 1:649, 2:1606–7).

Aubrey can sometimes be vague, and it is the annotator's task to address his imprecision. As this implicitly involves putting words into an author's mouth, it is important to choose the right sources. In the Life of Ralph Kettell, Aubrey writes that the elderly president of Trinity College, Oxford, "dragg'd with one foot a little, by which he gave warning (like the rattlesnake) of his comeing. Will: Egerton (Major Generall Egertons younger brother) a good witt, and Mimick, would goe so like him, that sometimes he would make the whole Chapell rise-up imagining he had been entring-in." The note on the rattlesnake was as follows: "A Virginian rattlesnake was among the exhibits at the Oxford Anatomy School at this period . . . while 15 Brazilian rattlesnake skins were displayed in the Repository of the Royal Society. The rattle, explains their cataloguer, gives 'timely notice of their approach,'" and I reference Nehemiah Grew's *Musæum Regalis Societatis* (1681) (*BL* 1:179, 2:1015). The mention of the Oxford rattlesnakes may remind the reader that Oxford was amassing such natural historical specimens, and that Aubrey is placing Kettell himself among these desiccated curios. There are other observations of the rattlesnake by members of the Royal Society, including Evelyn's very detailed comment on the live ones he saw at the house of George Joyliffe in 1657. But Evelyn says that the rattle was "a providential caution to other creatures," a comment which is alien to Aubrey's open-ended and almost secular way of thinking. So, I kept the note short and saved Evelyn's comment for more discursive treatment in another publication.[12] Aubrey had made donations to the Royal Society's repository and had also been asked to help prepare the catalogue.[13] Thus, Grew's wry and worldly comment might have shaped Aubrey's in some way; certainly it seemed closer to his intended meaning than Evelyn's, as well as to the date of composition of *Brief Lives*.

Aubrey's editors have always had to give his work more support than is usually appropriate, and in my commentary I used so much material from his manuscripts that I was often interlacing his words with my own. I tried to make this a harmonious relationship, and I hoped to avoid drowning out Aubrey's voice. Editing is a rhetorical art as well as a scholarly discipline, and I wanted not only the text, but also my notes and introduction to catch the feel of the texts, to be saturated in their language and tone, and to entice readers to explore them further.[14]

NOTES

1. John Aubrey, *Brief Lives* with *An Apparatus for the Lives of our English Mathematical Writers*, ed. Kate Bennett, 2 vols. (Oxford: Oxford University Press, 2015), i, xci (hereafter *BL*).

2. Anthony Wood, *Historia et Antiquitates Uniuersitatis Oxoniensis* (Oxford: Sheldonian Theatre, 1674), Anthony Wood, *Athenae Oxonienses*, 2 vols. (London: Printed for Tho. Bennet at the Half-Moon in S. Pauls Churchyard, 1691).

3. Andrew Clark, ed., *"Brief Lives," chiefly of Contemporaries, set down by John Aubrey, between the Years 1669 & 1696*, 2 vols. (Oxford: Clarendon Press, 1898), 1:7–8.

4. John Aubrey, *Miscellanies* (London: Printed for Edward Castle, next Scotland-Yard-Gate by Whitehall, 1696), 113–21.

5. MS Aubrey 9, fol. 28v.

6. Arthur MacGregor, ed., *Tradescant's Rarities: Essays on the Foundation of the Ashmolean Museum 1683 with a Catalogue of the Surviving Early Collections* (Oxford: Clarendon Press, 1983), 297–98; Kate Bennett, "John Aubrey's Collections and the Early Modern Museum," *Bodleian Library Record* 17 (2001): 235–36.

7. *BL* 1:cxlii; Oxford, Bodleian Library, MS Ashmole 1829, fol. 78.

8. John Aubrey, *The Natural History and Antiquities of the County of Surrey*, ed. Richard Rawlinson, 5 vols. (London: Printed for E. Curll in Fleet Street, 1719); Paul Baines and Pat Rogers, *Edmund Curll, Bookseller* (Oxford: Clarendon Press, 2013), 136.

9. Society of Antiquaries, London, SAL/MS/817/9, fols. 25, 30.

10. *Saturday Review* 18 (October 8, 1864), 461.

11. MS Aubrey 9, fol. 34.

12. *The Diary of John Evelyn*, ed. E. S. de Beer, 6 vols. (Oxford: Clarendon Press, 1955), 3:200.

13. Thomas Birch, *The History of the Royal Society of London*, 4 vols. (London: Printed for A. Millar in the Strand, 1756), 3:159.

14. It is perhaps no accident that the opening and concluding essays in this collection declare annotation to be a "rhetorical art." Indeed, it is.

CHAPTER 2

❧ Annotating Dryden, Southerne, and Defoe

Maximillian E. Novak

In the following pages, I describe from my personal perspective my activities as an annotator of various editions when I was an active professor at the University of California, Los Angeles. This is an admittedly subjective result, but the results speak for themselves, and perhaps my experiences may be of use to others embarked on similar projects.

I have to admit that my concept of annotating a scholarly edition was probably more elaborate than that of some fellow editors on the California Dryden edition, but we all knew that it was to be an edition of a great writer and would not be duplicated any time in the near future. It had been conceived as part of the gift to UCLA in 1934 of the William Andrews Clark Memorial Library, with its magnificent collection of Dryden's works. Professors Edward Niles Hooker and H. T. Swedenberg of the English Department brought out the first volume decades later in 1956. Hooker's brilliant annotations to his edition of the critical works of John Dennis (1939) served as a model. In their day, such editorial projects were sometimes derided as "factories." Such a term hardly suited the editorial work on the California Dryden. Until the final meeting over the introductions and annotations, we seldom came together.

I was surprised recently to see myself described as an "editor" in an Amazon entry. I am not certain how that happened. "Writer of Scholarly Annotations" is not a proper title, but I would consider that a more accurate description of my work. Editing often describes the word-by-word comparison of texts—a task I have never enjoyed. Writing annotations involves attention and learning—everything that scholarship should be about. For me, the main problem with annotating classic texts, such as the writings of Dryden or Defoe, was the feeling of interrupted learning. After weeks, perhaps even months, of work on a single problem, all that knowledge often must be encapsulated into a few sentences. In the end, the information necessary to the reader must be the important point. Even in an edition such as the California Dryden, which allowed full explanations of literary and historical matters, the necessity to move on to the next note and then the next was disappointing. In editing Dryden's *All for Love*, for example, I read everything available, both ancient and modern, about Antony and Cleopatra. By the end of my research, I had accumulated so much material on them that I thought I must surely write a book, but of course I never did. My task was to provide the reader with knowledge in a relatively succinct manner, not to write a study of these fascinating lovers and their time. Nevertheless, as a scholar my pleasure lay in gaining as much knowledge about my material as possible.

Volume 10 of the Dryden presented some unique problems: a Shakespeare adaptation, *The Tempest*; a sex comedy, *An Evening's Love: or, The Mock Astrologer*; and a heroic play, *Tyrannick Love*. The challenge was daunting. The encounter between Dryden and Shakespeare alone should have been irresistible to any scholar with a genuine interest in the period. Dryden and Davenant had changed a play that already, in its original state, had a masque and songs into a form that some years later, under the hand of Thomas Shadwell, approached what eventually became thought of as the "Operatic *Tempest*."[1] It was perhaps the most popular of Shakespeare's plays during the Restoration and eighteenth century. Davenant had undoubtedly sketched out the additions to the play involving various inserted materials—the man who had never encountered a woman in parallel with Miranda, a sister for Miranda, another for Caliban, as well as a doubling of the shipwrecked sailors from two to four, since this kind of increase was his specialty; however, many of the important changes in the poetic text were undoubtedly the work of the younger Dryden assisting the then poet laureate.[2] Given my work on *Robinson Crusoe* and its island possibilities, I felt that I was well positioned to deal with Shakespeare's themes, including the revolt of the sailors and servants—a concept that had its origins in an actual shipwreck on Bermuda during Shakespeare's time. I also felt comfortable in dealing with the position of Caliban in relation to Prospero with all its colonial ramifications. Other matters, such as the "weapon

28 | Notes on Footnotes

salve" that saves the life of Hippolito, involved research into contemporary science and the Royal Society.[3]

Of course, I had the benefit of the massive work that had been done on Shakespeare from the eighteenth to the twentieth century. The "Shakespeare Variorum" drew together much of this commentary; but not all.[4] Johnson's edition of Shakespeare had already served as a kind of variorum for the eighteenth century. Notes such as those by Frank Kermode in the Arden edition provided invaluable ideas.[5] In addition to these annotated editions, there were dozens of essays treating Shakespeare's play. What Dryden may have thought of it in 1667 was perhaps most essential for my purposes, but I had to be continually aware how much I was peering through the haze of history and historical scholarship.

The William Andrews Clark Library permitted me unheard of resources. I was able to work with copies of all the Shakespeare folios spread out in front of me, along with the quarto of the Dryden-Davenant text. When I needed to refer to a problem in, say, contemporary medicine, I was allowed to browse through the stacks of seventeenth-century volumes on that subject without any supervision. During this period, the California Dryden (as we thought of it) and the Clark Library functioned almost as a single unit; new additions to the collection were made mostly in areas involving the Dryden Project. I mention this because by the present rules of the Clark and many other rare book libraries, the annotations that I did would have been nearly impossible. Perhaps a more efficient modern scholar would find online materials as valuable as browsing through the stacks of a library with their real books and pages. This would never be my case. As I suggest later in this essay, the chance discoveries that were available through the books at the Clark were sometimes as valuable for my annotations as the more direct information for which I was searching.

In the hands of Dryden and Davenant, *The Tempest* became *The Enchanted Island*, a very different play from Shakespeare's masterpiece. My annotations always had to keep in mind the history of the play, which was not performed (more or less) as Shakespeare composed it until the middle of the nineteenth century. In 1667, Shakespeare's name would not necessarily be one to draw audiences to the theaters; to the contrary, it might have warned theatergoers that this was an old-fashioned play written by someone from the "Last Age." Dryden delivered a wonderful tribute to Shakespeare in the prologue in terms of the artist as a genuine magician and as someone who produced his plays out of the natural genius that was the basis of his greatness. In place of the original,

Dryden offered the kind of art claimed by the writers of Restoration drama. Some modern critics, such as Hazelton Spencer, reflected a feeling that Shakespeare's genius was God given and those who had made changes in his plays were guilty of a form of violation.[6] To the contrary, the playwrights of the Restoration tended to regard the drama of Shakespeare, Ben Jonson, and even the then still popular John Fletcher as embarrassingly primitive. Contemporary French tragedy and comedy along with Spanish plays were considered far more suitable. In annotating the newly constructed *Tempest*, I had always to keep in mind the relative nature of taste. Dryden and Davenant were not writing to desecrate the tomb of Shakespeare but rather to construct a successful play suitable to the taste of their time.

Annotating *An Evening's Love: or, The Mock Astrologer* involved understanding what I was to call "sex comedy" in terms of the original Spanish play, and more specifically the French comedy from which it was more directly derived. It also involved working with two foreign languages. Dryden's play was far more earthy than either of the earlier plays, written as it was in the early days of the court of Charles II, a time of considerable sexual license. Dryden was not reluctant to join in with this new spirit of comedy, but unlike his later play, *Limberham*, with its bawdy, farcical display of sexual encounters, *An Evening's Love* has considerable charm. Dryden apparently had competent knowledge about astrology. I did my best to understand his various references as well as I could, but as much as I read about the subject in contemporary manuals, I may still have missed some of the subtleties. I did much better with Dryden's discussion of comedy in the preface, one of his more interesting pieces of literary criticism.

The final play of this volume, *Tyrannick Love*, was a Saint Catherine play and a rhymed heroic drama. Dryden later spoke of the contrast between the saint and the emperor Maximin as a particular moment in his artistry. Maximin was a figure of power, a defiant, almost "romantic," hero in his evil. Dryden had set the tone for such a character with his figure of Almanzor in *The Conquest of Granada*, but Almanzor was essentially virtuous. Maximin is a tyrant, and his love for the saint is filled with ambiguity. He dies after ordering the execution of Catherine, defying the gods. Dryden was always tempted by the opportunity to argue in rhyme, and the contrast among the pagan philosophers brought in to argue against Saint Catherine's Christian beliefs forms a centerpiece of the play. The rhymed heroic play may have been doomed, but it gave Dryden an opportunity to show off his considerable talents as a poet and was a pleasure to annotate.

30 | Notes on Footnotes

Shortly before completing this volume and undertaking the next volume of Dryden's plays, I was asked to help with volume 17 of the California Dryden. Most of the volume was dedicated to Dryden's literary criticism, with the magnificent *Essay of Dramatick Poesie* as its most important work. Samuel Monk, the main editor of the volume, was unwell at the time, and Earl Miner, who was the most active director of the edition, suggested that several of us might lend a hand. This was a volume of criticism, and I agreed to help with some of the annotations. My largest task involved the annotations to the attack on Elkanah Settle by Dryden, Shadwell, and John Crowne with the title *Notes and Observations on the Empress of Morocco* (1674). While Crowne later attempted to take credit for most of the commentary in this work, it was obvious that Dryden, with the most profound credentials as a literary critic of the three, exerted the strongest influence throughout. Dryden's argument was that Settle's concept of the rhymed heroic play was so flawed that it almost constituted a parody of the form. Settle replied in a manner that was effective enough, pointing to some of Dryden's own absurdities. While it would be too much to say that the debate (along with the parodic *The Rehearsal*) killed off the rhymed heroic play, it is certainly true that it hardly lasted out the decade. The introduction and annotations gave me the opportunity better to understand Dryden's often shifting critical ideas. If his *Essay of Dramatick Poesie* had used the skeptical method of dialogue in dealing with English, French, and Greek dramaturgy, the *Notes and Observations* set forth some of what he found wrong with contemporary drama and what he considered bad poetry.

Between completing this volume and my next Dryden volume, I undertook a less ambitious edition of *Oroonoko*, Thomas Southerne's version of Behn's novella.[7] Once more I was faced with the problem of adaptation. Southerne added a subplot with two women searching for husbands as a complement to Oroonoko's love for his Imoinda. The period of the rhymed heroic play had passed, but Behn had made her African prince into someone advancing noble concepts of freedom and heroism in a situation involving his enslavement amid the very unheroic merchants who represent the worldly principles that appear ready to replace him. In annotating this text, I had to be aware of the way that Southerne paralleled his portrait of the heroic prince with that of the two women and their desire for some kind of status in their world, characters very much out of witty Restoration comedy. In addition, I knew that the play had been adapted several times later in the century to suit abolitionist sentiment. In writing my annotations, I thought it important to balance these three views—that of Behn's original work, Southerne's adaptation, and the later concept of the play. With David Rodes taking care of the text, I was free to explore the ideas behind this interesting work. At one point in Southerne's play, the two women make a direct connection between the plight of women in English society and that of Oroonoko and the other slaves and do their best to help the enslaved prince. How was one to annotate a play written at a time with so many intellectual currents? It was not easy.

Shortly thereafter I agreed to do two of the plays in volume 13 of the California Dryden, plays much indebted to Shakespeare: *All for Love: or, The World Well Lost* and *Troilus and Cressida*. The first was in no sense an "adaptation" of Shakespeare; it was Dryden's play on the theme of a heroic way of behaving that he felt was disappearing from his world. Still, I had to go over the play word by word to capture what echoes there were of Shakespeare's play, and I found many. But in stating on the title page that it was written in Shakespeare's "stile," Dryden intended to convey the idea that it was written not only in the manner of Shakespeare himself but also in that of his contemporaries. This meant that the highly metaphoric language of that period, both dramatic and lyric, influenced the manner of his writing. As my annotations revealed, there was almost as much of Samuel Daniel's poetic imagery from his play on *Cleopatra* (1594) as there was of Shakespeare. Like Dryden, Shakespeare had displayed his Antony and Cleopatra as heroic lovers, but no one could quite imitate Shakespeare's Cleopatra in her complex playfulness, scheming, and grace. Dryden had a different goal, a classical tragedy. His characters seem always already trapped by the fate that awaits them. It is noteworthy that Dryden's play *All for Love* (1677), or some version of his, combined with segments of Shakespeare's *Antony and Cleopatra*, held the stage until the end of the nineteenth century.

I viewed this play and *Troilus and Cressida* as deeply political. Both were written at a time, the Exclusion Crisis, when Charles II was beset with enemies; the attempt to remove the Catholic Duke of York, the future James II, as a claimant to the throne was gathering steam. *All for Love* seemed to feature the king and his mistress, the Duchess of Portsmouth, as essentially having given almost everything, including the kingdom, to sustain their love. Hence Dryden's subtitle: *The World Well Lost*. Shakespeare's protagonists probably did not feel that the "World" was necessarily "well lost," but Dryden's seem resigned to their fate. They act as if they are in the grip of an inevitable force of history, and my annotations were balanced between borrowings from Jacobean drama, history itself, contemporary politics, and the various literary allusions that filled everything Dryden ever wrote.

32 | Notes on Footnotes

Between writing *All for Love* and his version of the Troilus and Cressida story, Dryden had a momentary literary conversion. Although his first reaction to Thomas Rymer's *Tragedies of the Last Age* (1678), an attack on Shakespeare as a barbaric writer, had been to defend Shakespeare's artistry, Dryden seems to have fallen under Rymer's influence temporarily.[8] As I suggest in my commentary and annotations, Dryden did not fail to understand what Shakespeare intended in producing a play such as *Troilus and Cressida*, but consciously rejected what, at the time, he considered to be the disorderliness of the Renaissance aesthetic, with its ingenious balances and contrasts. He wanted to show what Shakespeare might have written had he composed the play according to the dictates of someone like Rymer and contemporary French critics. This meant jettisoning Shakespeare's ironic, often bitter, view of his characters and attempting to restore the supposedly heroic elements surrounding those involved in the war made famous in Homer's *Iliad*. In addition to this attitude about "improving" the work, an attitude that infuriated later critics who regarded any revision of Shakespeare's work as a desecration, Dryden rightly noted that the version of the play as it appeared in the Shakespeare folios involved some major printing errors. He directed some severe remarks about this in his preface and prologue—remarks that have sometimes wrongly been taken as a more generalized critique of Shakespeare's genius. My job was to explain what Dryden thought he was doing and why his artistic decisions made sense in the Restoration literary milieu.

Although Dryden changed the story of Troilus and Cressida, as it had descended from Chaucer and Shakespeare, into a tragedy of misunderstanding in which Cressida is a virtuous and faithful heroine, still this play was indeed an "imitation," adapting entire speeches from Shakespeare, and thus unlike *All for Love* in this regard. As with annotating Dryden's adaptation of *The Tempest*, this often required line-by-line, word-by-word evaluation. Which folio was Dryden using at any particular time? Why did he make a particular change? In this case, however, unlike the motivations behind the changes in *The Tempest* (mainly attempting to make the play more amusing), the exact rationale for Dryden's revisions had to be considered from the standpoint of the aesthetic improvement that was intended. Dryden wrote a lengthy preface to this play, announced on the title page as "Containing the Grounds of Criticism in Tragedy." Annotating this involved careful alertness to nuance in Dryden's criticism. As with his *Essay of Dramatick Poesie*, Dryden was drawing on his vast knowledge of Greek, English Renaissance, and English contemporary drama, as well as the drama and criticism of France during the seventeenth century. As I show in my annotations, whole passages are translations from the French critic René Le Bossu (1631–1680), whose rewriting of Aristotle's *Poetics* exerted a powerful influence on him at the time. In addition, as mentioned previously, the critical remarks of Rymer played a large role in his attitudes. Dryden also adopted Rymer's moral stance to the effect that the author is responsible for whatever perceived immorality might be in a play. But Rymer is treated as a relatively secondary critic compare to another French critic, René Rapin (1621–1687), and what was taken to be Longinus's treatment of the sublime.[9]

"The Grounds of Criticism in Tragedy" was one of the most difficult texts I ever had to annotate. Dryden's knowledge was vast, and there is an intellectual excitement in this preface. As his enemies frequently pointed out, he loved to put together learned arguments. His particular enthusiasm for Corneille and Racine, along with a general fascination for contemporary French critics, leads him to a defense of classical drama—the unities of place, time, and action, morally clear statement, and characters who reveal little ambiguity in their actions. In the last decade of his life, Dryden came to acknowledge Shakespeare as a divine genius, but in the earlier decades of the Restoration such a judgment was in doubt. With the heady success of *The Conquest of Granada*, he had dismissed the achievements of the great dramatists of the English Renaissance as something of a fluke. The great French playwrights of the seventeenth century were acknowledged throughout the Continent for their genius, while prior to Voltaire's discussion of Hamlet's soliloquy decades later, Shakespeare was strictly an English phenomenon. Annotating Dryden's struggle with the seeming paradox that Shakespeare had somehow to be greater than the playwrights of his own time was a pleasure that only an edition such as the California Dryden could afford. Some annotations ran to more than a page with full quotations from the works that Dryden had used in formulating his own critical position.

Sometime in the 1970s, when Manuel R. Schonhorn decided to join me in starting an edition of Daniel Defoe, I wanted it to be annotated along the same lines as the California Dryden. My own work on Defoe had convinced me that he had read deeply in European history and thought, and when he had the time, he had taken to writing his own lengthy annotations to his works, including *Jure Divino* (1706), his attack on divine right as a political system, and *Caledonia* (1706), his poem in praise of Scotland. His *History of the Union* (1709) was also filled with annotations. Works such as *The Consolidator* (1705) seemed replete with obscure references to contemporary events. Surely these required full annotations, but to my surprise, I overheard a well-known editor of Defoe say that he did not think Defoe required any such thing. He went on to compare Defoe to the women novelists of the period, whose works, in his opinion, also required little annotation. This seems unfair to both Defoe and the women, many of whom were both knowledgeable and thoughtful. At any rate, I would hardly have participated in what became known as the Stoke Newington Edition of the Writings of Daniel Defoe had I thought of the author in those terms.

Had we had the energy and organizational skills of P. N. Furbank and W. R. Owens, we would not have allowed the edition to languish as it did. I was putting together my book on various aspects of Defoe's writings and attended to the edition only in my spare time.[10] And to our dismay, during this period university presses gradually lost interest in scholarly editions.[11] At the same time, deans and some chairs of English departments discouraged young scholars from participating in such projects. At the end, even so established an edition as the California Dryden had difficulty reaching completion. Only the heroic efforts of Vinton Dearing succeeded in bringing out the final volumes, including the massive twentieth volume, somewhat after the year 2000 announced on the title page. But although he was a superb textual editor, without the brilliant efforts of Alan Roper, who left the Dryden project after finding the attitude of the university administration discouraging, the quality of the annotations declined precipitously.[12]

Schonhorn and I were delighted, then, when Jim Bjork of Louisiana State University and Gabriel Hornstein of AMS Press expressed interest in the Defoe edition. Jim breathed energy into the project, and we turned to see what volumes we had in progress. Joyce Kennedy had provided careful texts for *An Essay upon Projects* (1697) and *The Consolidator*, but only a few notes, and I asked Michael Seidel to see what he could do. He added two brilliant introductions and expanded the notes considerably, but still not into the lengthy commentaries to which my work on the California Dryden had accustomed me. I decided to go beyond the duties of a general editor and in the end added a third more, at least, to the annotations.

This had nothing to do, I am certain, with adding unnecessary material to these volumes. For example, *An Essay upon Projects* was the product of Defoe's ingenuity as he looked back over the seventeenth century from three years before its end and considered what improvements might be made in his society. He was already thirty-seven years old and as a tradesman and speculator had involved himself in a variety of innovative schemes. He had gone through bankruptcy some five years earlier and apparently had some time to contemplate his own and the nation's economic situation. This was indeed what Defoe rightly called the *Age of Projects*.[13] Not the age of invention—that was to come later. But speculation on possible improvements in society? That was eminently the work of Defoe's time.

The main point that the annotations to Defoe's various projects wished to stress had to do with the historical context behind many of them. The notion of an academy devoted to keeping the language from falling into neologisms and various forms of techno-speak had its origins not merely in the work of Bacon and the beginnings of the Royal Society, where this was indeed one of its goals, but also in more obscure attempts at founding such academies. The academy for teaching women was clearly influenced not only by Mary Astell's *Serious Proposal to the Ladies* (1694) but also by a dozen other contemporary plans to educate women. The military academy, with its emphasis on manly exercise, was deeply involved in contemporary politics—in the support for retaining some semblance of William III's army at a time when the war in Europe was coming to a close with the Treaty of Ryswick (1697). But if some of Defoe's projects were not entirely original, they were never lacking in ingenuity. The Defoe who was recovering from bankruptcy is everywhere present, as is his concept of the projector, who, forced by "Necessity," uses his inventive powers to escape from economic disaster.[14] Autobiography, history, politics, economics, insurance, a workable system of roads, and social improvement were among the many subjects that required annotation.

Several passages in *An Essay upon Projects* remained puzzling, and it is not at all uncommon to have editors pass by such moments in their text in silence. That might seemingly benefit the reputation of the editor, but it does a disservice to scholarship. I think all editors will have to admit to some pieces of information they will be unable to find. A degree of embarrassment goes along with the job since one would assume that giving so much time and research to an edition would provide answers to the most difficult problems. And occasionally that is indeed the case; Defoe's *Consolidator* is replete with obscure references, but although it is shaped as an imaginary moon voyage, it is filled with allusions to contemporary events, from Peter the Great's visit to England to the debates in the English Parliament, as our annotative work helped us to discover.

Defoe apparently believed that readers enjoyed filling in such allusions in much the same way that moderns take pleasure in a crossword puzzle. Thus, he has an obscure allusion to the "Constable at Bow"—an allusion that neither I nor the other editors had been able to annotate. After many years, I discovered that Defoe was free-associating two separate events having to do with self-defense, which he believed to be an inalienable right. Defoe believed that if a person were set on by a gang of men attempting to impress him into the navy, he had a right to defend his life, even if he killed someone in the process. On May 29, 1702, William Blackmore, the Constable of Bow, was killed when he tried to prevent the pressing of a citizen. Despite numerous witnesses, the three men accused were set free. Then three years later, not long before the publication of *The Consolidator*, Defoe printed a letter in his journal, the *Review*, concerning a press gang that attempted to seize a number of men at Bow Street, Covent Garden, and a constable named Ford who was severely injured in what amounted to a riot. The letter provoked Defoe to argue his own position on self-defense. After an interval of twenty years I seem to have solved Defoe's puzzle quite accidentally by browsing through Defoe's *Review*. I am not certain if this is an argument for taking time with scholarly editions, but in some cases it does not hurt.

In 1996, I began writing the line notes for the three volumes of Defoe's *Robinson Crusoe*. The first two volumes, *The Life and Strange Surprizing Adventures of Robinson Crusoe* and *The Farther Adventures of Robinson Crusoe*, had gone through hundreds, if not thousands, of editions, usually printed together up to the end of the twentieth century. The materials involving geography had been extensively annotated by someone identifying himself as the *Naval Cron.*, which was a major help, but from the time that Jean-Jacques Rousseau had used Defoe's work as a central philosophical text in his writings on education and isolation, it had gathered a penumbra of possible meanings in politics, economics, social thought, and religion, making it a most exceptionable text in Western literature. Annotating these volumes was something like working with Dryden's Shakespeare imitations, but with those texts, I had mainly to deal with the ways in which Dryden appeared to understand Shakespeare. With the Stoke Newington Defoe, we were committed to treating a more elaborate set of meanings. I had already commented on some of these subjects in my books on Defoe's treatment of economics and natural law, but expanding the subject field and annotating the *Robinson Crusoe* volumes word by word was a wholly different matter.

If, as with the treatment of Defoe's fields of knowledge in Leslie Stephen's essay in *Hours in a Library*, we believed that Defoe had only a shallow knowledge of the ideas that informed his world, an equally shallow approach to annotating his writings would have allowed for relatively brief entries.[15] Anyone fully familiar with Defoe's writings, however, had to recognize just how much he knew about the world around him and about the books that treated that world. The period during which he wrote his major fictions (1719–1725) preceded a time when he was to write entire books on geography, economics, education, social conditions, religion, and occult subjects. Since he did not have a classical education, he did not have the kind of background in Greek and Roman literature that might be found in a Dryden or Swift, but as I have suggested previously, about modern subjects he knew a great deal. He was not a profound thinker, but as all his contemporaries appeared to have agreed, he seemed to have opinions about almost everything. He liked to proclaim the originality of his ideas and was averse to admitting any degree of indebtedness to contemporary authors, but if the thinkers of his time had written on a given subject, Defoe was likely to know about it. He was thoroughly familiar with Hobbes and Locke; his poetry reveals how carefully he had read in Marvell, Milton, and Dryden. Similarly, he appears to have known almost all his predecessors in writing fiction. He had a comprehensive knowledge of British and European history and contemporary politics; he followed the controversy between the Earl of Shaftesbury and Bernard Mandeville; he read *Tatlers* and *Spectators* of Addison and Steele; his *Consolidator* was in part a response to Swift's *Tale of a Tub*. The annotations should reflect the full sweep of Defoe's intellect and command.

The second volume, *The Farther Adventures of Robinson Crusoe*, engaged philosophical readers less completely, but it also may be said that, in turning Crusoe into more a spectator than an actor, Defoe made him an astute observer of the world. From the beginning, we are given an analysis of humans as ruled by their passions. First it is Crusoe himself, in a frenzy over his desire to travel back to his island. Then it is the passionate display of relief after Crusoe's ship rescues the passengers from a ship bound from Canada, followed by an interest in questions concerning starvation when they encounter another ship that has been becalmed, the passengers found in a state of starvation, and Crusoe records the exact feelings of a maid as she comes close to cannibalism. That some of these themes carry over from the first volume suggests that Defoe had thought further about their significance. One scene, in which Crusoe rescues natives from a burning village—the result of violence perpetrated against native peoples—is one example of the anticolonialism theme found in the Crusoe volumes. More common, however, are his fantasies of a colonial takeover of China and his outrageous actions in crossing Siberia. Thus, although Defoe certainly placed Crusoe in more places for remote adventures than in the first volume, the second is equally filled with complex themes and ideas.

The final volume, *Serious Reflections . . . of Robinson Crusoe*, was the least popular of the three, or, one might say, thoroughly unpopular. Defoe's readership wanted to see Crusoe dealing with Moorish pirates, cannibals, and fierce Tartars. Although Defoe has him offer arguments about many of the themes in the first two volumes, this was hardly a substitute for what readers wanted— scenes of paralyzing fear such as those involved with the discovery of the footprint, or moments in which the natural feelings of Friday are expressed as he dances about in joy at discovering that he and Crusoe have rescued his father. The popularity of such moments was often dramatized on the stage in pantomimes. But Defoe had apparently exhausted his imaginative powers in revisiting the character of Crusoe. Still posing as Crusoe, while hinting that Crusoe might be a surrogate for someone who resembled the still infamous supposed Jacobite spy Daniel Defoe, the author suggests that a series of essays presenting the ideas involved in the earlier Crusoe volumes might be even more desirable to the reading public than the earlier fictions. If Defoe held such hopes, he was sadly mistaken. Who would have thought that the thoroughly earthbound protagonist of the first volume would lecture readers on spirits floating in the atmosphere or on the sad state of Christianity throughout the world? The best that could be hoped for—and this was hardly beyond Defoe—was that future scholars might search through the work for Defoe's ideas on fiction, isolation, poverty, honesty, and religion, and for the odd flowering of his poetic impulse.

On the other hand, while narrative does not always lend itself to extensive annotation, the essays in *Serious Reflections* are full of annotatable material. Defoe was about to embark on an amazing period of his life—a period that would see him writing a series of brilliant novels, travel guides, an economic survey of the world, and a series of social and moral critiques of that same world. If aspects of the first two novels provide valuable material for annotations, even more interesting are the ways they look forward to the works he was about to write. His treatment of poverty as a semilegitimate excuse for a variety of actions that might be considered immoral forms an ethical basis for *Moll Flanders*, *Colonel Jack*, and *Roxana*. His survey of the economy of the world in *Atlas Maritimus* (1728) was foreshadowed by Crusoe's survey of the religious state of the world. And Crusoe's sudden emergence as a theologian was to find a wider field in his *New Family Instructor* (1727) and in his various books on occult subjects. In short, for anyone who was deeply involved in Defoe as a writer and thinker, annotating *Serious Reflections* had many scholarly pleasures.

I completed my annotations before the work of G. A. Starr appeared in the edition published by Pickering and Chatto. Starr had always been thoroughly attuned to Defoe's religious thought, and much of Defoe's text was involved with the religious controversies of his time. Shortly thereafter, Starr staked a claim that Defoe was the author of *Christianity Not as Old as the Creation* (1730)—a work he demonstrates is unquestionably written by Defoe, once more showing how well Starr understands Defoe's religious position in the 1720s. I regarded Starr's contribution as an opportunity to enrich my own research, to build on what I knew about Defoe's text. The result is, I believe, certainly better than my original annotations and, in the end, even better than Starr's excellent work. The experience was something like working with Dryden's Shakespeare imitations, at least the Shakespeare part—an encounter with excellent minds commenting on complex texts. Much as I do, Starr regards Defoe as an important writer and a complicated thinker, and comments at length on Defoe's musings over religious matters. Since a large part of *Serious Reflections* involved Defoe's encounter with the religious controversies of his time, Starr's knowledge was invaluable and complemented my own.

This was not a matter of plagiarizing Starr's notes but rather of doing what annotators are supposed to be doing—passing on knowledge to future scholars. This is what the scholars of my generation were taught to do. When I arrived at Oxford in 1955, I was delighted to discover that that great student of early seventeenth-century poetry Herbert Grierson was still working on scholarly problems into his nineties. At the beginning of the twentieth century, he had returned the "metaphysical poets" to their original status as brilliant improvisators in creating complex, thoughtful verse and in the process had succeeded in influencing the shape of modern poetry. By these means he had gained considerable fame himself. Such fame—the fame of a brilliant scholar—is unlikely for those producing volumes within multivolume editions; admittedly working on large editions has its drawbacks, all that thought and labor for an edition that might, in the end, be listed in catalogues under the names of the general editors rather than those of the editors of individual volumes.[16] When a young scholar asked me why I had bothered to spend my time in this way, I answered that for the scholars of my time, this was what we thought we were supposed to be doing. I confessed that for me there were always large ideas that intrigued me and that I felt needed to be worked out, a need satisfied through writing separate monographs and essays. But having contributed to the totality of knowledge about past literature through writing annotations? I could hardly express regret about that.

NOTES

1. See Maximillian E. Novak, "Elkanah Settle's Attacks on Thomas Shadwell and the Authorship of the 'Operatic *Tempest*,'" *Notes and Queries* 15 (1968): 263–65.

2. Scholars working in the English Renaissance will sometimes ascribe the adaptation solely to Davenant. Dryden states that Davenant suggested adding the notion of a man who had never seen a woman and that the "Comical parts of the Saylors were also his invention and for the most part his writing, as you will easily tell by the style." He was trying to compliment the recently deceased Davenant in the effusive manner of the age, but it is also clear that Dryden intended it to be understood that he did most of the rewriting of Shakespeare's play, even some of the low comedy that was Davenant's specialty. He also seems to suggest that he was fully capable of imitating Davenant's "style." See John Dryden, *The Works of John Dryden*, vol. 10, ed. Maximillian E. Novak and George Robert Guffey (Berkeley: University of California Press, 1970), 4.

3. At the time the theory of the curative powers of weapon salve was associated with the advocacy of Sir Kenelm Digby.

4. *A New Variorum Edition of Shakespeare*, ed. H. H. Furness, 11th ed. (Philadelphia: J. B. Lippincott, ca. 1892).

5. *The Tempest*, ed. Frank Kermode (London: Methuen, 1975).

6. Hazelton Spencer, *Shakespeare Improved* (Cambridge, MA: Harvard University Press, 1927).

7. This volume was part of the Regents drama series, published by University of Nebraska Press in 1976.

8. See Dryden's manuscript comments, *Heads of an Answer to Rymer*, in *Works*, 17:185–98.

9. See especially Dryden, *Works*, vol. 13, ed. Maximillian E. Novak and Alan Roper (Berkeley: University of California Press, 1985), 542–45.

10. Maximillian E. Novak, *Realism, Myth, and History in Defoe's Fiction* (Lincoln: University of Nebraska Press, 1983).

11. Southern Illinois University Press, which had agreed to publish the Defoe edition, bowed out, and after a brief expression of interest so did the University of California Press.

12. For an example of the extraordinary inventiveness and careful scholarship that Alan Roper brought to writing annotations, see his annotations to the John Dryden–Nathaniel Lee *Oedipus* in volume 13 of Dryden's *Works*.

13. Maximillian E. Novak, ed., *The Age of Projects* (Toronto: Toronto University Press, 2008).

14. Daniel Defoe, *An Essay upon Projects*, ed. Joyce Kennedy, Michael Seidel, and Maximillian E. Novak (New York: AMS Press, 1999).

15. Stephen appears to have been prejudiced in his view of Defoe by the latter's business interests. As editor of the *Dictionary of National Biography*, he excluded those whose fame depended on having made their fortunes as businessmen. For his essay, "Defoe's Novels," originally written in 1864, see *Hours in a Library*, 3 vols. (London: John Murray, 1917), 1:1–43.

16. For example, in footnotes and bibliographies, the *Works* of Dryden published by the University of California Press is usually accredited to H. T. Swedenberg, omitting the names of dozens of individual editors.

CHAPTER 3

ঌ Annotation in Scholarly Editions of Plays
Problems, Options, and Principles

Robert D. Hume

Compared with the mountainous heap of books and articles about establishing the texts of seventeenth- and eighteenth-century plays, poems, and novels that has accumulated over the last century or so, precious little ink has been spilt on the subject of how those texts should be introduced and annotated, although many sensible suggestions have been made in now-ancient articles by Arthur Friedman and Martin Battestin.[1] Friedman, for example, distinguishes between "notes of recovery" and "explanatory notes." The former supply information presumably known to the original audience but not to the present-day reader; the latter "attempt to make a work more intelligible by showing its relationship to earlier works" (118). Battestin endorses that distinction and agrees that insofar as possible the sources cited should be contemporaneous with the text being edited. He also makes some useful points concerning the "nature" of the text at issue, and the particular interests of the annotator. In the last forty years, however, precious little has been published in this realm, and a survey of some sixteen major editions of playwrights since the appearance of William Smith Clark's *Orrery* in 1937 suggests that if there are "principles" on which editions of long eighteenth-century plays should be annotated, they are not widely understood and applied. For a list of the editions, see the appendix.

I see plays as a special case, radically different in several ways from poetry or fiction. If written for performance, they involve the editor/annotator in

42 | Notes on Footnotes

issues of physical milieu (that is, the wing-and-shutter changeable scenery theater totally dominant in professional theater in England from 1661 until well into the nineteenth century). Other issues include staging, scenery, props, costume, and music. Perhaps most crucially, plays from this period demand attention to the original cast, and what the identity of the performers can tell us about the designed impact of the original production. In trying, then, to lay down some suggestions and guidelines for annotators, I want to address six distinct issues. First, the need to supply basic annotation of the content of the text itself. Second, the problem of addressing "external" and "performance" matters. Third, to demonstrate the need for very different emphasis and focus from author to author and play to play. Fourth, to consider the coordination of introductions with "explanatory notes" and material that does not fit comfortably into them. Fifth, to point out some cases that require special handling. And finally, sixth, to suggest a guiding principle of sorts.

(1) Internal annotation of text. At the most basic level, an annotator needs to explain the meaning of obsolete words and words that have changed meaning over time—what Friedman calls "notes of recovery." This can be more contentious than one might think. Battestin objects point-blank to reporting an *OED* definition: "Notes such as these in a definitive edition serve only to clutter the page and to betray the editor's pedantry, not to say his condescension toward his readers" (6). I completely disagree. The reader who knows the historical meaning need not look at the note, but the reader who needs it cannot be expected to be consulting the *OED* every few pages, let alone oftener. Moreover, not everyone has free online access to that resource. Reporting a brief gist of the *OED* definition saves many readers a huge amount of time and trouble, even if they do have ready access.

Let me indicate some of the kinds of explanatory annotation that may be needed beyond meanings of words. Reference to named persons (living or dead) should be illuminated with a brief identification. "'Tis I, *John Lacy*, have reform'd your Stage" in the prologue to Buckingham's *The Rehearsal* needs a note explaining that Lacy was a playwright and a major comic actor of the 1660s and 1670s who created the role of the ridiculous playwright Bayes (Dryden) in Buckingham's play. Allusions of many kinds need to be identified. In the same prologue, "A Posie made of Weeds instead of Flowers" recalls a passage in George Gascoigne's preface to his *Posies* (1575), and "King Cambyses vain" needs to be associated both with Falstaff's speech in II.v. of Shakespeare's *1 Henry IV* and with Elkanah Settle's recent play *Cambyses King of Persia* (1671)—annotating these allusions provides very necessary information.

Annotation in Scholarly Editions of Plays | 43

History of ideas: in act III of Congreve's *Love for Love*, Scandal says "*Solomon* was wise, but how?—by his Judgment in Astrology—So says *Pineda* in his Third Book and Eighth Chapter." Herbert Davis does supply a note: "A Spanish Jesuit, who wrote a commentary on Solomon, 1609" (267). This is helpful, but barest bones; D. F. McKenzie offers the reader 180 words on Juan de Pineda (1558–1637), quoting Sir Thomas Browne on his erudition and reporting Congreve's citation of him and Jeremy Collier's riposte to Congreve (1:531).

Social customs, allusions to dress, and the like: near the end of act I of Congreve's *Love for Love* there is a passing allusion to "*Steinkirk* Cravats." Herbert Davis offers a helpful bare-bones explanation: "Casually tied muslin neckcloth, named after the battle of Steenkirk, in 1692, where the French officers had no time to tie them properly."[2]

Law: for example, in V.ii. of Wycherley's *The Plain-Dealer*, the Widow Blackacre responds to Freeman's attempt to blackmail her into matrimony with a protest: "O stay, Sir, can you be so cruel as to . . . put it out of my power to sue in my own name. Matrimony, to a Woman, worse than Excommunication, in depriving her of the benefit of the Law" (*Plays*, ed. Friedman, 501). Rather than marry him, she offers to pay his debts and secure him "an Annuity of Three hundred pounds a Year." This passage is a crucial key to her litigious character. Of seven twentieth-century editions on my bookshelves, only *one* annotates this passage: "wives 'are wholly . . . at the Will and Disposition of the Husband. . . . The Wife can make no Contract without her Husbands consent, and in Law-Matters *Sine viro respondere non potest.*'"[3]

Special emphasis on the value of money is often needful. Present-day inflation means that then/now calculations shift every year. A less obvious but enormous problem is the basis chosen for equivalency calculation. Measuring-Worth.com is a serious tool operated by highly respected economists, but for the buying power of £100 in 1707 as of 2018 it offers four very different measures. The "retail price index" value calculates to £16,530, "labor value" to £209,600, "income value" to £275,100, and "economic share" to £2,681,000. The "labor value" is more than 12 times the RPI figure; the "economic share," fully 162 times the RPI figure. No single multiplier yields a meaningful equivalency for all goods or services. I have argued elsewhere that for a variety of goods and services a multiplier of anywhere from 100 to 700 is common, though the figure can go as high as 1200.[4]

Consider a particular case, Farquhar's *The Beaux Stratagem* (1707). Mrs. Sullen and her sister Dorinda have marriage portions of £10,000 (2:173, 216).[5] By my multipliers this amounts to somewhere between £2,000,000 and

£3,000,000 in present-day buying power.[6] Mr. Sullen's £3000 annual income would amount to somewhere between £600,000 and £900,000 today by my reckoning (II, 222). The £2000 that Cherry has in her possession and that Archer thinks might be spent in a "Year or two" (2:182–83) would have buying power of £400,000 to £600,000. The guineas given to servants as tips at 2:209 and 214 would now be worth something like £210–£315 each. If we do not understand the magnitude of a guinea, we miss Farquhar's point: his fortune hunters are throwing money around to make an impression. Excellent as the Kenny edition is, it offers no help whatever with these sums. It is also blank on two cruxes of some importance. At 2:211–12 Foigard bribes Gipsey with "twenty *Lewidores*." At this point we should have been given a note explaining "Louis d'or" and its value.[7] A far worse problem occurs at 2:166–67, where Kenny blindly follows a corrupt text. Explaining the adventurers' circumstances, Archer says, "let me tell you, besides Thousand, that this Two hundred Pound, with the experience that we are now Masters of, is a better Estate than the Ten we have spent." That two younger brothers should have had £10,000 to spend is wildly implausible.[8]

A very different problem, and not a tidy one, is represented by playscripts that are adaptations of earlier plays. This is a major issue with several of Aphra Behn's plays, and indeed many plays of the period are far from being original compositions. Should this merely be reported in a headnote or an appendix with a few examples of what is retained, what is changed, and what is added? Kenny did this with Farquhar's *The Inconstant* (1702), based on Fletcher's *Wild Goose Chase* (1621? pub. 1652). Alternatively, should deleted or drastically rewritten material be printed in footnotes or endnotes, as Harold Love and I did for the first three acts of Buckingham's version of *The Chances* (perf. 1664, pub. 1682), a reworking of Fletcher's original play of circa 1617 (pub. 1647)? To do what we did can be immensely helpful in allowing readers to see just how drastic the additions and deletions can be, although putting deleted material in the text (rather than in endnotes) can be very distracting.[9] In my view, how much to represent of the source play and whether the material goes in footnotes or endnotes has to be a judgment call, case by case.

(2) External and performance issues.[10] I want to insist very bluntly that one of the most critical functions of annotation of plays is to assist present-day readers in understanding the impact of casting on performance. Playwrights, especially professional playwrights, were usually consulted about the casting of their plays. Indeed, they very often wrote with particular members of a company in mind, as Garrick writes in a letter of 1775.[11] Allowing the

playwright significant say in casting appears to have been long-standing practice, particularly for experienced playwrights.

Consequently, the original cast very often sheds important light on the impact the playwright hoped the play would have in performance. Consider Horner in Wycherley's *The Country-Wife* (1675), about whom twentieth-century critics disagreed quite wildly.[12] Back in 1913 John Palmer saw the play as a comic romp unconnected to reality. In 1959, Norman Holland saw Harcourt and Alithea as a moral "right way" and Horner as a "wrong way," but that same year C. D. Cecil declared the play a comic celebration of a libertine ideal. In 1965, Rose Zimbardo read the play as a harsh and systematic satire on lust; a decade later, Anthony Kaufman saw Horner as psychologically sick, a latent homosexual whose womanizing is a neurotic compulsion. In 1970, Virginia Ogden Birdsall proclaimed the play an argument for the virtues of sexual liberation, with Horner as a representation of the "élan vital" and "the life force triumphant," "a wholly positive and creative comic hero . . . squarely on the side of health, of freedom, and . . . of honesty." Little consensus has emerged in the thirty-five years that have passed since Milhous and Hume surveyed this chaotic critical muddle.

I have seen the play performed with the great fornicator played as an eighteen-year-old fun-loving scamp; as a thirty-five-year-old hard-boiled libertine who has been seducing and abandoning women since puberty and will clearly go on doing so as long as he retains his sexual vigor; and as a fat, bald, greasy whoremonger who is seducing manifestly unattractive women. What was spoken was what the printed page shows, but its impact varied enormously with the casting of key parts. The original Horner was Charles Hart, who was fifty in 1675 but still playing lead roles in tragedies and the male half of the "gay couple" made famous in his pairing with Nell Gwyn in the later 1660s.[13] Contemplating the roles he played, and remembering Wycherley's own libertine life, I see no way to argue plausibly that *The Country-Wife* was designed as a satire on libertinism. Moreover, his extended mockery of female outrage about the play does not suggest that the original audience thought it was seeing a satire on Horner and his sex life.[14] Charles Hart played heroic parts and dashing libertines, and his being cast as Horner needs to be a major part of any latter-day assessment of how Wycherley understood his play.[15]

My second case concerns Farquhar's *The Beaux Stratagem*. Modern productions I have seen all presented the play as a jolly romp. But Farquhar appears to have been unhappily married, and the 1707 text contains substantive allusions to Milton's *The Doctrine and Discipline of Divorce* (1643; expanded 2nd ed. 1644).[16] As Kenny notes in her introduction, major deletions occurred even during the first run (Count Bellair disappears), and the textual history of the play during the eighteenth century reveals increasing cuts in the marital discord material. The first edition text is decidedly darker, and much depends on how Mr. Sullen is cast.[17] He is described in the dramatis personæ as "A Country Blockhead, brutal to his Wife," and he is, of course, a very rich man. To cast one of the company clowns (for example, William Bullock) as Sullen might have seemed incongruous, but Benjamin Johnson, Francis Leigh, or Richard Estcourt could have done well in a comic production concept. In fact, the role of Sullen was created not by a clown or lightweight comic actor, but rather by the formidable John Verbruggen. One of his fortes was warrior types and kings, in such title roles as Southerne's *Oroonoko* and Rochester's *Valentinian*, along with Bajazet in Rowe's *Tamerlane* and Alexander in Lee's *The Rival Queens*. He acted Iago against Betterton's Othello. For such a man to communicate "brutal to his Wife" would *not* be comic. To understand *The Beaux Stratagem* as Farquhar conceived it, one *must* picture Sullen as large, tough, and potentially violent, not as a harmless country buffoon. Obviously, that is not the only way the play can be staged (and it may hardly ever have been), but an interpreter needs to understand what Farquhar imagined when he wrote it.

The near-universal failure of even major scholarly editions of plays to offer basic help in the comprehension of the actors' "lines" and the importance of particular performers to the meaning and impact of the plays in performance is shocking. Of course, most of the people who do heavy-duty editing of plays are from departments of "English," not "Theater."

We are direly lacking casting information for Beaumont and Fletcher and their contemporaries. By the 1670s most first editions of plays do identify at least the performers of principal roles. Where we have cast information, we are remiss if we do not use it. As an example of variant possibilities, let me offer Congreve's *Love for Love* (1695).[18] A "humours" production amuses us with a gallery of fools and a pro forma outwitting plot, topped off with an outrageously romantic finale verging on burlesque. Alternatively, a "romance" production presents more believable people. We can enjoy the wit and humor, but the focus of the production is ultimately on Angelica's "test" of Valentine. Milhous and Hume offer substantially different casts for the two production concepts (283) but suggest that the actual 1695 production was something of a mélange because the actors' rebellion of December 1694 broke up the United Company, for which Congreve had written the play. Fewer than half the parts in either of our hypothetical production concepts were cast that way in the actual

Lincoln's Inn Fields production of April 1695. I very much doubt that the impact of that production was what had been in Congreve's mind's eye when he drafted the play. My point is that envisioning the impact of various casting possibilities, actual and hypothetical, helps us visualize very different production concepts and impacts.

(3) Different play texts may need radically different notes and ratios of annotation to text. A prime example is the difference between Wycherley and Congreve. They have often been viewed as closely related, coupled with Etherege as the foremost practitioners of "the Restoration comedy of wit."[19] All three are in fact quite atypical in comparison with many dozens of comedies of the 1670s and 1690s, and the comedies of those decades are seriously distorted when we read them under the delusion that they are essentially similar products of the same period.[20]

As a crude measure of annotation intensity and depth, I have measured in centimeters the amount of vertical space devoted to introductory matter, text of play, and explanatory annotation (but ignoring textual apparatus) in three of the editions detailed in the appendix—the Davis edition of Congreve, the Friedman edition of Wycherley, and the McKenzie edition of Congreve that replaced Davis in 2011. I must emphasize the fact that what matters in this comparison is the *relative proportion* of editorial matter in each edition, *not* the comparative totals in centimeters, which are, of course, affected by type size and leading. The Davis edition of *Love for Love* occupies (exclusive of textual apparatus) some 2052 centimeters of vertical space: 48 of introduction (2.3 percent), 1943.5 of play text (94.7 percent), and 60.5 of explanatory annotation (2.9 percent). Fifty-five of 108 pages contain *no* explanatory footnotes; the notes provided are usually only one or two lines. For its day, the Davis edition was not a bad one, though its text and textual apparatus were not up to the Greg-Bowers standard.[21] A little more than a decade later, Friedman's *Country-Wife* occupied 1823 centimeters of vertical space: 52 of introduction (about 3 percent), 1497.5 of play text (82 percent), and 273.5 of explanatory annotation (15 percent).

This comparison is even more to Friedman's advantage than the raw figures might suggest. Granting that he totally fails to address issues posed by the cast, there are very few aspects of the text that needed more explanatory annotation than he supplied. Wycherley has relatively few topical allusions; he was not a bookish man, and there is little complexity in the ideas his characters express. Congreve, to the contrary, offers a vastly greater challenge to his editor. Fortunately, D. F. McKenzie was able and willing to rise to that challenge (with a vast amount of added help from Christine Ferdinand, who spent more than a decade completing the edition and getting it through press). In the McKenzie *Works* (2011), *Love for Love* has a text running to 2265 centimeters, with an introduction of 120 centimeters, explanatory notes of 616 centimeters, and a twenty-one-page account of "Early Performers" running to another 340 centimeters. Play text itself amounts to 67.8 percent of the total 3341 centimeters, the introduction to about 3.6 percent, explanatory annotation to 8.4 percent, and the account of performers to 10.2 percent. Congreve was a highly cultured, erudite, widely read man. Had Wycherley undertaken the task of writing *Love for Love* it would not have started with "Valentine *in his Chamber Reading...* *Several Books upon the Table*" and advising Jeremy that "*Epictetus...* is a Feast for an Emperor... feast your Mind, and mortifie your Flesh; Read, and take your Nourishment in at your Eyes; shut up your Mouth, and chew the Cud of Understanding. So *Epictetus* advises." Comparison of McKenzie's vastly erudite attention to the intellectual contexts of Congreve's texts with Davis's occasional and minimal identifications is sobering. For example, consider a passing allusion in act III to "the naked Prince." Davis supplies three lines quoted from the Montague Summers edition (1923, 257); McKenzie supplies 174 words and a good deal of context, with citations of multiple sources of commentary and a reference in Southerne's *The Maid's Last Prayer* (1:527). I cannot imagine that McKenzie would have had any interest in tackling an edition of Wycherley. Conversely, I see no way Friedman could have attempted to do with Congreve what McKenzie triumphantly succeeded in doing. In annotative terms, the demands posed by Congreve's intellectual context exceed Wycherley's by several orders of magnitude.

Exceptional intellectual range on the part of the playwright is not a common problem in long eighteenth-century drama. Congreve is a unique case. Dryden has an uncommon allusional range that has been more or less successfully addressed in the annotations for most of the California Dryden volumes. A vastly more common problem is satisfactory presentation of source materials, most especially when the source is an earlier play. "Originality" in story, ideas, and words becomes increasingly important between the mid-seventeenth century and the end of the eighteenth.[22] As early as 1671 Dryden complains that he is "tax'd with stealing" all his plays, replying that "'Tis true, that where ever I have lik'd any story in a Romance, Novel, or foreign Play, I have made no difficulty, nor ever shall, to take the foundation of it, to build it up, and to make it proper for the *English* Stage."[23] Aphra Behn is a prime example of a playwright whose modus operandi is heavily adaptive. She had no hesitation in drawing directly from published English playwrights, taking over quite a lot of speech as well as plot design and characters.[24]

What are the obligations of the editor of a work "appropriated" and significantly rewritten or added to? Merely to mention the fact, leaving investigation and collation to readers, seems unhelpful. The "nature" of the use(s) of the source text or texts should be explained, as should the rationale that appears to underlie the excision or addition of various materials. In her endnote annotation of Farquhar's *The Inconstant* (1702), an adaptation of Fletcher's *The Wild Goose Chase* (1621? pub. 1652), Shirley Kenny prints numerous bits and passages from the original to allow readers to evaluate for themselves how Farquhar has both made use of and departed from his source. The endnote placement does not make comparison easy, but some of the passages are long enough to devour too much of too many pages of text. However, if most of the alterations are merely words or phrases, they can be printed at the bottom of the page of text, which is what Harold Love and I did with Buckingham's version of *The Chances* (1664; pub. 1682), an alteration of Fletcher's play (1617? pub. 1647). "A Note on the Presentation of the Text" explains the "somewhat unusual format adopted in this edition. Our main text presents the Buckingham version as it was first published in 1682. At the bottoms of pages we have printed variant readings in the 'Beaumont and Fletcher' Folio edition of 1647 (Buckingham's source), including some passages *in extenso* that were drastically rewritten. The reader may thus see exactly how Buckingham altered the original play. The source notes cease at the end of act III because the last two acts are independent of Fletcher" (*Buckingham*, 1:39). We followed a similar policy in handling excisions and rewritten passages in Buckingham's (?) *The Restauration*, where some notes occupy as much as a page and a half of small type, actually interrupting the continuity of the Buckingham text (e.g., 1:488–90).[25]

In my view, no general rule can be posited about how best to handle the explanation and presentation of a play's relationship to its source(s). In a case like Buckingham's *Chances*, the relationship changes quite drastically at the end of act III. The editor's object ought to be to make clear the nature of the relationship: How much material is retained essentially unchanged? How much is cut, how much is added by the adapter, and what can we deduce about the adapter's dramaturgical, moral, political, aesthetic, or topical motives? Of course, one does not have to agree with the adapter's motives or choices. Few critics have had kind words for Nahum Tate's *King Lear* (1680), but we should remember that Samuel Johnson found the death of Cordelia unendurable and preferred Tate's happy ending. We are free to differ, but we should recognize that there was a rational basis for what Tate did to Shakespeare's play.

(4) Part of the logic of explanatory annotation depends on how it is conceived in relation to introductory matter and backmatter. Some readers will faithfully slog through every page of a long introduction. Others will jump past it and (perhaps) return to it after reading the whole of the play. Others will simply ignore all introductory matter. Footnotes are more often and more easily consulted than endnotes, but a plethora of footnotes can create a thin trickle of text atop a massive and distracting foundation of explanation and documentation. Explanatory annotation on the heroic scale of McKenzie's *Congreve* or the Hume-Love Buckingham *Rehearsal* really must be supplied in endnotes. The Twickenham *Pope*, splendid edition though it was for its day, is notoriously footnote-heavy. The general editors of the Cambridge edition of Behn are encouraging generous annotation concisely delivered. Where a third of a page (let alone more) is devoted to explanatory annotation, readers lose all momentum if they are constantly jumping from the author's text to seek edification supplied by the editor. The disruption is even more severe if readers must turn to the back of the book. Should endnotes be signaled in the text, so readers know that "something" will be available some dozens or hundreds of pages further on? In *Buckingham* we give no signal on the page; a reader must turn to the end matter to see if help is provided. In a heavily annotated text, the probability is quickly established that readers will find help in the endnotes. If endnotes are merely occasional, then probably a footnote number (or some signal indicating a note elsewhere) is in order.

Sometimes seriously needed annotation just cannot be reduced to reasonably sized footnotes. There are two obvious solutions, both of which can be employed in the same edition. Whether the introduction precedes the play (as in the Hume-Love *Buckingham*) or is tucked in before the explanatory endnotes (as in the McKenzie *Congreve*), a one-line note can direct the reader to any extended discussion of issues raised in the introductory commentary. This is frequently the case in the Cambridge *Behn* and seems to be working well. A reader who has skipped the introduction and jumped straight into the text can turn back to the page indicated and get help. Alternatively, if the text required many relatively short footnotes, but also some alarmingly or impossibly long ones, a one-line footnote directing readers to a bulky endnote might be the best solution. No law says you cannot have both.[26]

(5) Occasionally, special cases arise. I offer "Buckingham's" *The Rehearsal* (1671; pub. 1672) as a notable example. It was of course a committee enterprise

in which Buckingham's role remains essentially speculative. The play is an exuberant burlesque satire on new plays in the London theaters' repertories after 1660, reportedly started before the closure of the theaters by plague in June 1665, but not brought to the stage until December 1671. It was published without authorial ascription and with no paratext (dedication, cast, and the like), though it does include an anonymous prologue and epilogue. A third edition appeared in 1675, adding numerous hits at new plays from the previous four years, though awkwardly integrated. Whether Buckingham or any of his helpers took part in concocting these additions we have no way to determine. In several respects, then, *The Rehearsal* presents an editor with unique challenges.

In our headnote, Harold Love and I devoted more than a thousand words to our "Principles of Annotation," opening our explanation by noting that "In annotating *The Rehearsal* our object has been to provide the reader with as much assistance as we can in identifying satiric hits and possible hits while not simply burying the text in a flood of remote parallels" (1:392). We started from the twenty-four-page *Key to the Rehearsal* that was published in 1704 and reprinted in the second volume of "Buckingham's" *Miscellaneous Works* of 1704–5, which catalogues numerous passages attacked in sixteen contemporary plays. Drawing a line between what appear to be direct allusions to specific passages in other plays and loose parallels cannot be done with complete confidence. Ultimately, however, we supplied a list of ninety titles cited in our annotations and identified nine of them as the principal and most obvious targets (1:626–28).

Major points that needed to be covered in our introduction included questions of authorship and collaboration, literary targets, political targets, the addenda of 1675, a stage history spanning fully a century (Garrick played the role of Bayes ninety times between 1742 and 1772), reception, and influence. Introduction, play text, and explanatory apparatus ran to a total of 190 pages. Of that total, 63 were introduction (33.2 percent), play text 58 pages (30.5 percent), and explanatory apparatus 69 pages (36.3 percent). These proportions are rather extraordinary, but necessary to supply the information needed by serious readers.[27] If anything, these figures understate the comparative proportions, since they ignore type size and leading.

"Political targets" proved a considerable complication. In his "Discourse concerning the Original and Progress of Satire" (1693), Dryden says, "I answer'd not the *Rehearsall*, because I knew the Author sate to himself when he drew the Picture, and was the very *Bays* of his own Farce: Because also I knew, that my Betters were more concern'd than I was in that Satire."[28] This passing comment was mostly ignored or occasionally puzzled over for nearly three centuries, but in 1974 George McFadden published a revolutionary rethinking of "Buckingham's" play.[29] The brown paper applied to Bayes's broken nose at the beginning of III.i. is illustrated in ways strikingly similar to the black nose patch affected by Buckingham's political rival and bête noire, Henry Bennet, Earl of Arlington. As McFadden and Margarita Stocker have demonstrated, if one looks beyond the blizzard of bits of literary ridicule and contemplates the content and implication of Bayes's fatuous play, there is much implicit commentary on the sorry state of England circa 1670. As we observed, "The ineffectiveness of the two-headed government, the court intrigues, and the swipes at military mismanagement add up to a picture of a kingdom in total disarray" (1:352). We also point out that the principal

> target of the literary ridicule [i.e., Dryden as Bayes] is a systematic embodiment of the Stuart kings' divine-right theory of monarchy. To rubbish Dryden was to lay waste to his propaganda on behalf of Charles II. Buckingham systematically builds a parallel between the State and Bayes's poetic kingdom, and the hostile commentary of Johnson and Smith on the latter applies equally to the former. Dryden's heroic plays, particularly *The Conquest of Granada*, represent "exempla" of the "political theory and action" that Buckingham wanted to attack: they therefore provide a perfect dual target in which one of the items attacked both invokes the other and provides camouflage. Bayes's play projects—on his part unintentionally—a mordant picture of chaos, incompetence, and instability. (1:352–53)

Buckingham's mockery of Dryden's rhymed heroic drama and silliness in many other plays may seem no more than spiteful ridicule and hijinks, "But if we look at the content of the mock-play and its relationship to current events and Stuart ideology, then perhaps we see a radically different enterprise."

Obviously, *The Rehearsal* remained popular for a century because of its exuberant ridicule of plays, almost all of which were forgotten in fairly short order. But in the context of 1665–85, *The Rehearsal* had potent, indeed toxic, political implications. In this case, the nonexplicit meaning was soon left behind. We should also be aware, however, that changing contexts can alter the way a play would have been understood by both performers and audience.

Thomas Otway's *Venice Preserv'd* (1682) provides a good example.[30] The play was staged in early 1682 in the aftermath of the Popish Plot and Exclusion Crisis. It was evidently seen as a Tory denunciation of Whig plotters, with the Earl of Shaftesbury pilloried as the senile foot-fetishist Antonio (a part of the action dropped early in the eighteenth century). Attempts to read the play as an allegorical representation of current political conflict (1678–82) have not been very convincing except to their proposers, and of course by 1685 the Whig-Tory parallels were essentially an historical irrelevancy. Given the enormous popularity of the play for more than the next century, topical application cannot have been all there was to it.

What a helpful annotator needs to explain to the reader is that with some relatively modest textual excisions, *Venice Preserv'd* can be (and has been) effectively performed post-1685 with at least five radically different production concepts featuring three different principals. Beyond the original topical Tory production, Aline Mackenzie Taylor points to no. 2, a "plaintive Jaffeir" tragedy such as Robert Wilks performed early in the eighteenth century. Taylor's no. 3 features Barton Booth's "violent Jaffeir." No. 4 features James Quin and Robert Bensley's Pierre as a republican idealist (an astonishingly far cry from 1682's Tory propaganda). In the Napoleonic era throes of 1795, this viewpoint was anathema, and the Lord Chamberlain banned the play—which led to an immediate and astonishing reversal in which in no. 5 Pierre becomes a traitorous villain. Finally, no. 6 makes the play a pathetic vehicle that features the sufferings of Belvidera. This was certainly the direction in which Sarah Siddons took the play toward the end of the eighteenth century—and quite possibly the way Elizabeth Barry tilted the original production of 1682. This wildly varied and sharply contradictory set of production concepts is a valuable reminder that a great deal can depend on casting and direction.[31] My point, very simply, is that one of the duties of an editor of dramatic texts with varied stage histories is to help latter-day readers understand the sometimes radically different performance potentialities in the text at issue. With very little textual adjustment, *Venice Preserv'd* has functioned effectively as a biting defense of authoritarian government but also as a strident call for rebellion against that authority. Whether Otway fully "intended" either of those meanings I am personally inclined to doubt. My sense of Otway's *Weltanschauung* is one of profound gloom and negativity. If I were designing a production concept for *Venice Preserv'd*, I would stress corruption and despair.[32]

(6) For me, the takeaway seems very clear. Any "one size fits all" principle of annotation cannot apply. Writers vary enormously in terms of the kinds of annotation required to make sense of their plays. Even plays by the same author can place utterly different demands on the annotator. *The Rehearsal* absolutely needs the numerous and bulky footnotes that consume fully 36 percent of the Hume-Love edition's vertical space, but *The Chances* can be very satisfactorily dealt with at about 10 percent. The intellectual richness of Congreve's texts requires extensive and lengthy exegeses of allusions and sources, where Wycherley's bouncy and effective (if superficial) plays make relatively minimal and obvious demands on the annotator. Compare any few pages of the Davis Congreve with McKenzie's, and one instantly sees that Davis was barely getting the job done.

The realm in which editors' failure has been most dire is in analyzing the significance of casting for comprehending the designed impact of these plays. The original cast will in a high percentage of cases reflect the aims and preferences of the playwright. Later casts often reflect changed or evolving notions of what the production is supposed to communicate to its audience. Until recently, addressing this issue was by no means a simple matter, but Highfill, Burnim, and Langhans's *Biographical Dictionary* radically changed that state of affairs.[33] In sixteen volumes running to 7052 double-column pages, the authors supply seriously researched (if, alas, undocumented) accounts of all theater-related performers and other personnel for the whole of our period. In most cases, one can get a rapid snapshot of the parts each performer took. This is an enormous time-saver for anyone attempting to reconstruct the performance concept and impact of many hundreds of now little-known plays. Anyone editing a performed play from 1660–1800 has an obligation to inform the reader of the sorts of roles each named performer is recorded in, citing a substantial assortment of particular parts.[34] Another area in which improvement is needed is in annotating the musical aspects of drama. There is substantial song and dance in plays of this period, and a surprising amount of the music survives in print or manuscript. Two editions that have been exemplary in printing and explaining the music are McKenzie's *Congreve* and Thomas Lockwood's three volumes of plays by Fielding.[35]

If I were asked for a fundamental principle which an editor of long-eighteenth-century plays should abide by, it would be very simple: adopt a modus operandi which recognizes the enormous diversity of these plays, and apply "logic," not "rules."

Annotation in Scholarly Editions of Plays | 55

APPENDIX: CHRONOLOGICAL LIST OF SIXTEEN MAJOR EDITIONS OF
LONG-EIGHTEENTH-CENTURY ENGLISH PLAYWRIGHTS SINCE 1937*

The Dramatic Works of Roger Boyle Earl of Orrery. Edited by William Smith Clark II. 2 vols. Cambridge, MA: Harvard University Press, 1937.
The Works of Nathaniel Lee. Edited by Thomas B. Stroup and Arthur L. Cooke. 2 vols. New Brunswick, NJ: Scarecrow Press, 1954–55.
The California *Works of John Dryden*, vols. 8–16. Berkeley: University of California Press, 1962–96. On vol. 13 see review by Hume, *Theatre Survey* 28 (1987): 91–93.
The Complete Plays of William Congreve. Edited by Herbert Davis. Chicago: University of Chicago Press, 1967.
The Plays of Richard Steele. Edited by Shirley Strum Kenny. Oxford: Clarendon Press, 1971.
The Plays of William Wycherley. Edited by Arthur Friedman. Oxford: Clarendon Press, 1979. See Hume, "William Wycherley: Text, Life, Interpretation," *Modern Philology* 78 (1981): 399–415.
The Plays of David Garrick. Edited by Harry William Pedicord and Fredrick Louis Bergmann. 7 vols. Carbondale: Southern Illinois University Press, 1980–82. See reviews by Hume, in *Journal of English and Germanic Philology* 80 (1981): 578–81; 83 (1984): 130–32.
John Gay: Dramatic Works. Edited by John Fuller. 2 vols. Oxford: Clarendon Press, 1983. See review by Hume in *Journal of English and Germanic Philology* 84 (1985): 271–73.
The Works of Thomas Southerne. Edited by Robert Jordan and Harold Love. 2 vols. Oxford: Oxford University Press, 1988. See Hume, "The Importance of Thomas Southerne," *Modern Philology* 87 (1990): 275–90.
The Works of George Farquhar. Edited by Shirley Strum Kenny. 2 vols. Oxford: Clarendon Press, 1988. See review by Hume in *Philological Quarterly* 68 (1989): 378–82.
The Works of Aphra Behn. Edited by Janet Todd. Vols. 5–7. Columbus: Ohio University Press; London: Pickering & Chatto, 1996.
The Dramatic Works of George Lillo. Edited by James L. Steffensen. Oxford: Clarendon Press, 1993.
Henry Fielding. *Plays.* Edited by Thomas Lockwood. The Wesleyan Edition of the Works of Henry Fielding. 3 vols. Oxford: Clarendon, 2004–11. See Hume, "Fielding's *Plays* and the Completion of the Wesleyan Edition," review article in *Huntington Library Quarterly* 75 (2012): 447–63.
Plays, Poems, and Miscellaneous Writings Associated with George Villiers, Second Duke of Buckingham. Edited by Robert D. Hume and Harold Love. 2 vols. Oxford: Oxford University Press, 2007.
The Works of William Congreve. Edited by D. F. McKenzie and prepared for publication by C. Y. Ferdinand. 3 vols. Oxford: Oxford University Press, 2011.
The Plays and Poems of Nicholas Rowe. Stephen Bernard, general editor. Vols. 1–3 of 5. London: Routledge, 2017. Hume review forthcoming in *Scriblerian*.

*I have excluded twenty-eight fat volumes edited by Montague Summers: the *Works* of Behn (6 vols.; London: William Heinemann, 1915), Congreve (4 vols.; Soho: Nonesuch Press, 1923), Wycherley (4 vols.; Soho: Nonesuch Press, 1924), Otway (3 vols.; Soho: Nonesuch Press, 1926), Shadwell (5 vols.; London:

Fortune Press, 1927), and Dryden's *Dramatic Works* (6 vols.; London: Nonesuch Press, 1931–32). Textually, they cannot be taken seriously, but the annotation of all but Behn is extensive, learned, and helpful. Granting that he is quirky and self-indulgent, I insist that Summers be taken seriously by anyone dealing with these authors. He was theater- and performance-oriented, and his knowledge was encyclopedic and wide-ranging. His erratic documentation is infuriating, but much may be learned from his introductions and notes. The apparatus in the California Dryden would have been far better had the editors been willing to demean themselves to the extent of following Summers's leads.

NOTES

1. Arthur Friedman, "Principles of Historical Annotation in Critical Editions of Modern Texts," in *English Institute Annual 1941*, ed. Rudolf Kirk et al. (New York: Columbia University Press, 1942), 115–28; Martin C. Battestin, "A Rationale of Literary Annotation: The Example of Fielding's Novels," *Studies in Bibliography* 34 (1981): 1–23.

2. *The Complete Plays of William Congreve*, 234 (cited in appendix). The note in D. F. McKenzie's edition (also cited in appendix) runs to 167 words with reference to surviving pictures, including one of Congreve himself wearing such a cravat and similar allusions in plays by Durfey and Vanbrugh (1:515).

3. William Wycherley, *The Plain Dealer*, ed. James L. Smith, New Mermaids (London: Ernest Benn, 1979), 168 (citing Edward Chamberlayne, *Angliæ Notitia: or the Present Stage of England*, 2 vols. [1676]). I find no note of any kind on this passage in the Summers edition of 1924, the generally praiseworthy edition by Gerald Weales (1966), Leo Hughes's Regents Restoration Drama Series edition (1967), Peter Holland's *Plays of William Wycherley* (Cambridge: Cambridge University Press, 1981), or the Oxford World Classics edition by Peter Dixon (1996). Most regrettably, there is not a word of annotation in Arthur Friedman's still-standard Oxford edition of 1979.

4. See Robert D. Hume, "The Value of Money in Eighteenth-Century England: Incomes, Prices, Buying Power—and Some Problems in Cultural Economics," *Huntington Library Quarterly* 77, no. 4 (2014): 373–416.

5. Parenthetical page references are to the Kenny edition of Farquhar cited in appendix.

6. By way of comparison, I note that as of December 14, 2019, MeasuringWorth.com gives an RPI equivalence of £1,653,000 and a "labor value" equivalence of £20,960,000 for £10,000 in 1707. So my range starts significantly above their RPI calculation, but way below their "labor value."

7. French coin introduced by King Louis XIII in 1640. On basic gold coins in Europe in the seventeenth and eighteenth centuries, see John J. McCusker, *Money and Exchange in Europe and America, 1600–1775* (Chapel Hill: University of North Carolina Press, 1978), table 1.2 at 11. In 1707, the value in British currency would have been about 17s, so the bribe amounts to £17. This is a whopping sum of money at a time when average annual household income in England was about £40. That Foigard should command such a sum is definitely surprising.

8. Various editions between 1707 and 1988 presented this passage in six different ways. For an admirably sober corrective, see Alan Roper, "How Much Did Farquhar's Beaux Spend in London?," *Studies in Bibliography* 45 (1992): 105–12. Roper argues convincingly that the passage should read, "let me tell you, that this Two hundred Pound, besides the experience that we are now Masters of, is a better Estate than the Thousand we have spent" (110). Attention to the monstrous magnitude of £10,000 in 1707 should long ago have prompted a closer look at what is plainly a corrupt text.

9. For example, the fifty lines we print from Fletcher on pages 94 and 95 occupy fully a page and a quarter of those pages and restrict Buckingham's version to just six lines of page 94.

10. "Performance history" generally derives from the daily performance calendar, *The London Stage, 1660–1800*, ed. Emmett L. Avery et al., 11 vols. (Carbondale: Southern Illinois University Press, 1960–68 [i.e., 1970]). It has enormous virtues, but also dangerous pitfalls and inconsistencies from, in part, the abominably incompetent synoptic *Index* compiled by Ben Ross Schneider Jr. (1979) represents a hazard to unwary users. For an extensive history and analysis of this thirty-five-year enterprise, see all fifty-four thousand words of Robert D. Hume, "*The London Stage, 1660–1800*: A Short History, Retrospective Anatomy, and Projected Future," *Electronic British Library Journal* (forthcoming).

11. *The Private Correspondence of David Garrick*, 2 vols. (London: Henry Colburn and Richard Bentley, 1831–32), 2:31.

12. For a detailed discussion of the radical critical disagreements about the fundamental nature and aims of the play, see Judith Milhous and Robert D. Hume, *Producible Interpretation: Eight English Plays, 1675–1707* (Carbondale: Southern Illinois University Press, 1985), chap. 3.

13. Hart's many heroes include Almanzor in Dryden's *The Conquest of Granada*, Alexander in Lee's *The Rival Queens*, the title roles in Dryden's *Aureng-Zebe* and Chapman's *Bussy D'Ambois*, Marc Anthony in Dryden's *All for Love*, and Othello. His dashing rakes in gay couple plays include Celadon in Dryden's *Secret-Love*, Ranger in Wycherley's *Love in a Wood*, Don John in Buckingham's *The Chances*, Philidor in James Howard's *All Mistaken*, and Palamede in Dryden's *Marriage A-la-Mode*.

14. For Wycherley's ridicule of women's response to Horner and Wycherley's "filthy Play," see *The Plain-Dealer*, II.i. (410–12, in the Friedman edition cited in the appendix).

15. No notes or commentary on the performers in *The Country-Wife* are to be found in Summers's edition, 4 vols. (London: Nonesuch, 1924), nor in Weales's *Complete Plays* of 1966 (cited in the appendix), nor in Friedman's edition of the *Plays* of 1979 (cited in the appendix), nor in Holland's edition of the *Plays* (cited in note 3). Summers's failure to characterize the actors' "lines" and identify principal roles is particularly odd since he was very knowledgeable about the performers. Other editions that offer no help whatever with the performers are Thomas H. Fujimura's Regents edition of 1965 and Dixon's World's Classics edition of Wycherley's plays (Oxford: Oxford University Press, 1996). The Revels edition by David Cook and John Swannell (London: Methuen, 1975) does supply four pages in appendix B helpfully devoted to identifying the performers and specifying some characteristic roles, and James Ogden's New Mermaid edition, 2nd ed. (London: A. & C. Black, 1991), manages to be surprisingly helpful in a single page of small type.

16. See Kenny's introduction and notes to the play in her edition of the *Works* (cited in appendix), citing Martin A. Larson, "The Influence of Milton's Divorce Tracts on Farquhar's *Beaux' Stratagem*," *PMLA* 39 (1924): 174–78.

58 | Notes on Footnotes

17. For a detailed discussion of these issues, see Milhous and Hume, *Producible Interpretation*, chap. 10.

18. The following discussion draws on *Producible Interpretation*, chap. 9.

19. For example, in books of the 1950s that remained highly influential for decades, most notably Thomas H. Fujimura, *The Restoration Comedy of Wit* (Princeton: Princeton University Press, 1952), and Norman N. Holland, *The First Modern Comedies: The Significance of Etherege, Wycherley and Congreve* (Cambridge, MA: Harvard University Press, 1959).

20. A point first forcefully made by A. H. Scouten in "Notes Toward a History of Restoration Comedy," *Philological Quarterly* 45 (1966): 62–70, and developed at length in Robert D. Hume, *The Development of English Drama in the Late Seventeenth Century* (Oxford: Clarendon Press, 1976).

21. See the very fair review by Karl H. Klaus in *Philological Quarterly* 47, no. 3 (1968): 364–65.

22. The first major, systematic denunciation of "plagiaries" appears in Gerard Langbaine's 587-page *An Account of the English Dramatick Poets* (Oxford: Printed by L. L. for George West, and Henry Clements, 1691). The standard account of changing attitudes toward originality in playwriting is Paulina Kewes, *Authorship and Appropriation: Writing for the Stage in England, 1660–1710* (Oxford: Clarendon Press, 1998). Kewes extends her commanding overview to the end of the eighteenth century in "'[A] Play, which I presume to call *original*': Appropriation, Creative Genius, and Eighteenth-Century Playwriting," *Studies in the Literary Imagination* 34, no. 1 (2001): 17–47.

23. Preface to *An Evening's Love*, in *The Works of John Dryden*, vol. 10, ed. Maximillian E. Novak and George Robert Guffey (Berkeley: University of California Press, 1970), 210.

24. Some examples are *Abdelazer* (1676) from *Lust's Dominion* (1600); *I Rover* (1677) from Thomas Killigrew's *Thomaso* (pub. 1664); *The Debauchee* (1677) from Brome's *A Mad Couple Well Matched* (1637?–1639); and *The Revenge, or A Match in Newgate* (1680) from Marston's *The Dutch Courtesan* (1605).

25. The text was not published until the third edition of Buckingham's works in 1715. It may or may not have been performed in the 1680s.

26. As an example, I offer John Downes, *Roscius Anglicanus, or an Historical Review of the Stage* (1708), ed. Judith Milhous and Robert D. Hume (London: Society for Theatre Research, 1987). The 1708 original ran to 52 pages, liberally stuffed with names, titles, and particulars. Our edition runs to 28 pages of introduction, 110 pages of text with 400 footnotes, plus 8 pages devoted to 8 endnotes, a two-page appendix listing "Key Dates and Events," 3 pages of textual notes, and 40 pages of index. Of the 110 pages containing Downes's text, 62 are devoted half or more to footnotes.

27. By way of comparison with a more normal case, I note that our edition of Buckingham's *The Chances* ran to 130 pages, of which the introduction was 38 pages (28.4 percent), play text was 80 pages (59.7 percent), music for a song 3 pages (2.2 percent), and explanatory apparatus a mere 13 pages (9.7 percent).

28. *The Works of John Dryden*, vol. 4, *Poems 1693–1696*, ed. A. B. Chambers, William Frost, and Vinton A. Dearing (Berkeley: University of California Press, 1974), 8.

29. "Political Satire in *The Rehearsal*," *Yearbook of English Studies* 4 (1974): 120–28. McFadden's political reading was considerably deepened and extended by Margarita Stocker, "Political Allusion in *The Rehearsal*," *Philological Quarterly* 67 (1988): 11–35.

30. For an authoritative survey of the play's wildly varied productions from premiere into the nineteenth century, see Aline Mackenzie's appendix listing "Key Dates and Events," 3

pages of textual notes, and 40 pages of index. *Next to Shakespeare: Otway's Venice Preserv'd and The Orphan and Their History on the London Stage* (Durham: Duke University Press, 1950). For six radically different ways to perform the play, see Milhous and Hume, *Producible Interpretation*, chap. 6.

31. Phillip Harth, in "Political Interpretations of *Venice Preserv'd*," *Modern Philology* 85, no. 4 (1988): 345–62, argues that the play is much less centrally "political" than most critics have thought it, and points to its basis in "an actual historical event," as reported in Saint-Réal's *A Conspiracy of the Spaniards Against the State of Venice*, translated from French and published in London in 1675. This is a salutary caution. Harth is quite right that *Venice Preserv'd* is nothing like an allegory of current events and conflicts in London, and he was a scholar one did not lightly disagree with, but he had no interest in performance history and simply ignores what can be learned from reports of performance about the text's astonishing malleability in the first 125 years or so of its stage life.

32. For one of the best accounts of Otway ever published, see Thomas B. Stroup, "Otway's Bitter Pessimism," *Essays in English Literature of the Classical Period presented to Dougald MacMillan, Studies in Philology*, e.s., no. 4 (1967): 54–75. On the truly ugly, nasty world presented in Otway's three sour comedies (which have been condemned or ignored by almost all critics), see Hume, "Otway and the Comic Muse," *Studies in Philology* 73, no. 1 (1976): 87–116.

33. Philip H. Highfill Jr., Kalman A. Burnim, and Edward A. Langhans, *A Biographical Dictionary of Actors, Actresses, Musicians, Dancers, Managers, and Other Stage Personnel in London, 1660–1800*, 16 vols. (Carbondale: Southern Illinois University Press, 1973–93). Published in eight installments. For an extensive review of the first two volumes, see Hume, *Eighteenth-Century Studies* 8 (1975): 510–17.

34. Enormously helpful as the *Biographical Dictionary* is in this regard, it is not a panacea. After about 1670 we usually know the original principals from the dramatis personae in the first edition of the published text. From the autumn of 1705 almost all patent theater performances are advertised in newspaper bills, though not always with cast, let alone a complete cast. In most cases, there is no evidence of who performed what role on a particular night. Furthermore, the *Biographical Dictionary*'s listing of parts for each actor or actress is usually selective, and sometimes highly so. For example, of Thomas Betterton it indicates he acted "at least 120" roles (2:90), but Judith Milhous has documented "183 *certain roles*," 131 of which Betterton created. See Milhous, "An Annotated Census of Thomas Betterton's Roles, 1659–1710," *Theatre Notebook* 29, nos. 1–2 (1975): 33–43, 85–94. Given the gaps in our knowledge, Betterton's total was almost unquestionably significantly higher. And given the enormous range of parts he took, his taking a part does not necessarily help us characterize it. Nonetheless, for a great many performers knowledge of their "line" can give us a pretty good idea of how a part was conceived.

35. The editors of *The London Stage* did a fairly miserable job with music. Only Hogan's part 5 (1776–1800) cites Edith B. Schnapper's monumental *The British Union-Catalogue of Early Music Printed Before the Year 1801: A Record of the Holdings of over One Hundred Libraries Throughout the British Isles*, 2 vols. (London: Butterworths Scientific Publications, 1957). Bafflingly, no use was made of Cyrus Lawrence Day and Eleanore Boswell Murrie, *English Song-Books, 1651–1702: A Bibliography* (London: Printed for the Bibliographical Society at the University Press, Oxford, 1940). I have rarely seen these major resources cited in scholarship since 1970. Since then some very important works have been published; I note particularly Roger Fiske's monumental *English Theatre Music in the Eighteenth Century* (1973; 2nd ed.,

London: Oxford University Press, 1986), and Curtis A. Price's extremely valuable *Music in the Restoration Theatre: With a Catalogue of the Instrumental Music in the Plays 1665–1713* (Ann Arbor: UMI Research Press, 1979). Relatively little use has been made of either by editors of editions of plays. Day and Murrie have been splendidly continued by David Hunter in *Opera and Song Books Published in England, 1703–1726: A Descriptive Bibliography* (London: Bibliographical Society, 1997).

CHAPTER 4

ᔆ Annotating Topical Satire
The Case of Swift

Stephen Karian

Topical satire is possibly the most challenging genre to annotate. The contexts of a topical satire are highly particularized and often obscure. It might not be sufficient for an annotator to have general or even specific knowledge of events and perceptions of events during a particular year; truly understanding a topical satire may require an annotator to assign the satire's composition to a particular week and then reconstruct the relevant contexts for that week. A topical satire's obscurity exceeds the typical obscurity that surrounds works written centuries ago, as many topical satires were deliberately obscure. They were sometimes written for a select audience, and the identities of targets were often hidden out of fear of prosecution or other retaliation.

Topical satire blends fact, rumor, innuendo, and lies. Satirists distort and fabricate all the time. They are not historians, and their assertions should not be taken at face value. At the same time, topical satire almost always has some basis in fact, and it depends on that factual basis for its power to hurt its victims.[1] An entirely invented attack can be shrugged off more easily than one that is grounded, however tenuously, in some truth. When the factual basis of a satire can be reconstructed, the annotator should try to distinguish among true, false, and distorted charges.

Annotators must therefore immerse themselves in contemporaneous accounts to try to recapture a reading experience as close as possible to the time when the satire was written and circulated. That approach aligns with some of the most frequently offered guidance regarding the principles of scholarly annotation. One influential discussion defined "notes of recovery" that enable a modern reader to "read a work with something like the same understanding as the author's contemporaries for whom the work was originally intended."[2] That general principle has been invoked by others: "the aim of annotation is to reconstruct what a passage meant to the author and his first readers," "the principal duty of an annotator is to attempt to enable his contemporaries to read a book as its original audience read it," and "the explanatory notes should enable the reader to read with something of the knowledge and understanding of the original audience or audiences."[3]

Yet, as Ian Small has noted, "the concept of an author's original readership . . . needs to be handled with caution."[4] Small observed that this putative original readership often consisted of multiple readerships with varying levels of knowledge, and that literary works could be crafted to address such multiple readerships, which might entail some readers being intentionally left in the dark. These points are especially applicable to the annotation of topical satire, as contemporary readers did not necessarily have the requisite knowledge fully to understand a satire's references.[5] As a result, whatever traces such readers have left behind do not always reflect the author's intended meaning.

But that does not mean that such misreadings should be ignored by the annotator. D. F. McKenzie posited that "any history of the book . . . must be a history of misreadings," and this perspective is helpful for the annotator of topical satire.[6] False identifications, guesses, confusions of one individual with another—all of these provide insight into the contemporary reception of a topical satire. Citing such contemporaneous misreadings in a scholarly edition provides the best basis for a present-day reader to reconstruct the complex and various milieus within which the satire circulated.

To be sure, such evidence of contemporary reception is often difficult to locate. But the more heated the controversy that gave rise to the satire in question, the more likely that some record of its reception has survived. This evidence comes in various forms: textual variants in printed and manuscript sources; blank-filling and other contemporaneous annotation; contemporaneous commentary, both published and private; responses, which might appear in separate pamphlets, response poems, or periodicals; and contemporaneous discussions about similar topics, including the rumors and lies that played a role in the satire. This last category refers less to the reception of a particular satire and more to the discourse surrounding the topics explored in the satire. All this evidence, brought to bear in an organized, detailed, and concise way, can illuminate what was previously obscure, and in so doing, can help us appreciate why a particular satire was constructed the way it was.

To illustrate how some of the above points work in practice, I draw on my experience editing Jonathan Swift's topical satires with my collaborator James Woolley for a four-volume edition of Swift's complete poetry being published as part of the Cambridge Edition of the Works of Jonathan Swift. I should note at the outset that our work on this edition was a collaboration at every level, which means it is often difficult or even impossible to reconstruct where the work of one ended and that of the other began. For the two examples in this essay, I initiated the research, though the soon to be published results of that research are very much the product of our combined efforts. Both poems are topical satires Swift wrote in 1711–12, at the height of partisan debates over the War of the Spanish Succession: *The Windsor Prophecy* and *Toland's Invitation to Dismal*.

Given the particular challenges in annotating topical satire and given the paucity of commentary on this topic, my hope is that this essay, though grounded in only two poems by one satirist, will be more broadly useful. Those engaged in annotating topical satire should also consult particularly skillful works of criticism that reconstruct a satire's relevant contexts; such critical pieces can sometimes be more helpful than a previous editor's annotations.[7]

Swift wrote *The Windsor Prophecy* in late December 1711 at a precarious time for the Oxford ministry, which was trying to end the War of the Spanish Succession. Swift had just published *The Conduct of the Allies*, a major pamphlet promoting the ministry's peace policy, but he began to suspect that the Queen's support was wavering and that owing to the Duchess of Somerset's influence, the Queen was poised to remove Robert Harley, the Earl of Oxford, as Lord Treasurer. Seeking to discredit the Duchess, Swift wrote *The Windsor Prophecy*, which implicated her in the assassination of her second husband twenty-nine years earlier and suggested that she would poison Queen Anne. As it turned out, Swift's inflammatory poem was unnecessary. The Queen was fully committed to the peace and to Oxford, which incidentally shows how little knowledge Swift had about the inner workings of the court and ministry that he wrote in support of.

We know a great deal about the early circulation of *The Windsor Prophecy* thanks to Swift's nearly day-by-day account in the letters known as the *Journal to Stella*. Swift had planned to publish the poem on Christmas Day, but was warned off by Abigail Masham, one of his sources for court information. The day after Christmas he called on her and she persuaded him not to publish the poem. He wrote to the printer to prevent publication, though dozens of copies had been printed and given to friends. The poem was therefore printed but not published, that is, it was not made public through sale. But word about this scandalous satire must have gotten out. As Swift wrote with a note of pride, "'Tis an admirable good one, and people are mad for it."[8]

Annotating this poem poses numerous challenges. Written for a select audience and employing the fiction of being a recently discovered ancient document, it relies on knowledge of court gossip in December 1711 that was probably not available to many of Swift's contemporaries. Though scholarly commentary has clarified its various references, one puzzle surrounding *The Windsor Prophecy* has remained unsolved, namely how this poem relates to three other poems published around the same time with similar titles: *The Windsor Prophecy* (1712; Foxon P459), *The Windsor Prophecy, Found in a Marlborough Rock* (1711; Foxon W527–8), and *The Oxford Prophecy, Fore-telling the Late Sudden Change at C—t* (1711; not in Foxon, ESTC n042184).[9] Did these poems prompt and even inspire Swift? Are they responses to Swift's poem, and if so, what if anything do they reveal about the contemporary understanding of it? Were they part of a mini-genre that was popular at the time, and if so, why was it popular? As far as I am aware, these questions have not been previously asked. None of the three poems is mentioned in the editions of Swift's poems edited respectively by Harold Williams and Pat Rogers, and they are not discussed by the few commentators on Swift's *Windsor Prophecy*.[10] Explaining exactly how such apparently similar works relate to the topical satire being annotated is among the tasks that annotators of this genre should try to perform.

The place to begin is a careful reading of each "prophecy" poem in its original edition. Of the three poems, the one most like Swift's in appearance is *The Oxford Prophecy*, which survives in a single copy at Indiana University's Lilly Library, shelfmark BV5091.R4 O98. Similar to Swift's *Windsor Prophecy*, *The Oxford Prophecy* is a half-sheet edition with a brief prose statement before the poem and an imprint that contains the minimal information "*London*, Printed in the Year 1711." However, unlike Swift's *Windsor Prophecy*, *The Oxford Prophecy* does not use black letter, and it has three marginal glosses for what should be obvious references. The first line that refers to "Seventeen hundred . . . joyn'd to two Ones" is glossed as "1711," which seems unnecessary. "One Island . . . that appears to the sight, / From the Clifts that rise in it all beauteous and *White*" is glossed as "*Albion*." And "a Subject whose Name by the by, / Shall begin with an *H*, and shall end with a *y*" is glossed as "*Harley.*" It seems as if this poem is trying to imitate not only a printed edition of Swift's *Windsor Prophecy* but also a hand-annotated copy of it. Because these glosses are unlocking secrets that require no key, one is tempted to think that *The Oxford Prophecy* is parodying one of these annotated copies. Yet that hypothesis seems unlikely because the poem shares Swift's political perspective. More likely, this awkwardly written poem is a piece of hackwork by an unskilled propagandist.

The Oxford Prophecy must have been written after the composition of Swift's *Windsor Prophecy.* As shown in the *Journal to Stella*, Swift wrote his poem on December 23, 1711, before Marlborough was dismissed on December 30. The subtitle of *The Oxford Prophecy* states that it was written after "the late sudden Change at C[our]t," which must refer to that dismissal and quite likely to the anticipated dismissal of the Duke of Somerset as Master of the Horse; both men are alluded to near the end of the poem.

The Oxford Prophecy was reprinted in Dublin under the title *Marlborough Remov'd, or, The Down-fall of a Great Favourite. With a True List of all the New Promotions and Removals at Court* (1711–12; Foxon M106). This printing omits the prose preface and replaces it with a list of the successors of Marlborough and others as well as the names of the twelve new peers that Queen Anne created to ensure the success of her peace policy in the House of Lords. The new title clarifies the poem's occasion and removes any suggested connection to Swift's poem, which in any case was probably even less available in Dublin than in London (one edition of Swift's *Windsor Prophecy*, Foxon S941, was possibly printed in Dublin in early 1712). It seems fair to say that *The Oxford Prophecy* draws from Swift's *Windsor Prophecy* but only in the sense of continuing the same propaganda effort to support the peace. It uses Swift's poem as a model in only a superficial way.

The second of these poems, *The Windsor Prophecy* (1712; Foxon P459), also survives in a unique copy, British Library 1850.c.10 (19). It is not at all clear why the poem bears this title; it is a beast fable with some suggestion of a political application but is not at all prophetic. The fable describes a fig tree that had sheltered many birds but was damaged by a thunderstorm, causing the birds to flee. After the storm passes, some of the birds, including the turtledoves, return to the tree, but kites and other birds of prey take shelter in a neighboring oak and try to draw the others to join them. The turtledoves and their comrades refuse, indicating that they prefer their original home, the fig tree, where they will continue to live even if it is damaged. The general moral about steadfast loyalty is clear enough, though its application to the events of late 1711 is not.

The poem was in fact not written in 1711. It was first printed in 1708 with the title "The Way of the World" in William Pittis's collection *Aesop at Oxford: or, A Few Select Fables in Verse* (1709 [1708]; Foxon P422; advertised in the *Observator* on November 17, 1708). In that printing, the poem concludes with a verse moral lamenting that "Few . . . in our Days, / A Patriot in Disgrace will praise." The poem was reprinted as a half-sheet in 1710 under the title *A Tale of a Disbanded Courtier* (Foxon P460) with the moral (here called "Application") adapted to refer to the recent trial of the firebrand clergyman Henry Sacheverell.

So, a verse beast fable first published in 1708 under one title and reprinted in 1710 under another title was again reprinted in 1712, this time as *The Windsor Prophecy* and without the moral. Why this title was chosen in 1712 is not altogether clear; the poem's contents reveal no connection to Swift's poem or to its occasion. Most likely the notoriety surrounding Swift's poem exceeded its availability, because the poem was not widely published, and someone decided to capitalize on this unmet demand. In this respect, this *Windsor Prophecy*—I hesitate to refer to it as William Pittis's *Windsor Prophecy* since he probably did not authorize this title—although prompted by the existence of Swift's *Windsor Prophecy* does not engage with it, and thus its connection to Swift's poem is even more tenuous than that of *The Oxford Prophecy*.

The third prophecy poem is *The Windsor Prophecy, Found in a Marlborough Rock*. This poem does contain a prophecy, ostensibly written on a scroll, recounting a tree that despite having been consumed by fire flourishes amid "Seeds of Dissention." A dove bearing an olive branch (evoking the flood account in Genesis) brings peace to a turbulent situation: "*Kites, Hawks*, and *Vultures*, all shall strive, / Against the Dove's Prerogative." Clearly the dove represents Queen Anne and the poem endorses her peace policy and opposes those who wish to continue the war. The analogy of the tree and birds—especially the dove, kites, and vultures—is strikingly similar to details in the fable of the "Pittis" *Windsor Prophecy*. It appears that the author of *The Windsor Prophecy, Found in a Marlborough Rock* read the half-sheet version of the Pittis poem, interpreted it as applicable to the current debate over the peace, and sought to provide a sequel of sorts.

Therefore, despite the ways in which these poems' titles echo Swift's *Windsor Prophecy*, only *The Oxford Prophecy* can be said to be written in direct response to it. Even so, it is a poor imitation, and one designed for a much more public audience than Swift's poem. While the content of the "Pittis" *Windsor Prophecy* does not respond to Swift's *Windsor Prophecy*, its publication does reflect the particular circumstances surrounding the unusual and highly limited way that Swift's poem circulated. Its existence also reinforces our belief that Swift's poem generated much interest and uncertainty, given its lack of availability. *The Windsor Prophecy, Found in a Marlborough Rock* responds directly to Pittis's poem, but not to Swift's.

Unraveling this complicated tangle of four poems does not in the end result in a lengthy annotation in our edition; our discussion consists of two short paragraphs in the poem's introductory note. In an edition of such extensive scope, we have tried to practice editorial restraint, which often means that the length of our comments does not reflect the scholarly labor involved. Pope criticized Dryden in *The First Epistle of the Second Book of Horace Imitated* (1737) for lacking "The last and greatest Art, the Art to blot." Part of the art of annotation is concision.

Another of Swift's topical satires that places great demands on the annotator is *Toland's Invitation to Dismal, to Dine with the Calves-Head Club* (1712). This poem has many topics that need to be explained: the Calves-Head Club, which allegedly celebrated the anniversary of Charles I's execution; the reputation of the republican John Toland; the Tory animosity toward Daniel Finch, 2nd Earl of Nottingham (the "Dismal" of the poem) for his defection to the Whigs over the Oxford ministry's peace platform; the tradition of preaching Thirtieth of January sermons to mark the anniversary of Charles I's execution; Horace's *Epistle* 1.5, which Swift here imitates; the identities of the many prominent Whigs attacked in the poem; and the contemporary bases for these attacks.

Some of these topics had been handled well by Harold Williams in his edition and by Frank H. Ellis in volume 7 of the Yale *Poems on Affairs of State*. Indeed, Ellis greatly improved on Williams's notes, but more work remained, especially regarding the Whigs being attacked. The poem implies that Swift is drawing on many derogatory beliefs about these individuals, especially regarding embarrassing aspects of their personal lives, but it does little to explain or justify these attacks, and, as a result, these individuals seem to function as mere names for most modern readers. This perhaps explains why I had found it difficult to appreciate this poem before setting out to annotate it.

68 | Notes on Footnotes

To learn more about the nineteen Whigs attacked in passing in the poem, I had to go beyond the annotations of Williams, Ellis, and Rogers. Most of the Whigs were peers, which means that they have profiles in the standard reference work *The Complete Peerage*, which turned out to be a valuable resource.[11] Although *The Complete Peerage* often focuses on factual information in the entries for each peer, the footnotes contain many items of juicy, even slanderous gossip about these powerful individuals, and they provide an excellent starting point for annotating that blend of fact, rumor, and gossip that I noted at the outset as being characteristic of topical satire from this period. Using *The Complete Peerage* as a starting point, following the bibliographical trail suggested by sources cited in the notes, and drawing on other sources, such as the recently published History of Parliament volumes on the Lords, I could expand on and in one instance correct the identifications made by other editors.[12] Doing so helped me answer several questions: Who was the Montagu attacked for his alleged lack of learning? Why did Swift think that Scarbrough was a coward, that Portland and Cleveland lacked intelligence, that Bolton lacked eloquence, or that Lincoln was poor?

The identification of Montagu in line 24 was an interesting puzzle to solve. Williams identified him as Charles Montagu (1661–1715), 1st Earl of Halifax, noting his role as a patron of letters, which hardly explained Swift's attack on his lack of learning. But Ellis, rightly in our view, claimed that Swift referred to this Montagu in an earlier line as "*Hal—*," that is, Halifax, which would make sense because Swift elsewhere referred to these Lords by their titles. In that earlier line, Halifax is attacked for being impertinent, and we could assemble ample evidence that Swift and others viewed him as such. The poem's scattershot effect also implies that Swift does not attack a person more than once, which would mean that he does not refer to the same person using different names. Williams apparently did not recognize that principle and was misled by Deane Swift's identification of "*Hal—*" as Henry Boyle. Swift in fact attacks Boyle later in the poem as "*B—l.*"

But if the Montagu in line 24 is not Charles Montagu, then who is he? Ellis identified him as John Montagu (1690–1749), 2nd Duke of Montagu, and although he offered a gloss about his lack of interest in learning, the identification was not especially compelling, in large part because of this Montagu's youth in 1712 and consequent lack of significance. A much more likely target is the lawyer Sir James Montagu (1666–1723), Halifax's younger brother, who voted against the Queen's peace policy in the Commons on December 7, 1711.

Annotating Topical Satire | 69

He was also the first speaker against Sacheverell at his trial, which prompted this mockery in *The Westminster Combat* (1710):

> The first that Assaulted was valiant Sir *James*,
> A Warriour of Famous Renown,
> Who fir'd a Volley of Words without Means,
> Then trembling sat himself down.[13]

Other Whigs in the poem had been reliably identified, but the bases for Swift's attacks have not always been explained. Williams tended to provide only basic information about each, and Ellis sometimes expanded slightly on Williams, but at other times failed to annotate at all. Rogers's notes were uncharacteristically minimal. Thus, questions remained about the justifications for Swift's insinuations about Scarbrough's cowardice, the stupidity of Portland and Cleveland, Bolton's lack of eloquence, and Lincoln's poverty. I will not go into extensive detail on each, but having pursued the bibliographical trails provided by multiple sources, we could show that: Richard Lumley, 1st Earl of Scarbrough, disobeyed William III at the Battle of the Boyne in refusing to advance against superior forces; Henry Bentinck, 2nd Earl of Portland, was mocked by Delarivier Manley in *The New Atalantis* for lacking intelligence; Charles Fitzroy, 2nd Duke of Cleveland, was mocked by many for being unintelligent; Charles Powlett, 2nd Duke of Bolton, was ridiculed by Lady Cowper in a way that implied his lack of eloquence; and Henry Clinton, 7th Earl of Lincoln, was widely viewed as one of the poorest members of the peerage. In short, there is sufficient and at times ample contemporary testimony that aligns with Swift's characterizations, as partisan as they are. What this research demonstrates is that Swift invoked facts about or at least typical perceptions of each of these powerful Whig Lords, and that his satirical slights would have been recognized by contemporary readers familiar with gossip about them. In short, our research clarifies the bases for Swift's attacks in *Toland's Invitation to Dismal*.

Yet one question remained: why did Swift write this particular poem when he did? We know from the *Journal to Stella* that he wrote it in June 1712, and the dating of June 26 on a copy of the first edition by the book collector Narcissus Luttrell establishes that it was published by that date.[14] That means it was published soon after the parliamentary session ended on June 21. But the poem is set on January 29, the eve of the anniversary of Charles I's execution. It seems unlikely that Swift was recalling a specific January 29, but only that he wanted to use the Calves-Head Club in his adaptation of Horace's epistle and doing so required a fictional setting for the poem on that symbolic eve.

The poem's early reception perhaps holds a clue for understanding Swift's portrayal of the Whigs. In the Whiggish *Observator* of July 5, 1712, Swift's poem is grouped with two other "villainous Papers . . . that have been cry'd in the Streets, or privately handed about": *A Full and True Account of a Most Horrid and Cruel Plot Against the Queen, at Kensington, on Wednesday Night Last* and *A Full and True Account of the Apprehending and Taking of Mr. Jacob Buskin, Mr. Joshua Churchil, and Andrew Bell Esq; Three Notorious Plotters Against the Queen*. The latter pamphlet cannot now be located; the former claims that the Whigs were attempting to assassinate the Queen. This alleged plot is also mentioned in another poem at the time, *Whiggism Laid Open: and the Loyal Church-man's Health* (Foxon W391, advertised in the *Post-Boy* on July 19, 1712). The *Observator*, not surprisingly, dismisses any connection between the Whigs and a plot against the Queen and accuses the Tories of being the true enemies of the monarchy and the nation.

An attempted assassination of the Queen would have been extensively covered by the periodical press at the time. Whigs and Tories would have rushed to signal their loyalty to the monarch even if they differed on the issue of the Hanoverian succession. Yet very little was in fact published on this alleged plot—or more precisely, we have uncovered very little about it. Therefore, it seems more likely that the plot itself was part of a Tory propaganda effort to undermine the Whigs by portraying them as regicides, and that Swift's poem may have been part of that effort. Its depiction of powerful Whig Lords as members of the Calves-Head Club may have been designed as a prelude to this broader propaganda effort. Alternatively, others used Swift's poem as an opportunity to make similar attacks. In either case, this alleged assassination plot against the Queen was part of the broader political context in which Swift's poem was originally read and merits being discussed in an annotated edition.

Although I am confident that our edition of Swift's poems considerably advances our understanding of them, I also acknowledge that more work remains to be done by future commentators and editors. In our fourth volume, we discuss more than four hundred poems that have been wrongly attributed to Swift. Though we have not edited them, we summarize what we know of each poem's occasion, purpose, and publication and attribution history. For some of the topical satires attributed to Swift, we have been unable to discover why they were written, whom they were attacking. For example, *The Garden Plot* (1709), published in a London halfsheet (Foxon G10), satirizes a dispute involving land owned by a man named Hall. Who is this Hall, what did he do to become the target of this satire, and when and where did this dispute occur? We have not found answers to these questions. But our lack of success here and elsewhere creates opportunities for others to continue the work of annotation. Each annotator strives to build on the accomplishments of predecessors in illuminating what has remained obscure. This collective effort, which connects annotators of the past, present, and future, is foundational for literary and historical scholarship, and provides endless opportunities for genuine discovery.

NOTES

1. For a useful demonstration of how a factual basis can inform the reading of topical satires, see J. M. Treadwell, "Swift, William Wood, and the Factual Basis of Satire," *Journal of British Studies* 15, no. 2 (1976): 76–91.

2. Arthur Friedman, "Principles of Historical Annotation in Critical Editions of Modern Texts," in *English Institute Annual 1941* (New York: Columbia University Press, 1942), 115–28; 118.

3. The first quotation is from Martin C. Battestin, "A Rationale of Literary Annotation: The Example of Fielding's Novels," *Studies in Bibliography* 34 (1981): 20. The second quotation is from Ian Jack, "Novels and Those 'Necessary Evils': Annotating the Brontës," *Essays in Criticism* 32 (1982): 323. The third quotation, which notably allows for the possibility of "audiences," is from James Woolley, "Annotation: Some Guiding Considerations," *East-Central Intelligencer*, n.s., 8, no. 1 (1994): 11.

4. Ian Small, "The Editor as Annotator as Ideal Reader," in *The Theory and Practice of Text-Editing: Essays in Honour of James T. Boulton*, ed. Ian Small and Marcus Walsh (Cambridge: Cambridge University Press, 1991), 201.

5. Regarding *Poems on Affairs of State: Augustan Satirical Verse, 1660–1714*, ed. G. deF. Lord et al., 7 vols. (New Haven: Yale University Press, 1963–75), Michael McKeon noted that "even as the modern annotations successfully enable us to read these poems with a working knowledge of their topical reference, they also must elevate us far above the level of understanding available to the average contemporary reader who read without benefit of explanatory notes" ("What Were Poems on Affairs of State?," *1650–1850: Ideas, Aesthetics, and Inquiries in the Early Modern Era* 4 [1998]: 366).

6. D. F. McKenzie, *Bibliography and the Sociology of Texts* (1986; Cambridge: Cambridge University Press, 1999), 25.

7. For Swift's topical satires, two articles especially come to mind: Pat Rogers, "The Rod of Moses and the Wand of the Prophet: Swift's Poem on 'Sid Hamet,'" in *Documenting Eighteenth-Century Satire: Pope, Swift, Gay, and Arbuthnot in Historical Context* (Cambridge: Cambridge Scholars, 2012), 7–21; and James Woolley, "Writing Libels on the Germans: Swift's

72 | Notes on Footnotes

'Wicked Treasonable Libel,'" in *Swift: The Enigmatic Dean: Festschrift for Hermann Josef Real*, ed. Rudolf Freiburg, Arno Löffler, and Wolfgang Zach (Tübingen: Stauffenburg Verlag, 1998), 303–16.

8. *Journal to Stella: Letters to Esther Johnson and Rebecca Dingley, 1710–1713*, ed. Abigail Williams (Cambridge: Cambridge University Press, 2013), 351–52 (December 24, 1711), 353–54 (December 26, 27), and 360 (January 4, 1712); 353 (December 27, 1711).

9. Foxon numbers are from D. F. Foxon, *English Verse, 1701–1750: A Catalogue of Separately Printed Poems with Notes on Contemporary Collected Editions*, 2 vols. (London: Cambridge University Press, 1975).

10. The editions referred to are *The Poems of Jonathan Swift*, ed. Harold Williams, 2nd ed., 3 vols. (Oxford: Clarendon Press, 1958); and *Jonathan Swift: The Complete Poems*, ed. Pat Rogers (Harmondsworth: Penguin Books; New Haven: Yale University Press, 1983).

11. G. E. C[okayne], *The Complete Peerage of England, Scotland, Ireland, Great Britain, and the United Kingdom*, new ed., 13 vols. (1910–59; reprint, Gloucester: Alan Sutton, 1987).

12. Ruth Paley, *The House of Lords, 1660–1715*, The History of Parliament, 5 vols. (Cambridge: Cambridge University Press, 2016).

13. *Poems on Affairs of State*, 7:433. Here, "without Means" is equivalent to "without meaning."

14. This copy of Foxon S911 is Newberry Library, Case 6A 159 no. 94.

CHAPTER 5

ॐ A Picture Is Worth a Thousand Words
Annotated Facsimiles as Ideal Editions

Shef Rogers

Like Swift's Academicians of Lagado, who spoke not words, but the things themselves, modern critics stand on the verge of a syntax of concrete ideas, which may endow English criticism at the end of the century with an awareness of the iconicity of text.
—RANDALL MCLEOD, "Un 'Editing' Shak-speare," *SubStance* 10/11 (1981/82): 38

It is disconcerting to realize that this comment, composed forty years ago, referred to the end of the twentieth century, by which time it was indeed possible to create affordable facsimiles (to its credit, Dover Publications engaged enthusiastically with the opportunity). Since then, technology has continued to advance to the point that it is not only possible to print affordable facsimiles, but possible to design books that can be published simultaneously in both paper and digital formats, while more sophisticated digital formats can enable reproduction of texts too physically large for affordable printing or texts printed in type too physically small for ready legibility in a standard-size printed format.[1] Yet I am not aware of any scholars proposing new editions in a facing-page format. This essay argues that literature of the eighteenth century is ideally suited to such a format, that such a format enables an editor to offer a clearer and richer set of annotations, and that such editions offer a practical solution

74 | Notes on Footnotes

to some of the key challenges of editorial theory that have arisen since McLeod's essay appeared.

One phenomenon only vaguely implied in the epigraph from McLeod is the increasing availability of photographic facsimiles. Since the early 2000s, very large numbers of books—either digitized from microfilm (though much of that work will probably be superseded by Google or other digitization programs) or through automated photography—have become readily accessible.[2] Scholars and students increasingly encounter texts as online digital facsimiles and are not necessarily put off by older type styles, though annotation is required to enable full appreciation of both the bibliographical and textual codes.[3]

These digital resources are particularly beneficial for the study of works published after about 1700, due to the emerging standardization of book design particular to different genres and to the codification of spelling, so that fewer words require modernized spellings or annotation for modern readers to understand them. As Nicolas Barker demonstrates in his heavily illustrated essay, across Europe "consciousness of appearances, and their aesthetic or attractive power . . . was not acquired in general until the eighteenth century."[4] By then it was possible to purchase commercially produced ornament blocks and typefaces and even hire skilled compositors and engravers from overseas, leading to the dominance of styles such as the Dutch Elzevir format and design. At the same time, printed texts became a part of everyday life through administrative forms, newspapers, and advertising.[5] Basic literacy became a necessary skill, and demand led to the creation of dictionaries, culminating in Johnson's *Dictionary* (1755), an expensive commission funded by a consortium of established publishers to meet a perceived market demand. Legislation from 1710 establishing copyright in printed texts encouraged the gradual professionalization of both publishing and literary authorship. All these technological, legal, and intellectual developments reduced the rate of language change and increased attention to the design and cost of books.

Thus the literary publications of the eighteenth century are well suited to a facing-page editorial format, an arrangement that permits enough space for the required annotation and discussion of textual history while the original printings are sufficiently standardized and printed in large enough point sizes to permit reproduction in a convenient page size. (Nineteenth-century texts dwindle toward smaller point sizes and indulge in an increasing diversity of display faces, making the facing-page format more challenging, though still suitable to many titles.) Traditionally, scholars have used facing-page texts for comparisons of originals with edited texts or transcriptions. Maynard

A Picture Is Worth a Thousand Words | 75

Mack's *The Last and Greatest Art: Some Unpublished Poetical Manuscripts of Alexander Pope* (University of Delaware Press, 1984) is a significant example, but one that reveals the format's limitations as much as its attractions. Anyone who knows the book will recall both its largeness (31 × 24 cm) and weight (1.77 kg), which results from the heavy art paper necessary at the time for reproducing grayscale images sharply. Digital printing now makes it possible to reproduce grayscale images of very high quality on standard printing paper. The main benefit of Mack's design is the ability to position the transcription and the facsimile in parallel, thus aligning the two versions. A facing-page edition permits similar alignment, ensuring that the reader can immediately identify the relevant annotation, rather than having to locate the corresponding footnote or search through a list of annotations at the end of the text or in a separate notes section. Annotation in this format creates a conversation—among the author, the text being edited, the reader, and the editor—rather than imposing a hierarchy and forcing the editor to interrupt the original with a footnote number and even at times to intermingle the author's original notes and the editor's commentary.[6] A facing-page edition operates on a horizontal axis rather than on the vertical axis of traditional scholarly editions, and exploits the natural affordance of the codex structure, the page opening.[7] The facing-page layout enables a reader to attend more fully to the text, to enjoy something much closer to the reading experience intended by those who produced the book.[8]

This argument is not purely a pragmatic one, however. The choice of the word "ideal" in my title alludes to an argument cited by Gabriel Egan against Terence Hawkes concerning the logic of creating composite facsimiles such as the Malone Society facsimiles and Charlton Hinman's First Folio, publications that selected images from multiple copies to obtain the best text for each forme of each sheet of the book. Hawkes had argued that these compilations were attempting to show what printers intended to make, not what was actually produced. He concluded that "You can't have a 'facsimile' of an idea." Egan poses a reversal of this claim, to assert that "only an idea, not its physical embodiment, can be the subject of a facsimile."[9] I take his claim to mean that the photographic reproduction is still only an idea of the physical original, but the advantage of the facsimile over a printed edition is that it captures the realization of many more of the ideas that go into the publication of a book—those of the author, the printer, the publisher—rather than just those of the author. Given that all books are essentially inert until performed by a reader, any format that enables us to come closer to the experiences of original readers

76 | Notes on Footnotes

is going to provide more insight than a text abstracted from its physical and social contexts.[10]

The other reason for claiming that facsimiles are ideal editions relates to the fundamental divide in editorial theory that has emerged and been much contested since about the time McLeod penned the essay from which I have taken my epigraph. Although this controversy has often been depicted as a divide between European and Anglo-American practitioners, I think it is more accurate to describe it as a divide between single-version and eclectic editorial approaches. As early as 1975, Hans Zeller had fired a broadside at eclectic editing.[11] Debate persists, but the most authoritative defense of eclectic editing remains G. Thomas Tanselle's *A Rationale of Textual Criticism* (1989), which argues that each distinct textual witness is a piece of evidence that, when analyzed in conjunction with all the other witnesses, enables an editor to prepare a text that is as close as possible to the work. In Tanselle's rationale, the work is truly an ideal, indeed a Platonic ideal, because no single witness can ever fully realize or embody the work. Such a view of the editor's labor is daunting, particularly when enumerated as painstakingly as it has been in the MLA's Committee on Scholarly Editions' guidelines.[12] That complexity, coupled with the success of examples from the work of both McGann and McKenzie demonstrating the benefits of attending to bibliographical codes and social contexts, has tended to encourage scholarly editions based on a single version of the text.[13] Proposing to base an edition on a single copy of a single version in a facing-page facsimile is simply the logical extension of this practice. While the reproduction of a single copy may risk neglecting printing variants across different states and issues of a version (though these can certainly be recorded in the facing-page annotation), it vastly enhances an editor's ability to engage with bibliographical codes and social contexts.[14]

A TEST CASE

This sample edition has been designed to demonstrate some of the benefits of the facing-page structure for editions. Three of the most widely available and intellectually respected modern editions of Swift's poem have been taken as counterexamples in support of the traditional edition: the Norton Critical Edition, edited by Robert A. Greenberg and William B. Piper (1973), the Penguin edition of Swift's poems, edited by Pat Rogers (1983), and the Oxford

Authors selections from Swift, edited by Angus Ross and David Woolley (1984). All are excellent editions by superb scholars, created in accord with defined financial considerations and publisher policies. Those same concerns would govern the publication in print of any facing-page edition, and readers and publishers will have to weigh the advantages and costs of this proposed format. This essay simply puts the case for those advantages and argues that the costs are affordable in print and even less of a concern in a digital format.[15]

In this sample, notes that parallel or are adapted from the Norton, Penguin, or Oxford editions are presented in a serif font. Notes original to this sample are in a sanserif font. I hope this distinction readily enables readers to distinguish the benefits of the facing-page layout. Those who consult the Norton edition will immediately notice that it does not print any space between verse paragraphs and that constraints of space allow for very few notes and result in the occasional couplet split across two pages (e.g., ll. 103–4). The Penguin edition records the breaks between paragraphs and avoids splitting couplets but separates the notes from the text by nearly 350 pages and intermingles Swift's own footnotes with the editor's annotation. The 1984 Oxford edition retains Swift's original notes to the poem as footnotes on the page, but records annotations at the back, separated by 150 pages. Williams's 1958 Oxford edition retains Swift's original notes as well as recording textual variants and Williams's own explanatory notes (or cross-references to notes to previous poems) at the foot of the page. In the interests of space, I have not recorded Williams's sigla of editions here, but any facing-page edition would record those details in the textual introduction.

This selection from "Rhapsody"[16] does not include subsequent sections of the poem that were censored prior to original publication and that have been restored in the Penguin and Oxford editions. If the example were extended, the facing page would supply the censored text and leave the facsimile as the original readers purchased it. This editorial policy would enable a student to see that even the existing text, which led to the arrests of several printers, was inflammatory, but still appreciate all of Swift's verses, some of which were rightly deemed unpublishable at the time.

78 | Notes on Footnotes

Spelling often modernized to "Rhapsody," "an effusive utterance or piece of writing, often disconnected or lacking in logical argument" (*OED*), but also with etymological echoes of Homeric verse recitation. Spelt as here, however, the title may also indicate a pun on the word "rap," meaning to strike, often as a rebuke. An anonymous 1734 retort to Swift appeared under the title *A Rap at the Rapsody* (Foxon R116).

A misleading imprint. This is the first edition of the poem and it was published in London, though contemporaries may well have read it as expressing Irish sentiments.

Huggonson had printed the *Grub-Street Journal* in 1731–32 with Samuel Palmer and was thus familiar with London literary controversies (Plomer, 229).

The price of the poem is not inexpensive (though in line with other folio poems). The associations with coffeehouses and pamphlet shops would have indicated to readers that it was a topical piece.

ON POETRY:
A
RAPSODY.

Printed at DUBLIN, and Re-printed at LONDON:
And fold by J. HUGGONSON, next to *Kent*'s Coffee-Houfe, near *Serjeant*'s-Inn, in *Chancery-Lane*; and at the Bookfellers and Pamphlet-fhops, 1733.
[Price One Shilling.]

This woodcut decorated initial A may represent Hercules with his club, having succeeded in his first labor, killing the Nemean lion. While printers did not necessarily select decorative blocks based on a work's content, the image supports Swift's argument that it is nearly impossible to be a great poet.

Edward Young, *The Universal Passion: Love of Fame*, a series of seven satires published 1725–28. Swift's reference slightly refocuses the theme.

Swift may have in mind John Dryden's epigram celebrating Homer, Virgil, and Milton as a literary triumvirate, over a period of millennia. The reference to "Bays" in the next couplet would then represent an acknowledgment of Dryden's own literary dominance in the previous generation of poets.

ON
POETRY:
A
RAPSODY.

<blockquote>
ALL Human Race wou'd fain be <i>Wits</i>,
And Millions miss, for one that hits.
Young's universal Passion, Pride,
Was never known to spread so wide.
Say <i>Britain</i>, cou'd you ever boast,——— 5
Three <i>Poets</i> in an Age at most?
</blockquote>

fights with] Hyde, *New Misc.*, 1735, 1736 combats F., 1745.

Genius—natural aptitude.

A hard-won empire stretching far to the east.

(4)

Our chilling Climate hardly bears
A *Sprig* of Bays in Fifty Years:
While ev'ry Fool his Claim alledges,
As if it grew in common Hedges.   10
What Reason can their be affign'd
For this Perverfenefs in the Mind?
Brutes find out where their Talents lie:
A *Bear* will not attempt to fly:
A founder'd *Horfe* will oft debate,   15
Before he tries a five-barr'd Gate:
A *Dog* by Inftinct turns afide,
Who fees the Ditch too deep and wide.
But *Man* we find the only Creature,
Who, led by *Folly*, fights with *Nature*;   20
Who, when *fhe* loudly cries, *Forbear*,
With Obftinacy fixes there;
And, where his *Genius* leaft inclines,
Abfurdly bends his whole Defigns.

Not *Empire* to the Rifing-Sun,   25
By Valour, Conduct, Fortune won;

Nor

84 | Notes on Footnotes

Circle—the globe.

This verse paragraph is indebted to John Gay's *Trivia* (Penguin, 872).

Hogarth's *Rake's Progress*, plate 4 depicts such a shoeshine boy in the lower foreground.
Bridewell—central London prison; Stews—red-light district.
Drop—"To let fall in birth," usually used of sheep (*OED v.* II.14). Swift used similarly ironic language in *A Modest Proposal* (1729) and extends the pejorative animal imagery (cf. *OED* , s.v. "litter" *v.* 7a), while also invoking the newer meaning of strewn rubbish (*OED n.* 4).

Blast—"To affect injuriously or perniciously with" (*OED v.* II.8c), nothing akin to inspiration.

(5)

Nor higheſt *Wiſdom* in Debates
For framing Laws to govern States;
Nor Skill in Sciences profound,
So large to graſp the Circle round; 30
Such heavenly Influence require,
As how to ſtrike the *Muſes Lyre*.

 Not Beggar's Brat, on Bulk begot;
Nor Baſtard of a Pedlar *Scot*;
Nor Boy brought up to cleaning Shoes, 35
The Spawn of *Bridewell*, or the Stews;
Nor Infants dropt, the ſpurious Pledges
Of *Gipſies* littering under Hedges,
Are ſo diſqualified by Fate
To riſe in *Church*, or *Law*, or *State*, 40
As he, whom *Phebus* in his Ire
Hath *blaſted* with poetick Fire.

 What hope of Cuſtom in the *Fair*,
While not a Soul demands your Ware?
Where you have nothing to produce 45
For private Life, or publick Uſe?

Court,

The three geographical and social divisions of society.

Cf. Psalm 119:51, "The proud have had me greatly in derision" (Oxford, 684).

Swift correctly notes the value of the position of poet laureate, but understates the status of Colley Cibber (1671–1757), who was a celebrity actor, successful playwright, and powerful manager of the Drury Lane theatre. He also happened to be a royalist at a time when many of the best writers were not sympathetic to the monarch or to Robert Walpole.
In Remainder—legal term for an interest in a property in future.
Attainder—legal term used figuratively to mean "stain of dishonour" (*OED*, 2b), implying that Cibber's appointment as poet laureate has made the title worthless.
59] *N.P.* F., 1745.
The combined pains of difficulty writing and of hunger.

61] *No break* F., 1745.
The reparagraphing at lines 59 and 61 in some of the later editions emphasizes the triumph of Cibberian dullness over the poet laureate and turns the mock-epic simile into a direct commentary on the poet's pains.

(6)

Court, City, Country want you not;
You cannot bribe, betray, or plot.
For Poets, Law makes no Provifion:
The Wealthy have you in Derifion;   50
Of State-Affairs you cannot fmatter,
Are awkward when you try to flatter.
Your Portion, taking *Britain* round,
* Was juft one annual Hundred Pound.
Now not fo much as in Remainder;   55
Since *Cibber* brought in an Attainder;
For ever fixt by Right Divine,
(A Monarch's Right) on *Grubfreet* Line.
Poor ftarv'ling Bard, how fmall thy Gains!
How unproportion'd to thy Pains!   60

And here a *Simile* comes Pat in:
Tho' *Chickens* take a Month to fatten,
The Guefts in lefs than half an Hour
Will more than half a Score devour.
So, after toiling twenty Days,   65
To earn a Stock of Pence and Praife,

                                          Thy

---

* Paid to the Poet Laureat, which Place was given to one *Cibber*, a Player.

Rogers notes that "the remainder of the poem is in the tradition of 'instructions,' . . . the common seventeenth-century way of organizing a satire" (Penguin, 872n72).

Prologues often purported to be anonymous, "from hand unknown."
Aurora's Light—clichéd poetic language for dawn.

(7)

Thy Labours, grown the Critick's Prey,
Are fwallow'd o'er a Difh of Tea;
Gone, to be never heard of more,
Gone, where the *Chickens* went before.　　　70

How fhall a new Attempter learn
Of diff'rent Spirits to difcern,
And how diftinguifh, which is which,
The Poet's Vein, or fcribling Itch?
Then hear an old experienc'd Sinner　　　75
Inftructing thus a young Beginner.

Confult yourfelf, and if you find
A powerful Impulfe urge your Mind,
Impartial judge within your Breaft
What Subject you can manage beft;　　　80
Whether your Genius moft inclines
To Satire, Praife, or hum'rous Lines;
To Elegies in mournful Tone,
Or Prologue fent from Hand unknown.
Then rifing with *Aurora*'s Light,　　　85
The Mufe invok'd, fit down to write;

C　　　　　　　　　　　　　　　　Blot

90 | Notes on Footnotes

Wipe—"A cutting remark; a sarcastic reproof or rebuff" (*OED n.* 3, citing this line).

Perhaps the printer was expected to print the word as "CAPITALS" (as in the 1734 Dublin edition) or possibly the line refers to names printed only with opening and closing letters, e.g., w————e, a method that risked readers supplying a variety of possible names. Either way, the reference extends the point that typography can enhance satiric intent.

Smoaks—"To get an inkling of, to smell or suspect" (*OED*, s.v. "smokes" *v.* 8a).

100 the Jest:] Hyde, *New Misc.*, 1735, 1736, 1745 a Jest. F.

(8)

Blot out, correct, infert, refine,
Enlarge, diminifh, interline;
Be mindful, when Invention fails,
To fcratch your Head, and bite your Nails. 90

Your Poem finifh'd, next your Care
Is needful, to tranfcribe it fair:
In modern Wit all printed Trafh, is
Set off with num'rous *Breaks*———and *Dafhes*———

To Statefman wou'd you give a Wipe, 95
You print it in *Italick Type*.
When Letters are in vulgar Shapes,
'Tis ten to one the Wit efcapes;
But when in *Capitals* expreft,
The dulleft Reader fmoaks the Jeft: 100
Or elfe perhaps he may invent
A better than the Poet meant,
As learn'd Commentators view
In *Homer* more than *Homer* knew.

Your

NOTES

1. I had originally considered using as an example the first publication of Pope's "Messiah," but even a very high-quality image of *Spectator* 378 (May 14, 1712), with its double columns of type, flanking shoulder note biblical references, and lower-quality paper, would have been a challenge to reproduce legibly on a page this size. A facing-page edition would draw attention to the Virgilian epigraph (not recorded in the Twickenham edition, though noted in the recent Routledge edition) and highlight the frequency of the poem's indebtedness to Isaiah, thereby sharpening the contrast of the elevated subject matter with the mundanity of the advertisements that fill the rest of the sheet.

2. One advantage of this return to facsimiles of original printings is that familiarity with older editions prevents such books from appearing merely arcane artifacts and thus ensures that literary scholarship avoids the taint of antiquarianism.

3. I have used the term "bibliographical code" (the page design and reader expectations that inform a reader's response to what is visible on the page) in its now established form as the complement to textual codes (the meaning of the words themselves). This distinction was developed most explicitly by Jerome McGann, though the concept was further extended by Don McKenzie to include the wider context of a book's production and circulation, what he termed the "sociology of the text."

4. Nicolas Barker, "Typography and the Meaning of Words: The Revolution in the Layout of Books in the Eighteenth Century," in *Buch und Buchhandel in Europa im achtzehnten Jahrhundert / The Book and the Book Trade in Eighteenth-Century Europe*, Proceedings of the Fifth Wolfenbütteler Symposium, ed. Giles Barber and Bernhard Fabian (Hamburg: Hausweddel, 1981), 126–65.

5. James Raven's *The Business of Books* provides the best overview of the rapid increase in reliance on printed forms in the eighteenth century. No comprehensive guide to newspapers and periodicals of the century is available, in part because the number of publications is so large and their range so diverse. And with all those publications came advertising, though there were also plenty of handbills and posters—relatively few of which survive—promoting commodities, announcing performances, or proclaiming government decisions.

6. The most complex and tangled example I know of such intermingling occurs in the Twickenham edition of Pope's *Dunciad Variorum*. When that volume was printed in 1943, the editor, James Sutherland, made a virtue of necessity in noting that Pope's "distinction between 'Imitations' and 'Remarks,' which involved his printers in difficulties which they never solved satisfactorily, has been ignored" (*TE* 5.5). Ideally, it should be left to the reader, as Pope left it, to judge whether the printers sufficiently distinguished the two categories of notes, but printing such a multilayered text as well as the editor's annotations on pages the size of the Twickenham volumes would no doubt have been prohibitively expensive, if not impossible. All the more reason for modern readers to appreciate the impressive skills of compositors in 1729.

7. A counterargument would be that the facing-page format disrupts the page-opening structure of the original, which I readily concede. An alternative to address this problem would be to print a text in landscape format, with commentary on the outer halves of each facing page, though such an arrangement might be easier to produce on screen than in print. No editorial choice is perfect, and even facsimiles always depend on choices to which editors should alert readers (see Sarah Werner, "Digitized Images: Why Are They So Weird?," October 19, 2019, https://sarahwerner.substack.com/p/digitized-images).

8. Although I do not have space here to explore facing-page formats in a digital context, I will note that such a design on screen obviates the awkward need to scroll to the foot or the end of a document to follow the commentary. For a valuable discussion of considerations that should inform digital editions, see Elena Pierazzo, "A Rationale of Digital Documentary Editions," *Literary and Linguistic Computing* 26 (2011): 463–77; and *Digital Scholarly Editing: Theories, Models and Methods* (Aldershot: Ashgate, 2015). The most widely used facing-page edition I know of is the Folger Library edition of the plays of Shakespeare. Although the text of the plays is modernized rather than a facsimile of a folio or quarto text, the facing-page design enables Folger to make its edited text freely available online with the separate annotation more easily updated when new approaches or insights need to be added. In the Folger editions, there are occasionally notes that are too long to be accommodated on the facing page; these are gathered at the end of the text with a cross-reference from the facing page.

9. Gabriel Egan, "Type-Facsimiles, Photo-Facsimiles and New Media: A Paper Delivered to the Conference 'Recovering Renaissance Drama: 100 Years of Malone Society Publications' at Corpus Christi College Oxford on 23 September [2006]," https://www.dora.dmu.ac.uk /bitstream/handle/2086/7018/GEganTypeFacsimile.pdf.

10. For a fuller consideration of the place of facsimiles within a text's bibliographical history, see Joseph A. Dane, "'Ideal Copy' vs. 'Ideal Texts': The Application of Bibliographical Description to Facsimiles," in *Abstractions of Evidence in the Study of Manuscripts and Early Printed Books* (Farnham: Ashgate, 2009), 77–94. Dane's concern is that facsimiles of a single copy can become the essential reference for an entire edition, particularly when the facsimile is a composite production reproducing each forme from a copy deemed to preserve the best state of that forme. I am not advocating that the facsimile should serve as the ideal text, but rather that it should provide the single base text around which the annotation is constructed to enable a reader to understand a text most fully.

11. Hans Zeller, "A New Approach to the Critical Constitution of Literary Texts," *Studies in Bibliography* 28 (1975): 231–63.

12. See https://www.mla.org/Resources/Research/Surveys-Reports-and-Other -Documents/Publishing-and-Scholarship/Reports-from-the-MLA-Committee-on-Scholarly -Editions/Guidelines-for-Editors-of-Scholarly-Editions. I recognize that these guidelines are not limited to advice for editors of eclectic editions and that they offer a wealth of valuable advice, but most of the complications in meeting the committee's standards arise from practices related to eclectic editing. The Committee oversees the Centre for Scholarly Editions (CSE), established in 1976 to continue the work of the Center for Editions of American Authors (CEAA), founded in 1963.

13. This discussion admittedly simplifies the recent debates in editorial theory. Most notably, it omits mention of the work of Peter Shillingsburg, to whom my use of the word "versions" is directly indebted. Shillingsburg's taxonomy for distinguishing the stages and realizations of a "work" has influenced library cataloguing structures and will thus ultimately become widely adopted. For a valuable overview of the history of editorial approaches, see Marcus Walsh, "Theories of Text, Editorial Theory, and Textual Criticism," in *The Oxford Companion to the Book*, ed. Michael F. Suarez, S.J., and H. R. Woudhuysen (Oxford: Oxford University Press, 2010), 156–63.

14. Critics have increasingly attended to physical features of the page, reproducing supporting images in their arguments. For studies that reveal the value of working from original copies even of much-studied texts, see, in addition to McLeod's brilliant "Un-'Editing'" essay on kerning and ligatures, Peter Blayney on the significance of marginal spacing in quarto plays,

94 | Notes on Footnotes

Keith Maslen on imagery in printing ornaments, and Janine Barchas on frontispieces and inclusions of music and other visual elements. Blayney, "Quadrat Demonstrandum," *PBSA* III, no. 1 (2017): 61–101; Maslen, "Samuel Richardson: Printer-Novelist," in *Approaches to Teaching the Novels of Samuel Richardson*, ed. Lisa Zunshine and Jocelyn Harris (New York: MLA, 2006); Barchas, *Graphic Design, Print Culture, and the Eighteenth-Century Novel* (Cambridge: Cambridge University Press, 2003). Annotation in facing-page editions would also familiarize readers with indicators of false imprints, the significance of spacing, particularly as a signal of relative status in the signature of letters, and the textual consequences of altering printing formats (folded lines, extra or reduced space). Although some elaborate scholarly editions include a list of words hyphenated across the ends of lines, none that I know of records these other visual details, in part because there is often no simple method for doing so, precisely because so much of the meaning is embedded in the visual perception of the page.

15. I have also drawn on the current authoritative Swift edition as the basis for the textual variants recorded: *The Poems of Jonathan Swift*, ed. Harold Williams, 2nd ed., 3 vols. (Oxford: Clarendon Press, 1958), 2:639–59. The Cambridge University Press edition of Swift's poems is currently in process. The editorial policy for the Cambridge edition is to select a single version as copy text for each poem, though the electronic archive will provide access to other versions. The cost of a volume will be at least £100, plus charges for access to the electronic archive. For a useful discussion of the considerations guiding the policies and publications of the Cambridge edition, see Linda Bree and James McLaverty, "The Cambridge Edition of the Works of Jonathan Swift and the Future of the Scholarly Edition," in *Text Editing, Print and the Digital World*, ed. Marilyn Deegan and Kathryn Sutherland (Farnham: Ashgate, 2009), 127–36.

Of course, editors have long dreamed of and, increasingly, often created layered editions that enable a reader to jump to any version as desired. However, the complexity of multiauthority editions results in users as likely to be lost as informed. Single-authority editions, on the other hand, probably do not warrant the time and technology required to link each line of a reading text with an associated set of images.

16. The manuscript pages were reproduced with permission from the University of Otago Special Collections' copy of the poem, call number DeBeer Ec 1733 S.

CHAPTER 6

❧ Annotating Pope

Marcus Walsh

Amongst modern scholars, it is normally considered the business of the editorial annotator not to interpret, but to explicate the literary text. Annotators are concerned with meaning, not significance, with exegesis, not criticism. Their role is to give the information required by modern readers to understand a text from a different age and culture, and so, in Melvyn New's suggestive and testing formulation, "to position the reader on the brink of interpretation."[1] Editorial scholia address points in the text, normally at the level of the word, phrase, or sentence. They do not aspire to provide overarching readings of the text, though they take into account the larger textual context.[2] These positions are stated in the editorial guidelines for the Oxford University Press edition of *The Writings of Alexander Pope*: "As annotators, the volume editors' task will be to select and adduce information which is precisely and evidentially relevant to the particular crux addressed. . . . Exegesis depends on the identification of the specific ideas and specific senses which were available to and actually used by Pope, and which are activated by the specific words he writes."[3] I am responsible, with Dr. Hazel Wilkinson, for editing the volume of the Oxford *Works* containing the four "Ethic Epistles," as well as the *Epistle to Arbuthnot*, two of the Horatian imitations, and a number of epitaphs and elegies. An overriding policy of the Oxford edition is to use as copy, where appropriate, the text of poems as published in Pope's own authorized collections, the 1717 and 1735

Works. Our volume is based (following declared editorial policy) on the text, and contents, of the second volume of the first of the 1735 octavo editions of Pope's *Works*.[4]

Pope's Epistles raise some significant editorial issues, textual and explicatory. They were extensively rewritten during extended periods of composition, added to, redacted, and reordered, as not only the surviving manuscripts, but also the printed versions, show. Pope's own comments and footnotes to these poems, as well as the continuing process of revision evidenced by the autographs and printed texts, need to be evaluated and raise some questions of intention.[5] (Pope himself was the first annotator of his poems, and not only of the *Dunciad*.) Pope's lexis, and use of lexis, can be distinctive; it is often unfamiliar to a modern reader and raised questions even for his contemporaries. His poems engage closely with an early eighteenth-century social, political, and cultural world that requires detailed and apposite reconstruction. There are literary, as well as personal, allusions to be identified and investigated. Perhaps especially in the poems which belong to his *opus magnum*, the large philosophic poetic project of the last fifteen years of his life, there are issues of ethics and aesthetics that require description and explanation.

Most of the difficult words and passages in Pope, as in other writers, may be explained by research. They are, as George Steiner has called such difficulties, *contingent*: "what we mean by saying 'this is difficult' signifies 'this is a word, a phrase or a reference which I will have to look up.'"[6] Contingent cruces can be addressed by the ordinary discovery and application of pertinent evidence. Even in contingent cases, however, something more than "looking up" is involved. Evidence must be found, selected, and evaluated, for reliability, relevance, and explanatory power. And the nature of Pope's writing poses some of its own characteristic problems, taking the explicator beyond the "contingent."

For modern readers, the identities of the persons who appear in Pope's poems are often a barrier. Some of these characters are unnamed (and may or may not be identifiable with particular historical personages). Even where characters are named, it may be necessary for the annotator to weigh the evidence for competing candidates.

The numerous personal attacks in Pope's *Epistle to Arbuthnot* have a strong political tendency. Pope's targets here are preponderantly Whigs or Hanoverians of some kind or persuasion, many of them committed, some close to the centers of political power, some wielders of power themselves: Addison, Arnall, Bentley, Cibber, Dennis, Gildon, Halifax, Philips, Welsted. The political emphases of the poem might be illustrated by an apparently rather even-handed verse paragraph, accounting for the young Pope's entrance into his career as a published poet:

> But why then publish? *Granville* the polite,
> And knowing *Walsh*, would tell me I could write;
> Well-natur'd *Garth* inflam'd with early praise,
> And *Congreve* lov'd, and *Swift* endur'd my lays;
> The courtly *Talbot, Somers, Sheffield* read,
> Ev'n mitred *Rochester* would nod the head,
> And *St. John*'s self (great *Dryden*'s friends before)
> With open arms receiv'd one Poet more.
> . . . .
> From these the world will judge of men and books,
> Not from the *Burnets, Oldmixons,* and *Cooks*. (ll. 135–46)

Though this passage deals with Pope's early literary career and literary friends, it is not quite politically neutral. The list includes such Williamite and Whiggish figures as Talbot, Walsh, Garth, and Somers, certainly. It also, however, includes more politically visible and high-ranking figures of a different and less safe persuasion. It is striking that Pope is sufficiently pious, or foolhardy, to name early patrons who were recognized, by the time he first published this poem in 1734, as dangerously Jacobite in deed and reputation: Granville, Bolingbroke, and Francis Atterbury, bishop of Rochester.

These were well-known figures. The three men named in the last line of the passage are rather more obscure, however, and less certainly identifiable. Who were "the *Burnets, Oldmixons,* and *Cooks*"? Pope's footnote to the published poem tells us that these were "Authors of secret and Scandalous History." The surviving autograph manuscript of the poem is more informative, and more specific. Here notes written in Pope's own hand name these authors as "The Bp of Salisbury who writ ye History of his own Times," the "Author of ye scandalous History of ye Family of ye Stuarts," and the "Author of a Party history intitled The *Detection* of y^e *Reigns* of Charles. 1. 11. &c."[7] These autograph notes are powerful, if not conclusive, textual evidence of intention to mean. "Bp of Salisbury" clearly identifies Gilbert *Burnet*, author of *Bishop Burnet's History of his own Time* (2 vols., 1724–34), which Burnet himself referred to as his "secret history." Burnet was a Whig in politics, and closely associated with William III. Twickenham (4:106), however, suggests Pope had in mind Sir Thomas Burnet, the bishop's youngest son, who edited the second volume of Burnet's *History* and was a Whiggish associate of Addison.[8] John *Oldmixon* wrote, among other Whig histories, the hugely contentious *History of England, during the Reigns of the Royal House of Stuart* (London, 1730). *Cook* points to Roger Coke, *A Detection of the Court and State of England, during the Reigns of K. James I. Charles I. Charles II. and James II.* (1696); Twickenham thinks the reference is to Thomas Cooke (1703–1756), poet, pamphleteer, and translator, who had caused offence to Pope in his *Battle of the Poets* (1725), and *Scandalous Chronicle* (1726) but was not, unlike Gilbert Burnet and Oldmixon, an "Author of secret and Scandalous History." Twickenham suggests that here Pope "is measuring the great men who were his friends against the little men who attacked him"; Pope's autograph note, and the footnote added by him to the poem's first full print publication, suggest rather that his primary targets in this line were well-known and controversial Williamite and Whiggish histories. Here our interpretation of the poem as a whole, our sense of its personal and political emphases, must be shaped by how we resolve a particular issue of personal identification and the weight we place on textual evidence, in the autograph draft and the printed editions of the poem, in the words of the poet himself.

Most "literary" texts involve the editor in identifying literary allusion. The *Epistle to Arbuthnot* opens with a line that raises some questions about the nature and function of allusion, the nature of intention, and the duties of the annotator: "Shut, shut the door, good *John!* Fatigu'd I said." This is a famously direct and dramatic opening, Pope's tormented instruction to John Serle, his servant, gardener, and friend. There may, however, be another, less obvious, more playful, and more literary conversation going on here. In Dryden's *Essay of Dramatick Poesie*, Crites, arguing for poetic decorum, protests, "What is more unbefitting the majesty of verse than to call a servant, or bid a door be shut, in rhyme?" Did Pope intend an allusion to Crites's injunction? Pope certainly knew Dryden's *Essay*. It is more than striking that within three of the five feet of a pentameter line he contrives to violate both Crites's prohibitions. On the other hand, Pope does not make the reference explicit. It is an echo, not self-evidently an allusion. We cannot know psychological intention; we cannot know what was in Pope's head. We can deduce from textual evidence his intention to communicate a meaning in shared and shareable words. Here it seems to me the textual evidence of the reference is striking, but not demonstrative. An annotator points out the analogue, only; much virtue in *cf.*

Numerous authoritative, or at least partially authoritative, documentary witnesses exist for Pope's major poems. There are multiple printings, in many cases differing very substantially in the content that is included, and in how it is arranged. In some cases, any possible printed copy text is preceded by the publication of fragments; in almost all cases, any possible copy text is followed by printed texts incorporating authorial revisions. Manuscripts survive, sometimes no more than a solitary page, sometimes authorial drafts with heavy revisions, or drafts by amanuenses with heavy authorial revisions, or transcripts from Popeian autographs. It is the policy of the Oxford edition not to include manuscript variants in the historical collation.[9] We shall certainly, however, communicate what we find of significance in manuscript, more especially in autograph, sources. And, crucially, we shall use autographs where they provide evidence of interpretative value.

In practice, bibliographical and interpretative questions are interwoven, as editors of literary texts have always understood. A word in the "Sporus" passage from the *Epistle to Arbuthnot* raises just such issues:

> Satire or sense alas! can *Sporus* feel?
> Who breaks a butterfly upon a wheel?"
> Yet let me flap this bug with gilded wings,
> This painted child of dirt, that stinks and stings,
> Whose buzz the witty and the fair annoys,
> Yet wit ne'er tastes, and beauty ne'er enjoys. (ll. 307–12)

"Bug" is without exception the reading of the fifth line of this verse paragraph in the numerous lifetime printings of *Arbuthnot*, almost all of which have some degree of textual authority. However, "bug" is marked for replacement in Pope's autograph by the word "fly" in a surviving copy of the 1736 octavo *Works*.[10] Pope's autograph marginalia in this copy were clearly intended as corrected readings to be followed in some future printing. What might guide a modern editor's response? The bibliographical evidence is strong but points in two directions. Pope's autograph correction carries authority; on the other hand, so does the fact that neither this nor his other marginal emendations in this copy were incorporated in any lifetime edition after 1736. The bug persists. To what extent is textual choice to be affected by issues of meaning, by the semantic articulation of the line? A number of contemporary usages, pertinent and likely activated in this passage, were available to Pope. *Bug* carries the general sense of a small, nuisance insect or larva. More specifically, a caterpillar could be termed a "bug": Shaftesbury writes in *The Moralists* of "The Bug which breeds the Butterfly."[11] *Bug* could also mean, yet more to the point here, "A self-important, pompous, or conceited person; a pre-eminent or powerful person" (*OED*, s.v. "bug" *n.* 1. 2; earliest example 1536). Despite these several appropriate meanings of the word, however, the metaphor develops in ways that clearly continued to trouble Pope: neither bug nor caterpillar itself has gilded wings, and neither buzz, or stink, or sting.[12] "Fly" is less at odds with "butterfly," and Pope may have liked the alliterative consonance with "flap." Crucially, "fly" allows an easier transition of the metaphor into the bluebottle of the following lines. The coherence of the passage plainly matters, but the alternative readings here do not divide straightforwardly into sense and nonsense, coherence and incoherence. The choice between the readings is not cleanly decided by the textual and semantic evidence. This annotator retains the reading of the printed copy text, adduces Pope's autograph marginalium, and points out what senses of "bug" were available to Pope and consistent with the sense of the passage, and leaves the reader to interpret the evidence.

Pope's poetry is characterized by an extraordinary range of diction and his exploitation of the peculiarity and power of the carefully chosen word. His poems present many instances of necessary *lexical* clarification. In discussions theorizing about scholiastic procedure, the glossing of single words, often by reference to contemporary (or more specifically authorial) parallels, and especially by reference to historical dictionaries such as the *OED*, is usually thought of as only explanatory, a matter merely of "looking up." Even in simple cases, however, lexical explanations may involve a significant interpretative element. At the least, the annotator must discriminate among possible dictionary senses. Often the peculiarity of a word is less than obvious; the annotator searching for such cruces, like the editor searching for textual errors, is (to steal and adapt Housman's words)[13] a dog searching for hidden fleas. The lexical flea once found, and the identity of the flea established, the meaning of the passage may be changed, or expanded, or enriched. So, in the *Epistle to Arbuthnot*:

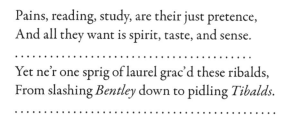

Ev'n such small critics some regard may claim,
Preserv'd in *Milton*'s or in *Shakespear*'s name. (ll. 159–68)

Having in the previous verse paragraphs lashed such Grub Street antagonists and rival poets as Dennis, Gildon, and Hervey, Pope here turns his attention to the new philologists, "each wight who reads not, and but scans and spells."

"Slashing *Bentley*" of course nails Richard Bentley's just-published edition of *Paradise Lost*, characterized by its marginal conjectures, and the "desperate hook[s]" within which Bentley had sequestrated readings and passages he thought to have been the product of a meddling early editor. "Slashing" is a military metaphor. "Pidling Tibalds" is Lewis Theobald, author of *Shakespeare Restored, or, A Specimen of the Many Errors as well Committed as Unamended by Mr. Pope* (1726). Theobald's detailed analysis of particular cruces in *Hamlet* is informed throughout by his knowledge and admiration of the methods of Bentley's historicizing classical scholarship. As the 1734 text of *Arbuthnot* put it, Theobald is one of the "piece-meal critics." Like other annotators, he deals in fragments, not whole meals.

Especially intriguing, however, in this couplet are the rhyme words, which apparently provide (to appropriate W. K. Wimsatt's phrase) a weaker "relation of rhyme to reason" than we expect of Pope. The rhyme might seem both cheap and comic. It is a two-syllable rhyme, highly unusual in his writing. As always, Pope reduces Theobald to "Tibald." Wimsatt indeed remarks that "Poor 'Tibald' was not a 'ribald.'"[14] The rhyme has more to say, however, and Theobald perhaps turns out to be more of a "ribald" than Wimsatt allows. "Ribalds" is a plural; it applies to Bentley as well as to Theobald, and to their wider scholiastic ilk. And the word "ribald" has several meanings. First, and most obviously, it refers to "a person of low social status," a rascal, a vagabond (*OED*, s.v. "ribald" *n*. A.1.a), or to "a foul-mouthed . . . person; one who uses offensive, irreverent, or scurrilous language" (*OED*, s.v. "ribald" *n*. A.2, citing this line). Johnson defines a ribald as "a loose, rough, mean, brutal wretch" (*Dictionary*, 1755; the examples include this couplet). The imputations of coarse language, uncouth behavior, and lower social status are appropriate to Bentley, the son of a yeoman farmer, who had been regularly accused of boorish incivility in his arguments with the gentlemen of Christ Church over the authenticity of the writings attributed to Phalaris. The imputations are less appropriate to Theobald, whose *Shakespeare Restored* offended Pope, but is free of Bentleian vulgarity. A search through the itemized listings of the *OED* shows, however, that "ribalds" has a third and more specific sense, still current in Pope's time, which skewers both men: "undisciplined camp followers or pillagers moving with ... the main body of an army, and sometimes acting as irregular soldiers ... hanger[s]-on" (*OED*, s.v. "ribald" *n.* 1a, 1.b, 2). "Ribalds" is richer in its implications, then, than the easy double rhyme might suggest. The rhyme bears out the burden of the couplet: unlaureled scholiasts Bentley and Theobald, like their philologizing fellows, are mere mercenaries, attendants on the armies of creative poetic genius, profiting illegitimately from their spoils, surreptitiously stealing their glory. Rhyme is related to reason after all.

A critical discussion of this couplet might say more than this. It might remind us that Bentley had been imaged in Swift's *Battel of the Books* as Thersites, most scabrous of camp followers, arguing with "the *Modern* Chiefs" over rights to the spoils of battle, and then attempting to kill "two Hero's of the *Antients* Army, *Phalaris* and *Aesop*," as they lay "fast asleep."[15] The critic might discuss how Pope here draws on a familiar topos of the Ancients and Moderns controversy. An explanatory footnote in a twenty-first-century edition of the poem, on the other hand, might do no more than list and evidence the peculiar and pertinent sense of the word "ribalds," and merely mention Bentley's thersitic role in Swift's mock-heroic *Battel*; to cite the lexicographical evidence and identify a likely intertext might be thought sufficient to place the reader "on the brink of interpretation."

There is, however, a fly in this scholiastic ointment, introduced by Pope's persistent tendency to adapt and revise his poems in manuscript and in print. In the fragmentary text of this passage printed in the 1727 Swift/Pope *Miscellanies* (though in no authorized printed edition of the whole poem, from its first separate folio publication in 1734 through to the end of Pope's life and beyond), Theobald is paired not with "slashing Bentley" but with "sanguine *Sew*—," that is, George Sewell, editor of Shakespeare's nondramatic works, published as a seventh, unsolicited, additional volume (1725) to Pope's *Shakespeare*. In the reading of the *Miscellanies* fragment, "ribalds" cannot therefore refer to Bentley, and cannot invoke Swift's *Battel*. Pope's replacement of Sewell's name with Bentley's was certainly motivated primarily by the appearance in 1732 of Bentley's edition of *Paradise Lost*; the change in target may reasonably be said to activate the older and specific meaning of "ribalds" in the passage.

There is a larger question of intention here. We have no direct access to what was in Pope's mind at the different times of the poem's composition and revision. An annotator cannot safely, here or anywhere, assert psychological intention. We do, however, have access, via surviving texts, to what he wrote and authorized for publication; we have access to his meaning intentions as embodied in the shareable language, syntax, and reference of his text. We have access also to broader intellectual contexts; here, especially, the library of themes and tropes that Pope and Swift used in connection with the new philological literary scholarship. The hypothesis is not in the end provable or falsifiable on the available textual evidence. Though common in the Middle Ages, the specific usage of "ribalds" to mean camp followers is rare in early modern writing.[16] (More usually, the word applies to blasphemers, rebels, rioters, and thieves.) Nevertheless, the pertinence of the word "ribald," in an available usage, to the sense of this passage, placed as it is in a prominent rhyming position, is reasonably strong evidence of intention to mean.

Some words used by Pope raise larger issues for explanation, and interpretation. Weighing the different possible denotations of the word "ribalds" is a relatively simple case. *OED* gives just seven subsenses, and though there is certainly some overlap among them, "ribald" as "camp follower" is distinct, and strongly related to the tenor of the passage in the *Epistle to Arbuthnot*. Using a lexicon such as *OED* can be more problematic, and may inevitably involve more interpretative judgment, in instances of what William Empson designated "complex words."[17] The standard historical dictionary format of listed senses, under a single or several categories, with illustrative quotations under each sense, provides an informative and helpful point of reference, but has its limitations. As Empson points out, in relation to the *OED*, a list of definitions under a headword in a dictionary may make redundant distinctions among the word's senses.[18] In any local use in a piece of writing—particularly in the dense, condensed writing of such a poet as Pope—the different senses of a word may interact. Even the *OED* may not capture all the historical nuances of a word's usages, or trace (as a thousand instances recorded in *Notes and Queries* confirm) the earliest usage of a word or demonstrate its full chronological range or its different senses, which may not be capable of clear differentiation. In real usage some words have rather clear, discrete, even technically specific meanings in their context in the poem. In such cases, to cite a dictionary definition is in itself explanatory (though other forms of evidence may also be helpful). Complex words, on the other hand, may be specific at a particular crux, but commonly blend different "dictionary" meanings.

Complex words (in Empson's sense) are a significant issue in Pope's *Epistle to Burlington*. *Burlington* was first published as a separate poem in 1731, with a title beginning *Of Taste*. . . . The title was changed[19] to *Of False Taste* . . . in "The Second Edition," published in 1731 (on the half-title page), and the three folios published in 1732 (on the title page). "Taste" as a concept is a focus of

Pope's attention and analysis throughout the poem. "Taste" as a word was and is complex. The word appears only half a dozen times in this poem of some two hundred lines, and almost always as a compromised term: a less intellectual and more physical relish, a voguish ostentation, a precocity and affectation. In the opening lines Pope wonders that the prodigal

> should waste
> His wealth, to purchase what he ne'er can taste?
> Not for himself he sees, or hears, or eats;
> Artists must chuse his Pictures, Music, Meats. (ll. 3–6)

"Taste" here is presumably *OED*, *v.* t. 8: "To like the taste of (usually *figurative*); to relish, approve of, enjoy, like, take pleasure in; in earlier use sometimes in neutral sense: to appreciate." The prodigal's aesthetic pleasure and understanding is here diminished and demeaned by its association with the physical senses. Elsewhere, taste is reduced to merely modish and profligate show:

> What brought Sir *Visto*'s ill-got wealth to waste?
> Some Dæmon whisper'd, "*Visto*! have a Taste." (ll. 15–16)

The nature-loving Sabinus wanders with joy through the natural scene of his growing woods; more fashionably,

> His Son's fine Taste an op'ner vista loves,
> Foe to the *Dryads* of his Father's groves. (ll. 91–92)

Neither of these last two uses can be simply illuminated by adduction of a dictionary definition. Nor do Pope's own footnotes to particular points in his satiric poem provide a positive or defining view of taste: "Abuse of the Word *Taste*," "the ill taste of those who are so fond of Evergreens," "the Principles of a false Taste of Magnificence," "false Taste in Books," "false Taste in *Music*," "And in *Painting*."

The word "sense," another complex word raising significant problems of meaning and definition, occurs four times in the body of the verse in *Epistle to Burlington*, never in any simple way for the five physical faculties. At its first appearance "sense" comes in a notably questionable shape, as a faculty essential to both architecture and landscape gardening:

> Something there is, more needful than Expence,
> And something previous ev'n to Taste—'tis *Sense*:
> Good Sense, which only is the gift of heav'n,
> And tho' no science, fairly worth the seven:
> A Light, which in yourself you must perceive;
> *Jones* and *Le Nôtre* have it not to give. (ll. 41–46)

In this account (to give voice to which Burlington himself is recruited), "*Sense*" is given priority over "*Taste*," and is represented as an internal faculty, a divine gift at least equal to other sciences, an inner light which cannot be acquired by study even of the two leading authorities in the two arts with which the poem is concerned. A primary meaning of "sense" in these lines is probably "ability or taste in matters of artistic judgement" (*OED*, s.v. "sense" *n.* 20); but "*Sense*" is here a complexly connotative usage. Pope's insistence on the internal nature of the faculty suggests that *OED*, s.v. "sense" *n.* 13 may also be operative: "A faculty or power of the mind or (in early use) the soul, such as imagination, reflection, memory, etc., often explicitly or implicitly contrasted with the bodily senses." Later in the poem Pope tells us that "*Sense*" is "of ev'ry Art the Soul" (line 65); where "ability or taste in matters of artistic judgement" appears to be the primary sense again, as it is when the landscape designer is advised that

> 'Tis *Use* alone that sanctifies Expence,
> And Splendor borrows all her rays from *Sense*. (ll. 177–78)

The collocation with "*Use*" suggests that the still-familiar usage of "sense" to refer to natural and practical intelligence, the ability to make sound judgments (*OED*, s.v. "sense" *n.* 11), may also be in play.

"Sense" is presented as a positive value in all of these instances and is therefore perhaps more susceptible than "taste" to local annotation, drawing more or less reliably on more or less appropriate subsenses provided by the historical dictionary. Nevertheless, Pope's uses of both of these complex and problematic words for aesthetic and moral conceptions can be open enough to puzzle explanation. Dr. Spencer Cowper promptly interrogated Pope on the subject of *taste* and *sense*, implying the obscurity of the relation between the terms, the vagueness of the two concepts, and the solipsism of both:

> what is't
> This thing thou boastest of so much, this TASTE?
> ....
> —'tis what I know, but cannot well describe;—
> How then shall meaner Souls this TASTE imbibe?
> —A Rule there is most certain, and but One,
> What is't?—'tis Sense—what Sense, dread Sir?—My Own.[20]

Modern scholiasts might not fully share Cowper's gleeful doubts, but could, in their effort to provide their reader with some illumination, be tempted to some fellow feeling. Because Pope's uses of these complex words are less than fully defined in their local settings, the attempt to determine or expand Pope's verbal meaning with a local *scholium* runs the risk of encountering just that local semantic imprecision that Cowper so tellingly lampoons. Yet some form of local *scholium* is necessary; a separate glossary of complex words would struggle to specify the meaning of such words in all their several places.

If an editor is to shed light on "taste" and "sense" as words and concepts in *Burlington*, it is necessary to take into account the larger discourse of the poem, and the particular discursive and cultural contexts within which Pope was writing. If individual uses of the word "taste" in the poem do not in themselves provide, or together amount to, a defined concept or complex of concepts, the poem as a whole might nevertheless be thought implicitly to delineate what Pope sought to communicate on the subject. The reader's apprehension of the poem in its parts and its whole—the reader's interpretation—may be aided by the annotator's clarification of the instances that lie behind, and construct, Pope's larger conceptions of true and false taste. The following lines, for instance, are the first in the poem in which Pope addresses Burlington himself. Here he briefly celebrates Burlington's architectural principles and achievements, and lampoons the abuses of those principles by the wealthy fools on whom heaven has visited "a Taste":

> You show us, *Rome* was glorious, not profuse
> And pompous buildings once were things of Use.
> Yet shall (my Lord) your just, your noble rules
> Fill half the land with Imitating Fools;
> ....
> Reverse your Ornaments, and hang them all

On some patch'd dog-hole ek'd with ends of wall,
Then clap four slices of Pilaster on't,
That, lac'd with bits of rustic, makes a Front.
Shall call the winds thro' long Arcades to roar,
Proud to catch cold at a *Venetian* door. (ll. 23–26, 31–36)

The lines are susceptible to targeted annotation, which potentially clarifies the relation of these specifics to true and false taste. Burlington here exemplifies true taste, particularly through his architectural designs, researches, and leadership. He has shown his contemporaries a truer sense of Vitruvian and Palladian architecture through his own publications, through his sponsorship of the writings of his followers,[21] and through his own architectural practice. Line 24 may refer to his plans for institutional buildings, of which two were built: Westminster School dormitory (1722–30) and York Assembly Rooms (1731–32). His designs, private as well as public, exemplified for Pope the belief that architecture according to Vitruvian and Palladian principles should be designed for its intended function, and should be intellectually and morally, as well as visually, coherent. Pope agreed that utility and convenience are key desiderata for good buildings; the stress here and elsewhere in the poem on the value of "use," and the association of "use" with true taste, recall Shaftesbury's insistence that *Beauty* and *Truth* are plainly join'd with the Notion of *Utility* and *Convenience*, even in the Apprehension of every ingenious Artist, the *Architect*, the *Statuary*, or the *Painter*."[22] The "imitating Fools" attempt what they do not understand; the importance of proper architectural rules, and the lamentable frequency of their misuse and misapplication, was a standard trope, in the writings of the eighteenth-century British Palladians, and of Palladio himself: "they who shall read these my books, may be able to make use of whatever will be good therein ... that one may learn ... to lay aside the strange abuses, the barbarous inventions, the superfluous expence ... that have been seen in many fabricks."[23] To clap "slices of Pilaster" on some wretched building is an offence against decorum and architectural logic: a coherent Palladian frontage requires true structural columns. Colonnades, connecting the central block with wings at each side, as at Houghton, are a familiar feature of the Palladian country house; open colonnades are appropriate to the balmy Veneto, but a dysfunctional abuse in windy Britain. So "taste" in architecture, and its opposites, might be shown to be articulated in these verses.

A second and broader defining context for "taste" is to be found in English exploration of and debate about the concept in the years when Pope was forming his own views. Delineation of that context requires the larger space of a headnote or appendix. Extended discussion of "taste" as an aesthetic, and ethical, faculty appeared in England early in the second decade of the eighteenth century, most significantly in Shaftesbury's *Characteristicks* (1711) and in the essays of Addison, particularly in *Spectator* 409 (June 19, 1712).[24] Shaftesbury deals with issues of religious belief, the arts, ethics, and aesthetics.[25] No particular crux in the *Epistle to Burlington* points directly to him, but the context provided by him and other authors on the subject of taste provides a pertinent guide to Pope's poem, on which an annotating editor might credibly draw.

Shaftesbury argues for a politics of true taste, led by the knowledgeable and polite. A true taste is acquired through study of the best classical and modern models by "lovers of art and ingenuity, such as have seen the world, and informed themselves of the manners and customs of the several nations of Europe," and have "searched into ... their architecture, sculpture, painting, music and their taste in poetry, learning, language, and conversation." Taste is based on nature; the aim of the man "who by pains and industry" has "acquired a real taste in arts ... is not to bring truth and nature to his humour; but . . . to accommodate his humour and fancy to their standard." By the exercise of such tastes "he understands how to lay out his garden, model his house, ... appoint his table." Nature's standard includes principles of regularity, form, and function which apply to all the arts; it is impossible "to advance ... in any ... taste of outwards symmetry and order, without acknowledging that the proportionate and regular state is the truly prosperous and natural in every subject."[26] True taste is a matter not only of aesthetics, but of ethics. Taste in music, for instance, demands knowledge of harmony, for "harmony is harmony by nature, let men judge ever so ridiculously of music," and "Virtue has the same fixed standard. The same numbers, harmony and proportion will have place in morals and are discoverable in the characters and affections of mankind."[27]

Shaftesbury's thoughts on taste have some evident resonances for the *Epistle to Burlington*. Pope similarly insists on study of the best classical and Renaissance models of architecture. For Pope, taste is not individual and solipsistic, but based, as he too conceived it, on "truth and nature," and on such a basis the man of taste understands how, or how not, "to lay out his garden, model his house, . . . appoint his table." Like Shaftesbury, Pope stresses in his poem the importance of regularity and symmetry in architecture, and the necessary connection of those values both with nature and with the virtuous and sociable life.

The problems the annotator of Pope faces are, in George Steiner's sense, "contingent." They are susceptible to the identification and proper application of closely pertinent evidence. The annotator constructs local explanatory hypotheses, valid to the degree they are supported by the evidence, and capable of falsification.[28] Pope's more complex and philosophical words and concepts require more discursive responses, often drawing on broader cultural, as well as local textual, contexts and evidence. Pope's elaborate and drawn-out habits of revision, the survival of multiple autograph drafts and printed texts, pose questions of explication as well as of textual choice. Neither category of non-contingent difficulty need lead the annotator to any extreme of skepticism. Textual plurality is not equivalent to textual indeterminacy; the surviving textual witnesses are multiple, but discrete. Responsible textual editors and annotators make informed choices and evaluations among those discrete witnesses. Ambiguity in verbal meaning is not equivalent to indeterminacy in verbal meaning.[29] Contextualizing discursive explanations is not mere speculation but, where supported by relevant documentary evidence, constitutes larger hypotheses, similarly open to validation and falsification, though they teeter on the edge of larger-scale interpretation and, perhaps without great danger, are more likely to fall over that brink.

NOTES

1. Melvyn New, "'At the Backside of the Door of Purgatory': A Note on Annotating *Tristram Shandy*," in *Tristram Shandy: Riddles and Mysteries* (London: Vision Press, 1984), 15–23.

2. I discuss the relation of local meanings with overarching meanings, and the significance of that relation for interpretation, in "Swift, the Church, and Religion: The Sermons, the *Tale*, and the Critics," in *Reading Swift: Papers from the Seventh Münster Symposium*, ed. Janika Bischof, Kirsten Juhas, and Hermann J. Real (Paderborn: Brill, 2019), 343–60.

3. *Guidelines*, December 2019, 17. The founding general editors are James McLaverty (now general editor emeritus) and Michael Suarez; they have been joined by Henry Woudhuysen, Paul Baines, Valerie Rumbold, and myself.

4. Our copy text is ESTC T5399; R. H. Griffith, *Alexander Pope: A Bibliography* (Austin: University of Texas Press, 1922), G388.

5. By the word "intention" I refer throughout not to the author's internal and unknowable mental state (Karl Popper's "second world" of mental states or acts), but to the author's intention to create communicable meaning by setting words down in discursive forms

110 | Notes on Footnotes

(Popper's "third world" of human discourse; Popper, *Objective Knowledge*, rev. ed. [Oxford: Oxford University Press, 1979], 162–63). My use of "intention" approximates to the second of Michael Hancher's three kinds: "*active intention*, or the intention that what one writes mean (and be recognized to mean) something" ("Three Kinds of Intention," *Modern Language Notes* 87 [1972]: 791–802).

6. George Steiner, "On Difficulty," in *On Difficulty and Other Essays* (Oxford: Oxford University Press, 1978), 26–27. Steiner's three other classes of textual difficulty—"modal," "tactical," and "ontological"—require, to a lesser or greater degree, interpretation, rather than explication.

7. *Last and Greatest Art: Some Unpublished Poetical Manuscripts of Alexander Pope*, transcribed and ed. Maynard Mack (Newark: University of Delaware Press, 1984), 425. Cf. below, Michael Edson's discussion of the problematics of identification in eighteenth-century satire.

8. See Alexander Pope, *The Correspondence*, ed. George Sherburn, 5 vols. (Oxford: Oxford University Press, 1956), 3:33–34.

9. Pope's autograph revisions in the surviving manuscripts are extremely complex and pose a serious challenge to clear and adequate reporting. In the case of *An Essay on Man*, for example, it would be impossible to construct a record readily comprehensible to the reader, even if space in our printed volumes was not limited. Our approach is flexible, however, and where manuscript variants are significant and capable of description, editors will decide whether to include them in the historical collation. In any case, volume editors will include discussion of the manuscripts as they judge it appropriate, and will discuss important manuscript variants (including those recorded by Jonathan Richardson or Warburton) in the explanatory notes.

10. Alexander Pope, *Works* (1736), II.90. British Library C. 122.e.31.

11. Shaftesbury, *Moralists* (1709), II.iv.127; cited in *OED*, s.v. "bug" *n.* 2.I.1; see Anthony Ashley Cooper, 3rd Earl of Shaftesbury, *Characteristics of Men, Manners, Opinions, Times*, ed. Lawrence E. Klein (Cambridge: Cambridge University Press, 2000), 285.

12. Johnson defines "bug" as "a stinking insect bred in old houshold stuff," cites Pope's couplet, and remarks that, in this his sole example, "wings are erroneously ascribed to it" (*Dictionary*, 1755).

13. A. E. Housman, "The Application of Thought to Textual Criticism," *Proceedings of the Classical Association* 18 (1921): 67–84.

14. W. K. Wimsatt, "One Relation of Rhyme to Reason: Alexander Pope," *Modern Language Quarterly* 5 (1944): 323–38.

15. Jonathan Swift, *A Tale of a Tub and Other Works*, ed. Marcus Walsh (Cambridge: Cambridge University Press, 2010), 160–62.

16. For a clear instance, see Richard III's oration to his troops before the battle of Bosworth, as narrated by John Speed: "What are [Henry Tudor's] followers but a sort of fainting runagates . . . onely braggers without any great deeds, . . . Ribaulds without reason, . . . neuer seene in the Front of a Battell" (*The History of Great Britaine under the Conquests of ye Romans, Saxons, Danes and Normans* [London, 1611], 724).

17. William Empson, *Structure of Complex Words* (London: Penguin, 1995).

18. Empson discusses the problematics of the list format of historical dictionaries in *Structure*, 391–413; cf. 86–87.

19. Probably at the prompting of Aaron Hill, in a letter to Pope of December 17, 1731 (Pope, *Correspondence*, 3:257; cf. 3:268).

20. *Of Good Nature. An Epistle Humbly Inscrib'd to his G—ce the D-ke of C——s* (London, January 22, 1732), 11–12.

21. Notably, Burlington's own *Fabbriche antiche disegnate' da Andrea Palladio Vicentino* (1730), William Kent's *Designs of Inigo Jones* (1727), Isaac Ware's *Designs of Inigo Jones and Others* (1731), and Robert Castell's *Villas of the Ancients Illustrated* (1728).

22. *Characteristics*, ed. Klein, 414–15.

23. *The Four Books of Andrea Palladio's Architecture*, trans. Isaac Ware (London, 1738), A1ᵛ. In the preface to *Fabbriche Antiche*, Burlington himself complains that no other age "has ever shown a greater disposition for costly building, nor has produced more ignorant pretenders, who have guided others out of the true lines of so beautiful an art" (trans. Morris R. Brownell, in *Alexander Pope and the Arts of Georgian England* [Oxford: Oxford University Press, 1978], 305).

24. Pope could also have come across *Taste. An Essay* (1732), selected and translated into English from the *Traité des Etudes* (Paris, 1726–31) of the French Jansenist historian and educator Charles Rollin.

25. Pope had read at least parts of the *Characteristicks*. He alludes to Shaftesbury's "The Moralist" at *Dunciad* 4:487–88. Pope's response to Shaftesbury has been extensively discussed by modern scholars in relation to *Essay on Man*.

26. "Miscellaneous Reflections on the Preceding Treatises and Other Critical Subjects," in *Characteristics*, ed. Klein, 405, 408, 409, 414–15.

27. "Soliloquy, or Advice to an Author," in *Characteristics*, ed. Klein, 157.

28. I have discussed hypothesis formation in annotation in my article "Hypotheses, Evidence, Editing, and Explication," *Yearbook of English Studies* 29 (1999): 24–42.

29. "Most verbal meanings are imprecise and ambiguous, and to call them such is to acknowledge their determinacy" (E. D. Hirsch, *Validity in Interpretation* [New Haven: Yale University Press, 1967], 44–45).

CHAPTER 7

❧ Uninformed Readers and the Crisis of Annotation

Michael Edson

Several of the preceding chapters have followed a familiar formula for editorial self-reflection, "This is what I did and why I did it."[1] My chapter does something different. Unlike most of the authors in this volume, I am a user rather than a maker of explanatory notes, and, as an outsider, I realize the reflections to follow may be a target for criticism. One need only look to "The Editorial Imagination," a recurring feature in *Essays in Criticism*, to see how often debates about editing involve only editor-insiders, and how frequently these editor-insiders chastise noneditors who challenge procedures of annotation.[2] Since I consider annotating satires that divide readers into insider-outsider, expert-amateur camps, it is worth mentioning from the start how discussions of editing are not free from such divisions. In the 1980s, for example, attacked by proponents of deconstruction and social editing, textual scholars felt called on to defend the editing profession, casting their antagonists (sometimes fairly) as ill-informed outsiders. As I suggest, the preference for explanatory notes reflecting informed, insider reading from the past aided this defense of a profession in crisis, though this preference might be reconsidered today.

For annotators working with knowledgeable past readers in mind, eighteenth-century satire presents a problem case: many topical satires enlist various devices—blanks, initials, pseudonyms—to obscure the persons or institutions attacked. As Claire Lamont has suggested, the central aim of annotation is to "remove" obscurity or inaccessibility. But are all problems of access equal?[3] The inaccessibility of satire is neither always an accident of time nor a product of law; as Andrew Benjamin Bricker has shown, be-dashed names rarely helped avoid libel charges, and satirists continued using them long after this inefficacy became clear.[4] Such obscurity was instead often intended, I would argue, to contribute to what Sean Silver has identified as satire's policing of "boundaries between in- and out-groups."[5] This claim challenges the idea embodied in decades of scholarly editions with exhaustive contextualizing annotation: that satirists aim at expert or insider readers, and only such readers can fully appreciate the intended message or experience. By treating satiric innuendoes as if archaic words, once obvious but no longer so, and by identifying them for modern readers, annotators today tend to overlook the possibility of deliberate inaccessibility. While annotators should not withhold information, nor decline to identify some allusions on the basis of likely unintelligibility in the past, I want to suggest they reconsider how to explicate blanks and allusions without implying their solutions were obvious and without difficulty for early readers. Using Samuel Garth's *The Dispensary* (1699) as an example, I argue that satire hardly requires understanding every allusion, and that the feelings of deficiency or exclusion prompted by blanks and initials may add to understanding. Annotators need to consider how explanatory notes can obscure the play of access and exclusion in satire, a dynamic in which sometimes not knowing could be both intended and central to the intended takeaway.

At least since F. W. Bateson declared that annotation recovers "what [texts] mean[t] to their author and his original readers," annotators have sought to balance authorial intention and historical reception.[6] One forceful advocate of this both/and approach was Martin Battestin. Writing in 1981 about Fielding's novels, he identifies explanatory notes as retrieving for an editor's contemporaries "what a passage meant to the author and his first readers."[7] Most subsequent rationales are variations on Battestin's. For Ian Small and Marcus Walsh, the annotator renders modern readers "as 'competent' as the original intended readership, by making available again a once-shared 'linguistic and literary expertise.'"[8] Paul Hammond, in his Dryden edition for the Longman Poets, defines annotation as providing "information which would have been available to well-informed Restoration readers."[9] Linda Bree and James McLaverty view annotators as explaining what "may well have been obvious at least to some of the author's original readers."[10] Even as they rectify modern ignorance of history and the classics, annotators of eighteenth-century works depend on some concept of past readers. But note the shift in focus: where Battestin pursued actual readers, these later annotators turn to intended, informed readers.

While the intentionalism of these rationales might be questioned, I narrow my own disagreement to the use of informed past readers as the model for what annotation re-creates for modern users of editions. Specifically, I question three editorial assumptions: (1) authors only intend writings for informed readers, (2) only informed readers interpret as intended, and (3) annotation helps later readers achieve the intended understanding by providing information. While this concept of intention does, in fact, work in most cases, problems arise in annotating satires featuring blanks and similar obstacles. When such devices were no longer found effective at avoiding libel, why did satirists continue to use them? Does understanding a satire require recognizing all or most of the disguised targets? To reconsider what counts as "informed" or "competent" reading in satire is a timely pursuit: many writers best known for satire are at this time either receiving a new annotated edition (Byron, Pope, Swift) or awaiting an update (Butler, Churchill, Garth).

At this point, one might turn to Swift's *Importance of the Guardian Considered* (1713) for a rebuttal: blanks and like devices did not frustrate comprehension because they concealed what was obvious to everyone. Presenting such devices in the traditional way, as a means to avoid libel charges, Swift emphasizes the all-knowingness of satire's original readers: "First, we are careful never to print a Man's Name out at length; ... *So that although every Body alive knows whom I mean*, the Plaintiff can have no Redress in any Court of Justice. Secondly, by putting Cases; Thirdly, by Insinuations; Fourthly, by celebrating the Actions of others, who acted directly contrary to the Persons we would reflect on: Fifthly, by Nicknames, either commonly known or stamp'd for the purpose, *which every Body can tell how to apply*" (emphasis mine).[11] However much his protestations anticipate those of modern annotators, Swift's twice declaring that "every Body" can recognize satire's victims seems misplaced, and not merely because the career of his colleague Pope was one long struggle against contemporaries misconstruing his satiric targets. Evidence suggests that innuendo eluded many readers, at least on the first pass. In a 1699 letter to Thomas Tanner, William Adams wrote, "As to the Satyr you mention of Dr. Garth's [*The Dispensary*], I've seen it: but understand it not perfectly. You must in your next letter give me a kind of Key &c."[12] Of Manley's *New Atalantis* (1709), Thomas Hearne observed that the satire "was not easily understood" without "the key that was handed about."[13] Keys do pursue profit or publicity under cover of explanation, but Adams and Hearne imply that keys also addressed real deficits of understanding. Incomprehension even befell authors' friends. John Wilkes groused in 1764 about "obscurities" in his friend Charles Churchill's satires, and Swift reversed his earlier position and claimed the 1728 *Dunciad* baffled both himself and readers "twenty miles from London," where "no body understands hints, initial letters, or town-facts."[14] It is hard to imagine a real reader closer to an intended reader than Swift was for Pope, yet Swift struggled. Combined with marginalia in surviving early copies of satires by Dryden, Manley, and others—which show contemporaries failing to identify targets or identifying them incorrectly—the above testimonies suggest not only that authors and early readers often diverged in their interpretations but also that blanks did disguise and targets were not always obvious.[15]

The overrating of reader competence has not gone overlooked by scholars, though it has not yet had much influence on explanatory annotation. Steven N. Zwicker notes the scholarly tendency "to impute encyclopedic knowledge to readers in the past."[16] As Michael McKeon observed two decades ago, the vast explanatory notes to the Yale *Poems on Affairs of State* (*POAS*), far from catching up the late moderns to the early ones, in fact "elevate" today's readers beyond the "understanding available to the average [Restoration] reader who read without benefit of explanatory notes."[17] How many past readers would have noticed more than a few dozen of the hundreds of parallels and allusions identified in recent editions of Swift's *A Tale of a Tub* or Manley's *New Atalantis*? As Robert D. Hume observes, "No reader of the time would have been able to supply more than a smattering of the identifications, even when the poems were new. To presume that these works were readily intelligible to their original readers is a serious error."[18] Yet annotators today continue to presume such intelligibility in a qualified way: admitting that many actual readers would have been ignorant, they tend to view intended readers as ideal, all-knowing, and since these readers also guide modern practices of annotation, explanatory notes supply what these ideal readers supposedly understood, including the identities behind the blanks and asterisks. One might counter that *POAS*, as mainly coterie verse, does not reflect the greater accessibility of the public satires of Pope and Swift. Yet as confusion within Pope's own circle over his targets implies, satiric references were never fully transparent, even to insiders.[19]

With all this contrary evidence, writers would not have expected highly informed readers alone. My belief is that satirists knew the capacities of readers and sometimes turned gaps in their knowledge to advantage. Otherwise, the

116 | Notes on Footnotes

jokes in some satires about incomprehension and failure would make little sense: in his *Vernoniad* (1741), for example, Fielding taunts readers as "egregiously ignorant of History who cannot fill . . . up" his poem's blanks.[20] Samuel Johnson's "common reader" had no special learning and would not have lived up to the expectations for intended readers that Dustin Griffin attributes to the Twickenham Pope editors: "The present-day reader, in the Twickenham view, needs to know not only where Pope refers to the South Sea Bubble or to Walpole's mistress but that Addison stands behind Atticus, and Hervey behind Sporus, *since Pope expected his first readers to see the originals*" (emphasis mine).[21] It seems doubtful that Pope expected such perfection for every blank in every satire. Surely understanding was less important in some cases than in others, as in the 1728 *Dunciad*, where occasionally struggling with blanks only proved that the dunces were both forgotten and forgettable. For all the uproar over the real-life equivalent of Timon in the *Epistle to Burlington* (1731), Pope continued to disguise many targets in his *Imitations of Horace* (1733), risking further misreading and incomprehension. Satirists apparently expected or desired that some would struggle or fail to identify some targets, making these struggles or failures part of the intended experience.

The essay that best illuminates the rationale for annotators' focus on expert, intended readers is Ian Small's "The Editor as Annotator as Ideal Reader." Though an editor of nineteenth-century works, Small handles issues of access and reader competence in the same way as recent editors of eighteenth-century texts. In his essay, Small immediately dismisses the possibility of a "perfectly competent reader" in the past for whom all allusions and meanings were available.[22] The impossibility of this reader makes problems for annotators who, like Battestin, work by reconstructing the competence of actual, historical readers. Citing the dialect in Emily Brontë's *Wuthering Heights* (1847), Small asserts that we cannot know if some writings were meant to be intelligible for every early reader, leaving those annotating according to actual, historical readers in a bind: annotate for readers who understood, or for those who did not? Small takes seriously that writers may at times intend less than complete understanding, leading him to conclude that providing modern audiences with the information possessed by "readers which the author had, or could have had, in mind" (206) is the only real option for scholarly annotators.

The persistence of something like Small's approach in recent eighteenth-century editions may make it look more persuasive than it actually is. The problem is that such rationales struggle to escape the ideal, all-knowing reader they claim to reject. The reason for this is not simply that informative annotation looks unjustified if authors intended to reach some uninformed readers. The larger reason is complexity: while providing a general sense of intention, available evidence often gives little guidance on local issues, such as how satiric blanks should be identified, and which blanks were intended to be challenging or obscure. While Small admits that authors can intend incomprehension, not knowing comes in more degrees or varieties than knowing. At least as presented in scholarly editions identifying every possible reference and innuendo, knowledge comprises total mastery, whereas readers might be ignorant about some, but not all, the gutted names. How can one annotate for the latter? Without an all-knowing, intended reader, grounding explanatory annotation on a concept of intention fails to offer more stable, determinate meanings than an audience-based approach. Best to admit that ignorance may have been meant for some while still annotating texts with the more determinate, informed historical reader in mind.

The dominance of the intended, expert reader as the basis for annotation must be seen in the context of editorial responses to certain challenges in the 1980s, when our current rationales for annotation developed. Small seems to gravitate toward intended, expert readers because he views knowledge about actual readers as too mushy, too variable, compared to the more solid, objective world of intended readers and intention. Writing in the 1990s, Small was not alone in shrinking from the perceived subjectivism and variability of reader-based approaches: attacked by proponents of deconstruction, reader-response criticism, and social editing, which substituted to varying degrees readers for authors and readings for fixed meanings, editors had reasons to be suspicious. Small, for example, goes out of the way to dismiss deconstruction as having no place in editing (191). Audience-based annotation was less easily dispatched: like the social editing of Jerome McGann and others, which extended intention to the acts of readers, audience-based annotation could be seen to confuse objective explication with subjective interpretation. As the many rebuttals of McGann appearing in the 1990s imply, the social editor's collusion with the theorist-outsiders deserved a stronger rebuke; the distinction between theory and editing needed reiterating, lest social editing endanger the concepts—intention, meaning, and literature—central to editing's professional status and authority. Traditional editors saw social editing introducing insuperable difficulties into text editing: if the author's final version was no more authoritative than versions adjusted by friends or later publishers, editors would be forced "to reproduce everything written, literally every mark on every page."[23] Small

118 | Notes on Footnotes

perhaps fears the same crisis in annotation, where all identifications, no matter how irrelevant or wrong, would go into footnotes because some ill-informed early reader made the association with a satiric innuendo.

The question today is whether annotators should continue to distinguish intention- from audience-based annotation for reasons that may now seem outdated. Social editing no longer stirs controversy; editors no longer need to fend off deconstructionists. Eighteenth-century disguised satire is one instance that would benefit from blending of intention- and audience-based approaches to annotation. Blanks, initials, and nicknames solicit reader involvement; even if satirists had one target in mind or preferred some identifications to others, these devices leave the responsibility of identification to readers. Clever readers can find unintended innuendo or allegory anywhere, and annotators are hardly required to explicate such private associations. But blanks and like devices are textual spaces where *significances* become *meanings*, in E. D. Hirsch's usage of the terms, and editors might acknowledge this more when annotating. Of course, satirists sometimes regretted the results—think of Pope's dismay with the applications of Timon—but they kept at it because, I would suggest, failing to fill some blanks or to recognize targets could send important signals to readers. Annotating such devices therefore requires allowing that intended readers may not always be informed readers, and that difficulty, failure, ignorance, and exclusion may have been at times part of the intended experience. To illustrate these claims, I discuss below Garth's *Dispensary*, which demonstrates one of the larger sorts of understanding that can arise from local failures of comprehension. Eager to defend the medical profession, Garth uses such failures to define what makes a professional and, along the way, fictionalizes a historical event with some resemblance to the perceived crisis in the field of editing in the 1990s.

Again, the idea that annotation supplies later audiences with the knowledge of intended readers runs into problems when authors intend parts of their writings to be inaccessible, at least to some. Such tactical inaccessibility, I argue, though central to Garth's mock-heroic satire, drops from view in the notes in the standard 1970 edition by Frank H. Ellis, who explicates the poem's medical terms and its ninety or so concealed topical references. Annotators have always struggled with texts meaning different things to different readers, including texts or portions of texts being for some readers meaningless, however meaning is defined. While Small acknowledges that authors can aim at different readers simultaneously, for him the author's and therefore annotator's preference is with knowing readers, whose knowledge allows for the fullest appreciation of the author's intention. While Garth does aim at fellow doctors supporting the free clinic project of 1698 memorialized in his title, the readers best able to grasp what scholars have seen as Garth's primary purpose—to defend professional boundaries and illustrate the dangers of not doing so—are probably those, including apothecaries, near the edge of these boundaries, those who do not know, or who struggle to recognize, some of the poem's many medical, classical, and topical references, knowledge of which confers professional status and expertise.

The 1698 dispute between the London apothecaries and the Royal College of Physicians over the dispensary was just one episode in a longer crisis. From its founding in 1617, the Society of Apothecaries was firmly subordinated to the College, whose members diagnosed patients, prescribed remedies, and licensed apothecaries to sell medicine. Class divides reinforced professional ones: classically educated at Oxford or Cambridge, the physicians dismissed the apothecaries as profit-driven shopkeepers ignorant of "the traditional teachings of Galen and Hippocrates." During the 1660s, however, apothecaries began diagnosing and treating patients, even claiming to do these jobs better than physicians.[24] The physicians in turn tried to restrict apothecaries from accessing medical knowledge. In 1687, the College first directed that prescriptions sent to apothecaries no longer include directions for usage. Then, it forbade members to "reveal or divulge the[ir] Secrets" to the apothecaries, including knowledge of treatments and symptoms.[25] Finally, the College proposed a dispensary, which would take business from the apothecaries. Though focusing on the clinic, Garth's poem participates in this longer-running defense of expertise against those who held that experience trumps education and credentials. One wonders what Garth would think of the many self-declared experts online today.

Not content to sit by while the dispensary made them victims of what we might describe as labor casualization, the apothecaries persuaded their allies in the College to impede the project. It is this disloyal few, the "apothecary physicians," for whom Garth, a College member and supporter of the clinic, reserves his fiercest attacks in *The Dispensary*, published in May 1699. Like the editors of a later time, who saw in social editing's embrace of theory a threat to the field of editing greater than that posed by theory alone, Garth regarded the physicians' embrace of the apothecaries as more dangerous to the profession than the apothecaries themselves. Garth's intention is clear. Through his satire he seeks to quell the same strife that he had attempted to heal two years earlier, in his 1697 Harveian oration, a speech to the College in which he pled for a "return again to unitie" in their ranks. There, he had appealed to a shared professional identity and authority, reminding listeners not to forget their "Interest as Fellowes of this Colledge," lest they allow the apothecaries to take their jobs.[26] Garth repeats his appeal in *The Dispensary*, both in its preface, where he shames the apothecary physicians for selling out "the Dignity of their own Profession," and in the poem, where he presents their collusion as part of a larger devaluation of expertise portending a public health catastrophe.[27]

The form of *The Dispensary* forces on its readers the insider-outsider, expert-layperson dichotomies endangered in the world beyond the poem. I do not mean chiefly Garth's mock-heroic form, though this contributes. In narrating low or trivial events in elevated, comically inappropriate terms, mock heroic naturalizes social and professional hierarchies: the many collapsed distinctions and false equivalences in *The Dispensary* emphasize the need to respect ranks and distinctions. The formal element I mainly have in mind is Garth's use of blanks, technical terms, and mock-classical pseudonyms, which alert readers to their own place in a system of differential knowledge and divided labor. Following Ellis, who restores letters Garth omitted from names and explains both Garth's targets and his medical terms, scholars can miss the point: the struggle and sometimes failure to grasp portions of *The Dispensary* is central to the poem's intended effect. Scholars working from Ellis's edition not only present Garth's targets as obvious, but also treat their identification as unrelated to Garth's enforcing of distinctions on those who would ignore them.[28] But Garth surely knew he would reach some readers without all the topical and technical knowledge to understand. What did these readers take from the poem? In denying the apothecaries access to knowledge and excluding their hands-on experience from the realm of true expertise, the College defended its own authority by restricting access to information. Likewise, Garth confronts his readers with the limits of their knowledge, thereby reminding them of their place on the expert-novice divide.

At first glance, Garth's blanks and pseudonyms, like those in so many satires from the century to follow, sell the illusion of access to restricted knowledge. Consider two passages, the first describing the library of the apothecary-physician Carus in canto 4, the second narrating a part of the battle between apothecaries and doctors in canto 5:

Uninformed Readers and the Crisis of Annotation | 121

And up these shelves, much *Gothick* Lumber climbs,
With *Swiss* Philosophy, and *Danish* Rhimes.
And hither, rescu'd from the *Grocers*, come
M—— Works entire, and endless Rheams of *Bloom*.
Where wou'd the long neglected *C*——*s* fly,
If bounteous *Carus* should refuse to buy? (page 47; cf. Ellis ed.,
   4.130–35)

From *Stentor*'s sinewy Arm an Opiate flys,
And straight a deadly Sleep clos'd *Carus*'s Eyes,
Chiron hit *Siphilus* with *Calomel*,
And scaly Crusts from his maim'd Forehead fell.
At *Colon* great *Japix Rhubarb* flung,
. . . .
Scribonius a vast *Eagle-stone* let fly
At *Psylas*, but *Lucina* put it by. (page 67; cf. Ellis ed., 5.191–200)

The problem is that passages like these never disclose all; readers draw identifications from their own stores of information, something easy enough for
physicians or those frequenting their circles. However, for outsiders such
passages only stir feelings of ignorance, exclusion, and inequality. Ellis's filling
in the blanks in the first passage ("*More*'s Works entire, and endless Rheams
of *Bloom*") is a more obvious instance of what his notes identifying Stentor
et al. in the second passage also do: they diminish awareness today that some
experience of not knowing, momentary or continued, was intended.[29] As
formal restrictions on access, these pseudonyms and similar devices remind
readers of the bounds of their knowledge and, accordingly, of their place in
social and professional hierarchies. Struggling to identify the physician-
characters would remind readers that they themselves are not doctors. When
modern annotators make these obstacles disappear in the belief that intended
readers understood everything, they distort the intention they claim to recover.
This is not to suggest that annotation is warping or oppressive and therefore
needs to be discontinued; rather, annotators just need to do more to indicate
which references were more or less likely intended to be recognized by some
or all past readers.

Modern annotators are not simply doing what the early makers of keys to
satire did. Appearing as late as 1714, the printed keys to *The Dispensary* at best
reduce, not eliminate, inaccessibility. Of the poem's ninety or so potentially

identifiable innuendoes, surviving keys identify no more than thirty-six. Further, the keys break their promise of access, sometimes introducing further obstacles, as one key did for Spadillio in canto 4: "A Footman, who has got an Estate: I suppose the Author means Mr. *A——— M———*."[30] The existence of such keys demonstrates less that Garth's actual readers (with or without keys) were informed than that many, as Adams confessed to Tanner, felt left out, even after consulting a key. Adams's experience was close to the intended one. In a letter to Arthur Charlett written soon after the poem's publication, Garth identifies twenty-one of its characters. Charlett may have requested assistance in a prior letter, but Garth seems to have anticipated Charlett's confusion, which would indicate Garth as intending some, even specialists, to be puzzled: "I have subscrib'd ye interpretation ye Town putts upon some names and abbreviations in a late Poem you have been pleas'd to reade."[31] Charlett was a doctor, though not a London one, so Garth had reason to include him in the joke—but without dissipating all the mystery. Also consider the copy at the Harvard Medical Library with marginal notations dated 1699 by a Henry Ffowns, which identifies sixty-five characters, including all but two of those Garth identified for Charlett, though in six instances Ffowns's identifications differ from Garth's.[32] Blanks may be left blank or misidentified for reasons other than difficulty or ignorance. But assuming that at least some of his omissions or variants do reflect a struggle to understand, Ffowns differs little from the less than perfect reader imagined in Garth's letter to Charlett.

What perhaps most divided readers of *The Dispensary* into experts and nonexperts never received notice in any of the printed keys: the classical allusions and medical terms. Consider the following passage, where a personified Envy chews the scrolls of Fame:

> And as the rent Records in pieces fell,
> Each Scrap did some immortal Action tell.
> This show'd, how fix'd as Fate *Torquatus* stood,
> That, the fam'd Passage of the *Granick* Flood.
> The *Julian* Eagles here, their Wings display;
> And there, all pale, th' expiring *Decii* lay.
> This does *Camillus* as a God extol,
> That points at *Manlius* in the Capitol.
> How *Cochles* did the *Tyber*'s Surges brave,
> How *Curtius* plung'd into the gaping Grave.

Great *Cyrus* here, the *Medes* and *Persians* join,
And there, the Glorious Battel of the *Boyn*. (2.25–36)

Most of these densely packed references are classical, and making sense of them in 1699 would have required reading Latin. The medium of both Garth's Harveian oration and the College's entrance exams, Latin had long served as a tool for class and professional differentiation. Latin was the main way in which doctors set themselves apart from apothecaries, few of whom had substantial knowledge of Latin or ancient medical works. Readers, including apothecaries, who struggled with passages like that above were invited to see their own lack of the expertise needed to claim the physician's mantle. Such passages reiterate the College's rebuttal of the apothecaries' ambitions: medicine was not a mechanic task, of diagnosis and treatment alone, but rather a liberal art. By identifying the allusions without reminding modern readers who in the past would have recognized them, Ellis diminishes Garth's intended point.

The same goes for Ellis's handling of Garth's references to medicines. Garth emphasizes how the apothecaries have little grasp of medical terms and treatments, as in the passage below, where the apothecary Horoscope makes a burnt offering while "mumbl[ing] o'er / Vile Terms of Art" in prayer:

With cold *Solanum* from the *Pontick* Shore,
The Roots of *Mandrake* and Black *Ellebore*.
And on the Structure next he heaps a Load
Of *Sassafras* in Chips, and *Mastick* Wood.
Then from the Compter he takes down the File,
And with Prescriptions lights the solemn Pile. (3.70–71; 81–86)

For Horoscope, medical "Terms of Art" become things, incantations used to help apothecaries sound like true experts, the result being, for Garth, malpractice and death. It seems more than coincidence, then, that his poem would mention many treatments while often leaving vague what they treated. For readers who knew little of what solanum or sassafras healed, the passage's obscurity reiterated the knowledge distinguishing doctors from nondoctors. In this respect, Garth's poem again replays the College's own efforts to monopolize knowledge by omitting certain information from prescriptions. Yet Ellis identifies the usages of solanum and the rest; while grasping Horoscope's ignorance about such medicines, users of Ellis's edition are exempted from Garth's apparent aim to have them share Horoscope's exclusion, which would reinforce the absurdity of his medical aspirations. While modern readers need to know that solanum was a real medicine with specific applications, supplying this information need not rule out also reminding modern readers that Garth may not have expected all his early readers to recognize this and the other medicines mentioned.

My claim here is not that intended readers failed to understand all or even most of Garth's classical allusions, medical terms, and obscured targets. Many readers had no trouble identifying these elements. Even readers without Latin knew about the classics from other sources, and nondoctors knew about medicines from taking them. In fact, all that was required to get Garth's point—that expertise matters, that doctors are specially qualified to do what they do—was a few instances of incomprehension across the poem, of feeling excluded, even temporarily. If a slightly less than "perfect" understanding made Adams clamor for a key, what would a reader like Ffowns, who identified just sixty-five of Garth's ninety targets, have felt? The problem of annotating *The Dispensary*, then, is less one of the knowledge conveyed than of its conveyance. Intended readers did not comprehend as quickly or as completely, without exertion or difficulty, as do modern readers with editorial notes. The struggle to arrive at a satisfactory understanding in 1699 increased readers' respect for medicine as an expertise, something Garth would have welcomed. In fact, the readers most likely to overlook this element of the poem are precisely the readers produced by Ellis's edition: totally informed readers, for whom the Latin allusions and technical terms are automatic and the identities of the characters all but obvious.

The poem's obstacles also held meaning for more knowledgeable insiders, including the apothecary physicians. Giving experts and insiders occasions to use their specialist knowledge in identifying blanks and allusions, satire builds group cohesion, reminding informed readers of what expertise they share. Thus, even as Garth ridicules the apothecary physicians, who by muddying the doctor-apothecary distinction imperil the authority of their field, his manner of ridiculing—through a mock-classical poem filled with technical language and topical references most familiar to physicians—compliments their learning and social position, as if to remind the renegade doctors of their difference from the vulgar apothecaries with whom they have lately leagued. Even if some physicians, like Charlett, struggled from time to time, the pseudonyms and terms made it easier for them to imagine other readers, apothecaries included, who were more ignorant than themselves, readers who grasped fewer of the poem's terms and targets, a failure that reinforced through contrast the doctors' own group identity. Since the physician-apothecary distinction already depended on reading—of Latin, of the classics, of symptoms—Garth uses inaccessibility to rebuild professional community through the reading of his poem.

Before I offer a few practical suggestions for annotating satire, two questions need to be addressed. First, in gently criticizing Ellis's explication of terms and references, am I suggesting we should stop annotating, or somehow annotate for uninformed readers? Not at all. My suggestion is to avoid endorsing the fiction of the all-knowing intended reader, who is an unintended by-product of the exhaustive annotations in scholarly editions, editions themselves shaped by a longer history of editors needing to defend and demonstrate their own expertise in the face of various challengers. Annotators should be alert to the possibility of writers sometimes having less than specialist readers in mind, a possibility with which Ellis, working in the 1960s from something like Bateson's rationale, is unconcerned.

The second question is broader: while what I say about annotation works nicely for my interpretation of *The Dispensary*, with professional distinctions as its subject, can this approach be applied to other satires? I would answer yes, obviously, in that I share Silver's sense of eighteenth-century satire, whatever its ostensible focus, as always creating or reinforcing distinctions of some kind. A satire such as *Absalom and Achitophel* (1681) not only argues for excluding some from political power but also depends for its own status as a state poem on the possibility of some readers being excluded from its secrets, a possibility that Dryden's allusions and pseudonyms introduce. Likewise, for the *Dunciad*, a satire dividing high from low culture, we have to suspect that Pope welcomed some failures of understanding: depending on context, confusion signaled either a reader's distance from or involvement in Grub Street. Any satirist in the long eighteenth century who assumes social, political, or professional distinctions, which is most of them—Whig and Tory, court and city, town and country, poet and hack—could intend concealed references to reinforce such divisions by reminding readers of what they did not know.

So, what are annotators to do? How can one supply information to make a satire accessible today when inaccessibility was at times intended? Declining to annotate is not an option, since satirists expected at least some readers to be informed. While the approach will vary depending on whether they aim their edition at students or scholars, annotators should do more to inform

126 | Notes on Footnotes

modern readers of the difficulty that some concealed references may have posed to readers in the past, even if modern readers cannot experience this difficulty for themselves.

To help inform today's users of scholarly editions about intended, uninformed ways of reading, I offer four suggestions to annotators:

1. Reproduce blanks and related typographic obstacles. By replacing these spaces with names, the annotator reduces a satire's appearance of exclusiveness or inaccessibility. Ellis's removal of the blanks is uncommon these days, but it persists in some student editions. Even if many of the targets were probably obvious, the absence in the text should be honored, and the identifications reserved for footnotes or backnotes.

2. Pair identifications with some brief explanation of what intended readers may have struggled with. By simply identifying all the targets for every possible allusion, the annotator may seem to suggest all were equally identifiable in the past. Annotators do occasionally insert phrases such as "The poet here refers to X, but whether many readers recognized this as X remains a question." Such phrases should be much more frequently used. The best way to determine what blanks and pseudonyms were more challenging than others is by looking to early copies with manuscript notations. The fewer readers who filled a blank, and the greater the disagreement shown when they did assign a name, the likelier they had difficulty. With this knowledge, annotators can then use available documentary evidence to determine if a satirist wanted or expected this concealed reference to be challenging.

3. Supply a fuller range of identifications from early copies with marginalia or other sources. This already goes on in a limited manner: the Twickenham Pope editors, for example, list variant identifications from Edmund Curll's *Dunciad* keys. However, this practice is inconsistently observed. The Longman Dryden ignores that the Duchess of Cleveland competed with the Duchess of Portsmouth in the minds of early readers identifying Bathsheba in *Absalom and Achitophel*.[33] Insisting that concealed references will have a single correct or intended identity overlooks the deliberate openness to variation and failure suggested by a satirist's choosing to conceal targets. Offering a larger sample of identifications made by past readers, and noting when they often offer no identifications, will counteract the implication that mis- or nonunderstanding in satire cannot at times be intended.

4. When using intended, ideal readers to identify targets, keep in mind other readers as well, and their failure to make proper identifications or any identification at all. Pope's identifications from his copy of *The Dispensary* at the Huntington Library, which Ellis cites in his edition, are extremely valuable, but there may be dozens of other annotated copies in rare book collections belonging to now forgotten readers who probably lacked Pope's knowledge. Consider including them. Their comments can be informative for weighing the areas of ignorance satirists may have depended on to make some readers feel excluded from the subjects or events treated.

These are just a few possible steps annotators can take to continue facilitating the understanding of eighteenth-century satire without leading later readers to think that every intended reader had encyclopedic knowledge or that satirists could not intend some local incomprehension to help readers comprehend a more global point. If *The Dispensary* shows us nothing else, it is that the use of initials and other devices for making social and professional distinctions has a long history in satire, and that the desire to make readers today informed insiders should not stop annotators from attending to the outsider created by disguised satire in the past, the uninformed reader.

NOTES

1. I adapt this phrase from D. C. Greetham's review of Ian Small and Marcus Walsh, eds., *The Theory and Practice of Text-Editing*, in *Text* 7 (1994): 466.

2. See Christopher Ricks, "To Criticize the Critic," *Essays in Criticism* 69, no. 4 (2019): 467–79.

3. Claire Lamont, "Annotating a Text: Literary Theory and Electronic Hypertext," in *Electronic Text: Investigations in Method and Theory*, ed. Kathryn Sutherland (Oxford: Clarendon Press, 1997), 49.

4. Andrew Benjamin Bricker, "Libel and Satire: The Problem with Naming," *ELH* 81, no. 3 (2014): 889–921.

5. Sean Silver, "Satirical Objects," in *The Oxford Handbook of Eighteenth-Century Satire*, ed. Paddy Bullard (Oxford: Oxford University Press, 2019), 373.

6. F. W. Bateson, "The Responsible Critic: A Reply," *Scrutiny* 19, no. 4 (1953): 320.

7. Martin C. Battestin, "A Rationale of Literary Annotation: The Example of Fielding's Novels," *Studies in Bibliography* 34 (1981): 20.

8. Ian Small and Marcus Walsh, eds., introduction to *The Theory and Practice of Text-Editing: Essays in Honour of James T. Boulton* (Cambridge: Cambridge University Press, 1991), 8.

128 | Notes on Footnotes

9. Paul Hammond and David Hopkins, eds., *The Poems of John Dryden*, 4 vols., Longman Annotated English Poets (London: Longman, 1995), 1:xxii.

10. Linda Bree and James McLaverty, "The Cambridge Edition of the Works of Jonathan Swift and the Future of the Scholarly Edition," in *Text Editing: Print and the Digital World*, ed. Marilyn Deegan and Kathryn Sutherland (Farnham, UK: Ashgate, 2009), 130.

11. Jonathan Swift, *English Political Writings, 1711–1714*, ed. Bertrand A. Goldgar and Ian Gadd (Cambridge: Cambridge University Press, 2008), 229.

12. Quoted in Richard I. Cook, *Sir Samuel Garth* (Boston, MA: Twayne, 1980), 64.

13. *Remarks and Collections of Thomas Hearne*, 2 vols., ed. C. E. Doble (Oxford: Oxford Historical Society, 1886), 2:292.

14. Wilkes to Churchill, August 27, 1764, in *The Correspondence of John Wilkes and Charles Churchill*, ed. Edward H. Weatherly (New York: Columbia University Press, 1954), 89; Swift to Pope, July 16, 1728, *The Correspondence of Jonathan Swift*, ed. Harold Williams, 4 vols. (Oxford: Clarendon Press, 1963), 3:293.

15. Alan Roper, "Who's Who in *Absalom and Achitophel*," *Huntington Library Quarterly* 63, no. 1/2 (2000): 98–138; and Stephen Karian, "Reading the Material Text of Swift's *Verses on the Death*," *Studies in English Literature 1600–1900* 41, no. 3 (2001): 515–44.

16. Steven N. Zwicker, "What Every Literate Man Once Knew: Tracing Readers in Early Modern England," in *Owners, Annotators and the Signs of Reading*, ed. Robin Myers, Michael Harris, and Giles Mandelbrote (Newark, DE: Oak Knoll, 2005), 78.

17. Michael McKeon, "What Were Poems on Affairs of State?," *1650–1850: Ideas, Aesthetics, and Inquiries in the Early Modern Era* 4 (1998): 366.

18. Robert D. Hume, "'Satire' in the Reign of Charles II," *Modern Philology* 102, no. 3 (2005): 344.

19. The Earl of Oxford, for example, had "difficulty in spotting allusions to members of his own circle." See James McLaverty, "Pope in the Private and Public Spheres: Annotations in the Second Earl of Oxford's Volume of Folio Poems, 1731–1736," *Studies in Bibliography* 48 (1995): 46–48.

20. *Contributions to "The Champion," and Related Writings*, ed. W. B. Coley, The Wesleyan Edition of the Works of Henry Fielding (Oxford: Clarendon Press, 2003), 566n.

21. Dustin Griffin, *Satire: A Critical Reintroduction* (Lexington: University of Kentucky Press, 1994), 116.

22. Ian Small, "The Editor as Annotator as Ideal Reader," in Small and Walsh, *Theory and Practice of Text-Editing*, 189 (hereafter cited in the text).

23. Marcus Walsh, "'Why Edit Anything at All?' Textual Editing and Postmodernism: A Review Essay," *English Literature in Transition, 1880–1920* 38, no. 2 (1995): 202.

24. John F. Sena, *The Best-Natured Man: Sir Samuel Garth, Physician and Poet* (New York: AMS, 1986), 25, 33.

25. Cook, *Sir Samuel Garth*, 55.

26. Frank H. Ellis, "Garth's Harveian Oration," *Journal of the History of Medicine and Allied Sciences* 18, no. 1 (1963): 19.

27. Ellis omits Garth's preface in his edition, so I quote from *The Dispensary: A Poem. In Six Cantos*, 3rd ed. (London: Printed and Sold by John Nutt, 1699), sig. A1ᵛ.

28. See, for example, Patrick J. Daly Jr., "Monarchy, the Disbanding Crisis, and Samuel Garth's *Dispensary*," *Restoration* 25, no. 1 (2001): 40.

29. Frank H. Ellis, ed., *Poems on Affairs of State: Augustan Satirical Verse, 1660–1714*, vol. 6, *1697–1704* (New Haven: Yale University Press, 1970), 4.133–34 (hereafter cited in the text).

30. *A Compleat Key to the Seventh Edition of the Dispensary* (London: Printed for J. Roberts, 1714), 19.

31. For a transcription of Garth's letter to Charlett, see Sena, *Best-Natured Man*, 168.

32. Harvard Countway Rare Books, PR3471.G3 D6 1699 c.1.

33. For identifications of Bathsheba, see Roper, "Who's Who," 108–9. For the Longman edition identification of Bathsheba, see Hammond, *Poems of John Dryden*, 511–12n.

CHAPTER 8

❧ Footnote Failure

Thomas Lockwood

If you are a scholar and have chosen to undertake the editing of an older literary text with explanatory notes, you have probably considered that this means having to push your way onto the same page with the author (if you are writing footnotes) and flag down the reader somewhere in the middle of the text long enough to hear what you have to say. With endnotes the interruption is a little politer, in that the reader can escape more easily—like ignoring the pub bore when he is talking from the other side of the room, rather than at the next barstool. But either way you are asking a lot. Maybe the reader is anxious to hear from you just at this moment you have chosen to talk—you may well hope so—but possibly not. Maybe what you have to say will light up the text and leave the reader feeling grateful, though again possibly not. The scholarly annotation is a peculiar critical intervention, with much room for trouble. Failure seems built into the convention of the explanatory note, since the aim of showing what a historical text means, where its meaning is doubtful or obscure, is inevitably compromised by the barriers of time and mentality in making what amounts to a translation. Not fatally compromised, necessarily, but the effort to explain does take place in a fallen world, where there is sometimes just no path back to the original meaning, or no way of knowing how the original readers might have responded. Even when you think you have got the right handle on a crux of meaning or reference beyond pure fact, it is rare to feel quite certain, or it ought to be rare. I am assuming here, by the way, that there is an evidence-informed meaning to be found, and that its recovery and explanation, however difficult or liable to failure, is the goal of annotation. That assumption might be challenged as a matter of theory, where editorial intervention itself is seen to make any objective determination impossible, but at the workaday level of annotation most editors, certainly including me, proceed as if there is an answer out there and their job is to find it.

It is a job made for failure, no doubt, but one too where failing better is always possible, though not so easy to define. Failing badly, on the other hand, is impossible to miss: getting facts wrong, explaining too much, editorializing, turning notes into interpretive essays, assuming too much or too little, weaponizing notes to attack enemies, using anachronistic sources, accepting predecessor annotations without checking them, getting the audience wrong. Most editors try to avoid obvious crimes like these, though in the fog of writing annotations it can be embarrassingly easy to wander into them. Once in print, the notes will look like they belong in the places they occupy on the page, but every editor knows that the bare unannotated text was a field of variable possibilities, which someone else, or even the same editor, might fill up differently. This is only to say that contingency runs deep in the trade of note-making, along with failure. In what follows, I am reflecting on what seem to me some of the more interesting challenges in editorial scholarship under those circumstances in which the text calls for an explanation that the editor finds not quite possible to make. I have my own record of failure to draw on and will start there.

UNPRINCIPLED ANNOTATION

In the late 1990s, I was asked to edit the drama volumes of the "Wesleyan" edition of Henry Fielding's works.[1] The Wesleyan University Press, which had begun the edition more than thirty years earlier, was by now a ghost, with Oxford having taken over. Both press imprints appear in friendly union side by side at the bottom of the dust jackets, but take the jacket off and the one real imprint reveals itself on the dark blue buckram spine. I came to my job with little relevant experience, apart from knowing something about Fielding. I had a few vain opinions about editing and how it ought to go, based on not much apart from reading footnotes I liked or (more often) did not like. I was most certainly not a textual editor or analytical bibliographer and had to learn

132 | Notes on Footnotes

what I did of those terrifying sciences on the job, but writing notes was something I felt I should be able to do. I never told myself it would be easy, but I did think I could manage to succeed so long as I was willing to put in the work—like Robinson Crusoe with his big boat, saying he would build it first and worry later about how to get it into the water. As it turned out, he never could.

Like a typical academic, I began by reading about the enterprise in books, but they did not give me quite what I wanted, which was practical guidance on how to do this work. I found the literature on editorial theory and scholarly editing illuminating, and some of the arguments engaging, but for the part of the work looming largest and most menacingly to me, in the annotation of these plays, I took counsel from those who had been there before and had written most directly about what to do and not do in formulating notes: particularly the classic attempts to put the rules of this work on a consensus footing, like Arthur Friedman's early essay on principles of historical annotation, Albert Hamilton's "The Philosophy of the Footnote," and Martin Battestin's widely circulated "A Rationale of Literary Annotation."[2] These treatments of the subject had emerged from a quiet but important little postwar struggle over what explanation, if any, the scholarly editor of a literary text should give the reader who might need help understanding what the author meant. Everybody mostly agrees now that explanatory notes belong there, but that is only because the nontrivial argument for leaving the text to speak for itself, with minimal interference from the editor, lost out. By the time I began work on the Fielding plays it was a given of the edition that I would be explaining things in footnotes. The two principles I took most to heart from Friedman and Battestin, as well as from my own reading of scholarly editions, were that notes should be supported from original research in contemporary sources only—no cheating with modern books or references—and that they had better not turn into little arenas for riding around on hobby-horses.

These rules give a valuable discipline to the work of annotation, so long as they are followed. But it is easy to rationalize suspending them. In his edition of *Tom Jones*, Battestin notoriously made space in the notes for his own interpretations of good nature, prudence, and providential justice as themes of the novel,[3] and then with impressive confidence brought this very criticism of his own editing into the "Rationale of Annotation" essay to show that what one reviewer had regarded as contestable literary interpretations having no place in an authoritative edition were in fact acceptable because the readers of such editions are sophisticated academics capable of judging for themselves and would appreciate the insights of an editor with superior knowledge of the author.[4] The line between informing and editorializing can be hard to draw, but not there. Another good rule is to say what you need to and stop. This one I did not take to heart. Near the beginning of the first play I set to work on, *Love in Several Masques*, one of the characters says something about "the Vapours." So I explained the vapours, with illustrations drawn from a deep well of conscientiously contemporary sources, not forgetting the period gender and class associations, until I had created a little sociomedical treatise taking up nearly a third of the page even in the Lilliputian size of the footnote typeface.[5] When I think of it now, James Thurber's little girl with her book report comes to mind: This book tells me more about penguins than I want to know.

The literature of annotation left me feeling doubtful that any principles or "rationale" of annotation could help much when it came time to decide where to put a note or what to put in it. Not that the principles can be ignored. Obviously, the note should take account of the intended audience, and should not serve as a cart for your own crank ideas. But the actual work of making notes winds along through so many practical decisions and details at textual ground level that it is hard to keep looking faithfully upward at the principles. There is something about this work, or maybe about those who end up doing it, that fills up the frame with trees, leaving the forest nowhere in sight. As an editor you are the captive of the text, which pulls you this way and that down a wandering track left by somebody else, such that one minute you are thinking about how early modern juries were empaneled, and the next about coach fare from Newcastle to Edinburgh in 1760, or whether your author ever read Tacitus. It has its appeal, this ride-along, but it can also atomize your thinking or dull your awareness of larger wholes.

In my house when I was in grade school there was a 1950 *World Book Encyclopedia*. I do not remember looking things up in it but instead would open volumes at random and begin reading. Perhaps by the same quirk of disposition I like the miscellaneous topic-mongering of annotation work for the very reason that the subject is constantly changing—something no other kind of academic scholarship will tolerate—while the puzzle-solving payoff stays the same. Like many editors I feel I learned much from my years in harness on the Fielding volumes, amounting to an eccentric education along *World Book* lines, but arguably useless outside its one-time application to the text that produced it. This peculiar form of learning, guided as it were merely by the preoccupations and intellectual reflexes of the author you happen to be editing, does have good value in that it cultivates an intuition for what does and does not signify on the page you have to edit. This is an underrated advantage for

134 | Notes on Footnotes

editorial efficiency, although it kicks in only after prolonged close exposure to the author. An editor may also come to an author, and perhaps most often does, already well prepared for explanation simply by a mental or temperamental affinity. Assigning a book review to somebody whose own work is of an opposite stamp can produce an interesting result, like Dr. Johnson writing about Swift. But it does not work with editing, where some sympathetic instinct for what the author means or wants to suggest or might be thinking or is joking about, page after page, is almost a necessary condition.

At an early stage of my career I had the good luck to fall into a friendship with the late Bertrand Goldgar, the distinguished scholar and editor of Swift and Fielding. He defined for me the power of this critical imagination, which he combined with an intellectual honesty and modest self-reckoning notably at odds with his learning and quality of mind. I got to know him when he was working on his edition of the *Covent-Garden Journal* for the Wesleyan-Oxford Works of Henry Fielding.[6] He was daunted by the whole project and liked to talk about just how daunted he felt—anxious, self-deprecating, hilarious—and though he knew his own considerable strengths there was no fake modesty in his accesses of self-doubt. He loved Fielding and had an extraordinary feel for the subtleties of his comic mentality. He had absorbed the period culture with a deep fluency, especially at the level of verbal expression, with a natural gift of historical imagination. He was also very funny.

In the *Covent-Garden Journal* of March 17, 1752, Fielding rehearses a story from Ariosto in which a husband discovers his wife in the arms of her lover, a scene Fielding interrupts with two lines of verse, as follows:

(Let me not name it to you, you chaste Stars!
And thou pale Moon, turn paler at the Sound!)

The two lines look like they must belong together, but they do not. The first is from *Othello*, as Goldgar notes,[7] while the other has nothing to do with that play and comes from nowhere he could find, despite obsessive searching. Did Fielding misquote something else from *Othello*? No, there is nothing close to these words, and anyway Fielding knew that play intimately. Did he just make it up? An editorial nightmare, ending in defeat. "The second line has not been identified," as Goldgar was finally forced to declare in the published note, sounding calm, but actually grinding his teeth and meaning (I happen to know) *Damn Henry Fielding to hell and that pale Moon with him,* or words to that effect. Try finding it yourself using books, without digital assistance. I can wait.

The point about my old friend Goldgar is this. Like many accomplished editors, he had what I take to be a vital condition of explanatory note-making, beyond any philosophy or rationale or principles, which is unflagging intellectual tenacity, and integrity, in getting at the truth of the text. Now I recognize that using the word "truth" here may be asking for trouble. I am not talking about interpretations of the text, but only about those questions of meaning or reference reasonably seen as having answers. The distinction is not always so clear, of course, but in many (not all!) cases where most would agree an explanatory note is needed, there is only one good or definite answer. "Thou pale Moon" is an example, from the crazy-making category. Here is a simpler and more typical one, from Fielding's comedy *The Modern Husband* (1732). When Lord Richly asks Mrs. Modern if she has seen the new opera, she says, "I cannot bear an Opera, now poor *La Dovi*'s gone." Richly replies, "Nor I, after poor *A la Fama*."[8] Who are La Dovi and A la Fama and where or why did they go? One is Francesca Cuzzoni, identified by the desperately fashionable Mrs. Modern with the air she sang in Handel's *Admeto* beginning "Là dove gli io giro," and the other is Faustina Bordoni, who sang "Alla fama dimmi il vero" in Handel's *Ottone*. They had last sung in London four years earlier and were then singing in Italy. Richly and Mrs. Modern go on talking about them in ways that call for a bit more explanation, but that is the gist of the editorial problem the text throws up here. It is certainly a question with an answer, requiring some searching, though nothing heroic—somewhere in between looking up a date and finding the "pale Moon"—and there really is just one answer. This is a familiar category of annotation, and a big one.

The constant editorial ground-bass of questions with answers may explain the limited effect critical theory has had on the operational habits of literary annotation. Its effect on editorial and textual theory is another matter—think of the socialization of texts, or the concept of authorial intention. For the actual production of explanatory notes, however, there is little difference in purpose or ideal result between the editing practices of 1950 and 2000. There are obvious differences of quality, from unimpeachable to sloppy, or of approach, as of chatty versus close-mouthed, but not so much of conceptual orientation. The reason would seem to be that the results are subject to verification—a date, a name, a source—and even in the many borderline cases where interpretation must play a role, as with a muted possible allusion to somebody or something,

136 | Notes on Footnotes

the result is based on evidence that can be tested or challenged as sufficient or not. It is not all questions with answers, but neither is it just questions. Literary interpretation thrives on questions, even fetishizes them. Literary annotation wants answers.

HACKING THE ALLUSION

We talk of a rationale of annotation for editors, but is there a rationale of allusion for authors? I find myself thinking about that if I linger over a quotation or reference in a text I am reading—let alone a text I am editing, where the lingering may reach unhealthy duration. What did the author have in mind with this quotation? And what would original readers have thought of it? Obviously, we cannot read their minds, but I think annotators will try anyway, even though a full understanding may be out of reach. A deep effort itself can still improve the quality of the editorial note, in historical discrimination and context if not also by an exemplary embrace of informed uncertainty. There is no good rationale of allusion any more than of annotation—a cluster of no doubt mixed motives is behind any allusion, such as to give the work a borrowed resonance, point a moral, insinuate an ironic parallel, show off a fund of learning (there the author and editor sometimes overlap), make a descriptive shortcut (Fielding entirely eliminates the labor of description by referring us instead to a Hogarth picture to see what Bridget Allworthy looks like).[9] Authors have their own habits of quotation or allusion, their own fields of reference and reading, which their editors necessarily learn to follow, sometimes logically, sometimes intuitively. To my mind the classic example of this kind of search through the author's own awareness is the subtle, patient analysis modeled by John Carroll in "On Annotating *Clarissa*," operating like a safecracker listening for the quiet clicks of the tumblers.[10]

In *The Absentee* (1812), Maria Edgeworth sometimes likes to repurpose within her own text quoted words too well known to need marking: Mrs. Dareville "gave full scope to all the malice of mockery, and all the insolence of fashion. Her slings and arrows, numerous as they were and outrageous, were directed."[11] Modern editors explain the allusion—how can they not—but might wish it could be ignored. Edgeworth also likes to import quotations marked or set off as such, as where her character Lady Isabel quotes (sarcastically) a line of verse about women so virtuously loving that they "feel every vanity in fondness lost."[12] The line is set off in the text but not identified, as if

Edgeworth expects her reader to recognize it. Maybe the original readers would, though I am not so sure. It comes from George Lyttelton's poem *Advice to a Lady* (1733), which got some later circulation through Dodsley's *Collection of Poems* (1748), but by 1812 would have had a very feeble pulse. Not for Edgeworth, though, who used the same line in *Leonora* (1806),[13] again without identification, and took some verses from Lyttelton's *Monody* on the death of his wife for the epigraph of *Belinda* (1801), this time identifying them. What matters for Edgeworth is that the quoted words she borrows be embedded within the thought they complete or continue in her own text, which means that (unlike the epigraph) the quotation cannot be identified without spoiling the effect. Presumably, she would expect or at least hope for her reader to appreciate the result, recognizing the borrowing and taking some pleasure in the unexpected application. What happens if they recognize those slings and arrows but not the line "feel every vanity in fondness lost"? We are down to mind-reading again, but it is hard to imagine it would matter much, to the excluded reader or to Edgeworth.

Frances Burney runs allusions or tags of verse into her narrative without identifying them while usually marking them as quotations, but these are mostly the belongings of educated period reading, like Shakespeare or Milton. Cecilia is "open as day to melting charity," from *2 Henry IV.*[14] And when she is asked if she is fond of public places she replies, "Yes, Sir, *soberly*, as Lady Grace says,"[15] which is a comic bit from *The Provoked Husband* (1728), still popular in repertory at the time and a reference Burney could have expected many of her readers to recognize. Charlotte Smith in *The Old Manor House* (1793) likewise seems sure enough of what her readers would know, or should know, when she makes a comparison with Sir Roger de Coverley fussing about his portrait gallery of ancestors,[16] but unlike Burney or Edgeworth she has an editor-friendly habit of spelling out sources, sometimes in a conscientious note. An asterisk after "The sylvan pen | Of rural lovers" takes us to the name of Thomson (though not the work) at the foot of the page, and elsewhere in the novel the quatrain she quotes beginning "Ye distant spires, ye antique towers" is felt to need identification as Gray's *Ode on a Distant Prospect of Eton College* (but would it have?), though not "It is the East—and Juliet is the Sun!" on the same page, for which surely nobody reading this book would need help.[17]

Not in 1793, anyway, and yet—consider this editorially treacherous circumstance in Fielding's *Tragedy of Tragedies* (1731), where the lovelorn Princess Huncamunca calls out, "O, *Tom Thumb! Tom Thumb!* Wherefore art thou *Tom Thumb*?" and Fielding as mock-editor glosses the line not with Shakespeare but with Otway's *Caius Marius* (1680): "Oh! *Marius, Marius*; wherefore art thou *Marius*?" Is that part of the mock-scholarship joke, with Fielding comically pretending ignorance of the line in *Romeo and Juliet*? The Otway citation is real, however, and it is by no means clear that the line we hear so unmistakably parodied in Huncamunca's voice was being heard that way in 1731. *Romeo and Juliet* had not been seen on a London stage since 1660, whereas *Caius Marius* was one of the overwrought heroic tragedies Fielding had in his burlesque sights, and in any case the line comes from the old Tom Thumb chapbook story, when his mother misses him (he has been swallowed by the cow) and calls, "Where art thou Tom? Where art thou?" In this case I was the editor attempting to explain what was going on here, and I more or less defaulted. I meant to sound authoritative and to cover the possibilities, but it amounted to an elaborate shrug.[18]

In Farquhar's *The Inconstant* (1702), when the hero Mirabel is confronted by the heroine's friend Bisarre, looking to upbraid him as a faithless lover, Mirabel starts talking to her in mockingly apposite scraps of Latin verses from Virgil's story of Dido and Aeneas. It is a funny scene: after reciting a few scorching words from Dido's raging denunciation as befitting himself, "Very true," he observes. Here is a case where it would improve life for the editor to have some handle on the rationale of the allusion—some idea of what Farquhar knew about what his audience would know. Mirabel quotes a somewhat disordered jumble of famous bits, like the line beginning "At Regina dolos" (iv.196), which some at the theater would certainly have recognized, though many would certainly also have not. Would they also notice the jumbling? The modern editor did (Shirley Strum Kenny), but there is just no telling quite where and how Farquhar thought he might get the laughs from his audience. So, we call it a known unknown, and leave the rest to charity.[19]

For anyone tracking the allusive habits and quirks of English-language novelists in the eighteenth and early nineteenth centuries, Walter Scott is the biggest beast. He was a great editor himself, of course, and brought to his novel-writing a heroic appetite like Fielding's for feeding his stories with scraps of literature and learning. Scott was at home imaginatively in the seventeenth and eighteenth centuries and thus ideally disposed for editing that literature. Even though his work in this form, on Dryden and Swift, obviously would not compare with modern editorial scholarship like that of the California or Cambridge editions, on the score of intuitive understanding it holds up notably. Scott the novelist can be editor-like about letting his reader know who or what he is quoting, but he will just as often take Fielding's approach and leave the reader, or future editor, to figure it out with no help. Sometimes, of course, he is himself the author of verses interpolated in the narrative without attribution. Sometimes he throws out a clue: "Which of your crack-brained Italian romancers is it," wonders the surprisingly well-read Fergus MacIvor in *Waverley* (1814), "that says, 'Io d'Elicona niente / Mi curo, in fe de Dio, che'l bere d'acque / (Bea chi ber ne vuol) sempre mi spiacque!'" Scott provides the reader with his own MacIvor-like translation at the bottom of the page ("I reck nought of your Helicon," etc.), but nothing about the source. The crack-brained romancer is Teofilo Folengo, from *Orlandino* (1526). In the same chapter, Scott has Fergus reciting some verses in French, written by Scott himself, who later noted, "This is a parody but of what I cannot well remember."[20] He often takes the editor's job on himself, filling in his own explanations where he knows the reader almost certainly could not follow, as with his glosses of the cant language in *The Heart of Midlothian* (chapter 30), or of Gaelic in many of the novels. With Scott we are at a limiting case where allusion and explanation run exuberantly together in the same channel, which, however, does not mean that the job of editing Scott's novels is made any easier. When he opens a chapter with an epigraph, as he nearly always does, and it comes from Shakespeare or Otway or Crabbe, he will say so (not always noting the work, however), but sometimes it will be simply "Old Song" or "Old Play," which supplies a long perspective in the application, and reminds us of Scott's antiquarian bent, but leaves work for the editor. Scott's rationale or rhetoric of allusion ideally might make it easier to determine questions of original meaning and likely reader response, by reason of the extra level of information he tends to provide, except that it is also necessary to edit or explain his own editorial interventions as well. They are part of the creative ensemble too and if anything may represent not a simpler but a more complex challenge for that reason.

How far can the well-meaning editor go in tracking down words that seem to belong to something or someone other than the author? Not words in quotation marks or clearly tendered as if brought in from outside, but nevertheless possibly alluding outward, so to speak. Here is an example, from *Mansfield Park* (1814). When the young Bertrams and Crawfords are trying to settle on a play for their home theatricals, Austen says that "neither Hamlet, nor Macbeth, nor Othello, nor the Gamester, presented any thing that could satisfy even the tragedians; and the Rivals, the School for Scandal, Wheel of Fortune, Heir at Law, and a long etcetera, were successively dismissed with yet warmer objections."[21] The expression having a faint life of its own here, unlike the other usages of the sentence, is "a long etcetera." It is not a quotation, is not important, and does not need explaining, but to some (or to me, anyway) it sounds like a borrowing. It has a little iambic movement and vitality you can appreciate by replacing "and a long etcetera" with "etcetera." It is hard to imagine Austen making such a flat-footed choice as that, but do the words she does choose belong to her?

Not exactly, as it turns out that the phrase goes back to a poem by Cowley called *The Chronicle: A Ballad* (1656), which sets forth an impressive memory roll of mistresses formerly in serial possession of the poet's heart, from the first (Margarita) down to the most recent:

> Then *Joan*, and *Jane*, and *Audria*,
> And then a pretty *Thomasine*,
> And then another *Katherine*,
> And then a long *Et caetera*.

Nineteen altogether, not counting the present holder or those ungallantly covered by the long et cetera. That locution caught on and was known to be Cowley's, at least until Cowley faded from living awareness by the middle of the eighteenth century, after which it persisted well into the nineteenth century on its own. The author of a sentimental novel called *The Assignation* (1774) speaks of "the long et-cetera of fine-spun sensations,"[22] perhaps without knowing the original. In Fielding's rude world, on the other hand, knowing the source meant the phrase could be given a bawdy turn, and sometimes was. For the politer age of Austen fifty years later it had been worn free of any unfit application.[23] After two centuries of modest idiomatic life, it disappeared.

All this is interesting, no doubt, but should it be a note in *Mansfield Park*? The reckless me would say yes, if only as a kind of editorial power move to show up Austen for choosing unawares (I assume) this jokey expression with its slightly tainted history. But why should she not choose it? Why should she know that remote association? It was an available period idiom. And what difference does it make? (This is the more sensible and sadder me weighing in: sadder, because it is looking like there will be no note after all.) It might be a close call, where most scholars nevertheless would probably decide against annotation—the editor of the Cambridge Austen volume gave it no attention, by the way—but perhaps it makes a good illustration of that never quite clearly visible dividing line between the literally noteworthy and the safely ignorable.

How many editors have entertained the criminal thought of silently walking away from a reference they were unable to identify or explain, without providing any note at all? Many, no doubt, including me. Some may even have done it (not me!), in a desperate gamble either that no one will notice (unlikely) or that anyone who does will assume it must be something too familiar to need explaining (also unlikely). For the editorial majority who face up to the defeat, the passive wording usual in such cases—"Not identified"—itself tells a sad story of wishing to be as far away as possible from the scene of failure. Where the unknown or unexplained something is more complicated than a name or source like the begetter of that "pale Moon," and the failure cannot be noted simply by the brutal "not identified," most editors will seize the opportunity to talk at more length about the problem as a kind of therapeutic self-care that also has the value of creating a framework for understanding exactly what remains unknown and what further evidence might make a difference. In my own experience with the saturated topical comedies of Fielding's final years at the Little Haymarket Theater, these gaps of explication would regularly open up, like breaks in an ice field only just a little too wide to reach across. *The Historical Register for the Year 1736*, for example, has a scene of Farinelli-maddened ladies of quality eagerly talking about a craze for little wax Farinelli dolls supposedly for sale in London. One of those watching from outside the rehearsal frame cannot believe it: "This must be Invention." The rehearsal play author, Medley, says otherwise: "Upon my Word, Sir, it's Fact."[24] Medley is practically begging his future editor for an explanation here, and the question is simple enough: Was that a fact? Medley stands in for Fielding, who has assembled this theatrical "register" of the cultural and political nonsense belonging to the year 1736, none of which otherwise is invented. However, I could find no evidence apart from the play itself to document the Farinelli wax-doll commerce. I would bet the evidence is out there somewhere, awaiting a better or luckier search. For the note that had to be written anyway I said there was no reason to doubt Medley, adding 150 words about wax figures exhibited for show in the period (but life-size, not dolls) with further comment on a suggestion insinuated in the follow-on conversation that the wax dolls were gratifying the ladies in a manner not fit to be mentioned, which scholarship obliged me to mention. I hoped the note had value, but it is also true that it amounted to saying, "I don't know."

Such are the inside jokes and allusions of these densely self-referential plays that some jokes or throwaway bits that scored with the original audiences will escape the modern editor altogether, unless somebody at the time should have

142 | Notes on Footnotes

written about it in a surviving record—which almost never happens. In some
cases, we have no idea even of what we may be missing, like Donald Rumsfeld's
unknown unknowns. But sometimes we do know and can do nothing about
it. In the character of the bastard modern Apollo in *The Historical Register*,
Fielding seems to be taking off the Drury Lane Theatre manager Charles
Fleetwood (though even that is not quite certain, as he sometimes also sounds
like Walpole). As this Mr. Apollo sits on his great chair surrounded by attendants, he is casting Colley Cibber's version of Shakespeare's *King John* and
doling out parts to the players, assisted by his prompter and deputy. When he
comes to the part of Robert Faulconbridge, he asks the Prompter, "What is
this *Robert*?" In the atmosphere of the moment, this can only be the opening
for a swipe at Sir Robert Walpole, whose first name got played on endlessly in
the political press. Mr. Prompter replies, "Really, Sir, I don't well know what he
is," adding, "he is no very considerable Character, any body may do him well
enough; or if you leave him quite out, the Play will be little the worse for it."
The joke there is clear enough. But not the next one: "*Peter* of *Pomfret*, a
Prophet—Have you any Body that looks like a Prophet?" asks Mr. Apollo. "I
have one that looks like a Fool," says Mr. Prompter.[25] This is so obviously a laugh
line, with the Prompter possibly also gesturing at one of the players, that it wants
explaining, but though it is clearly a joke, it hovers now hopelessly out of reach.
Who is he talking about? What does it mean that he looks like a fool? All once
so easily understood, now alas impenetrable, on my exertions anyway. I like to
believe that failing better, if not succeeding, is possible even in hard cases like
this, given more time and imagination for the search: but *ars longa*, etc.[26]

NOTES

1. Henry Fielding, *Plays*, ed. Thomas Lockwood, 3 vols., The Works of Henry Fielding
(Oxford: Clarendon Press, 2004–11).

2. Arthur Friedman, "Principles of Historical Annotation in Critical Editions of Modern
Texts," in *English Institute Annual 1941*, ed. Rudolf Kirk (New York: Columbia University
Press, 1942); A. C. Hamilton, "The Philosophy of the Footnote," in *Editing Poetry from Spenser
to Dryden*, ed. A. H. de Quehen (New York: Garland Press, 1981), 127–63; Martin C. Battestin,
"A Rationale of Literary Annotation: The Example of Fielding's Novels," *Studies in Bibliography*
34 (1981): 1–22.

3. See, e.g., Claude Rawson, "Fielding in the Dock," *London Review of Books*, April 5, 1990.

4. Battestin, "Rationale of Literary Annotation," 13–14.

5. Fielding, *Plays*, 1:34n3.

Footnote Failure | 143

6. Henry Fielding, *The Covent-Garden Journal* and *A Plan of the Universal Register-Office*, ed. Bertrand A. Goldgar, The Works of Henry Fielding (Oxford: Oxford University Press, 1988).

7. Ibid., 147n2.

8. Fielding, *Plays*, 2:245 and n. 2.

9. Henry Fielding, *The History of Tom Jones*, ed. Martin C. Battestin and Fredson Bowers, 2 vols., The Works of Henry Fielding (Oxford: Oxford University Press, 1975), 1.11.66.

10. In G. E. Bentley Jr., ed., *Editing Eighteenth-Century Novels: Papers on Fielding, Lesage, Richardson, Sterne, and Smollett Given at the Conference on Editorial Problems, University of Toronto, November 1973*, (Toronto: A. M. Hakkert, 1975), 49–66.

11. Maria Edgeworth, *The Absentee*, ed. W. J. McCormack and Kim Walker (Oxford: Oxford University Press, 1988), 36.

12. Ibid., 247.

13. Maria Edgeworth, *Leonora* (London: J. Johnson, 1806), 2:3 (letter 41).

14. Frances Burney, *Cecilia* (1782), ed. Peter Sabor and Margaret Anne Doody (Oxford: Oxford University Press, 1988), 2.4.129.

15. Ibid., 4.6.275.

16. Charlotte Smith, *The Old Manor House*, ed. Anne Henry Ehrenpreis (Oxford: Oxford University Press, 1989), 1.2.15.

17. Ibid., 3.4.272, 3.9.326.

18. Fielding, *Plays*, 1:564, 600n79.

19. The confrontation is in act 3, scene 2, and *"At Regina dolos"* is in the *Aeneid* 4.196; see *The Works of George Farquhar*, ed. Shirley Strum Kenny (Oxford: Clarendon Press, 1988), 1:434–35, 632.

20. For this and the preceding references, see *Waverley* (1814), chap. 23, ed. P. D. Garside (Edinburgh: Edinburgh University Press, 2007), 118, 564.

21. *Mansfield Park*, ed. John Wiltshire (Cambridge: Cambridge University Press, 2005), 154.

22. *The Assignation* (1774, 2:85). Republished in Dublin as *Harcourt* (1780), falsely ascribed to Frances Burney ("By the Authoress of Evelina").

23. For the allusion in Fielding, see *The Coffee-House Politician* (1730), in *Plays*, 1.432; the expression appears in sarcastic reference to Sacheverell, Swift, and other "Christian Heroes" in *Bishop Atterbury's and Bishop Smalridge's Reasons for Not Signing the Declaration* (1715), 13 (with thanks to Pat Rogers for that citation); and Eliza Haywood gives it a salacious tilt in *The City Widow* (1729), 25. Cf. the later examples in the *Oxford English Dictionary*, 2nd ed. (2c.).

24. Fielding, *Plays*, 3:423 and n. 3.

25. Ibid., 3:437 and n. 3.

26. Look it up yourself.

CHAPTER 9

🎣 The Angry Annotator Annotated

Melvyn New

Let it be confessed that when I stepped down after nine years as department chairman in 1988, at the age of fifty, one faculty gift to me was *The Portable Curmudgeon*. Thus, because we had never met, I had to admire W. B. Carnochan's dedicating his review of the ninth and final volume of the Florida Edition of the Works of Sterne to a discussion of the characteristic "testiness" of my editorial commentary.[1] That volume was published in 2014, so I had had a full quarter century to hone irritability; now, six years later, having become an outraged octogenarian, it seems time to investigate this career-long tendency, so perceptively noted by both colleagues and Carnochan. However, because savvy annotators strive to separate elucidation from interpretation, I offer here no Habermasian observations on my lack of social skills nor a Marxist screed against the commodification of my professorial talents at my industrial-model STEM institution.[2]

Rather I want to concentrate on the context that defines the work of a present-day annotator, the textual milieu in which we "live, move, and have our being." We most often think of annotation as an excavation of the past in terms of definitions and identifications, sources and analogues, the elucidation of words, objects, or places unfamiliar to a modern reader. All this labor, we assume, will contribute toward more informed commentary on any individual work, knowledge being more useful than ignorance in every academic discipline, so also in literary criticism. Thus, editors and annotators believe that their labors will matter to future generations of interpreting scholars.

The first encounter with this future will be the reviews of an edition placed into a scholarly world that the editor hopes is atremble with the expectation that an accurate text and informed annotation will be of immense value to interpretation. No longer will they affirm that Uncle Toby was injured at the Battle of Waterloo, as I have recently read; or that "The Unknown World" is "evidence" of Sterne's heretical thought, since editorial work has now proven that the poem is not his, but was authored by a devout Baptist minister sometime before 1728.[3] Similarly, having to stop in mid-thesis one's headlong argument that Sterne embraced a materialistic view of what he labels the "great—great SENSORIUM of the world" in order to account for Addison's *Cato* (1713) may interrupt the critic's free flow of imagination, but surely thankfulness for helping avoid a probable misconception will ensue.[4] With this intended helpfulness in mind, the first moment in which an annotator might become just a tad testy is when the reviewer, honest to a fault, admits he "does not have the knowledge to attempt any judgments" about questions of attribution that have "roiled the waters of Sterne scholarship for a long time" (Carnochan, 74).

As book review editor for the *Scriblerian* for some twenty years, I have queried some invited reviewers who declined a particular title because they were "too familiar" with the subject and therefore have opinions—who else is better qualified to review the book? Surely not someone unfamiliar with the subject matter, yet Carnochan was simply being honest where others do not admit to inadequacy, most especially reviewers of editions who write jacket blurbs instead. While reviews in upscale newspapers are not the same as those in academic journals, a recent review of *Letters of Oliver Goldsmith* (Cambridge, 2018) offers one indication of this confusion of blurbs with reviews: Claire Connolly in the *Irish Times* (March 27, 2019) writes that "the editors . . . have undertaken considerable original research in updating and adding to" Katharine Balderston's 1928 edition.[5] One might compare this evaluation to the review I wrote for *Eighteenth-Century Studies*, faulting the edition for not sufficiently updating or adding to Balderston, among its many failures.[6] Perhaps Connolly is sweet-tempered and I am ill-tempered, but I believe my review was the solid result of a process taught to me by means of an at times harsh review of the Florida *Tristram Shandy* written by the outstanding bibliographer

Hugh Amory, namely that a competent reviewer of an edition must know enough to replicate at least some portion of the editorial and annotative work before rendering a judgment.[7]

While careful reviews of scholarly editions are rare enough, they are almost never found for textbook editions. Perhaps this is deemed unnecessary because scholars should never use classroom texts for their scholarly citations, but the practice is widespread, so much so that monograph and journal editors no longer seem to require better sources. Essays on *Tristram Shandy* still appear with citations from the 1967 Penguin edition, despite its being superseded by an edition in 1997, based on the Florida text and notes. A Norton textbook edition of *Humphry Clinker* (2014) blurbed on the back cover as "finally a definitive, scholarly edition" is anything but that. The Georgia edition (1990), edited by Thomas R. Preston and O M Brack Jr., is the "scholarly edition" (scholarly editors shun "definitive," since their edition will rightfully be replaced by a future edition). Whether textbook editions should be reviewed is a question worth raising, but doing so might alert scholars to the danger of using a flawed text and annotations directed toward undergraduates when publishing what purports to be scholarly work.[8]

This problem has been compounded by the addition to the scholarly and teaching canon of many women authors unedited since their first appearance. Important issues in this regard are raised in a fine collection, *Editing Early Modern Women*,[9] so I will mention here just a few examples from direct experience. Pickering and Chatto published an edition of Haywood's *The Invisible Spy* (2014). This is, at best, a classroom edition, although priced at $99; its text is filled with errors, its notes comprise a totally inadequate 30 pages for 467 pages of text.[10] Its most serious problem, however, is Haywood's mediocrity, although it is curmudgeonly to say so. The *TLS* reviewer of the edition, for example, praised the work's "magnificent construction: sexy, sexless, knowing, inquisitive, pervasive and persuasive." My review suggested otherwise.

A second problem with editions of women writers elevated to canonical status emerged when I happened upon the Oxford edition of Edgeworth's *Belinda* (1994). Again, this is not a novel of great merit, but in this instance the editor produced an annotated text quite adequate for classroom use. What disturbed me, however, was Edgeworth's careful practice of using quotation marks to highlight quoted passages—and the annotator's failure to identify most of them. Since this edition was prepared before many online tools like ECCO and LION, it is unfair to fault the editor, but it does mean that scholars using this edition as their basis will have a distorted view of the novel if they fail to inform themselves that Edgeworth, steeped in eighteenth-century literature, builds her story with borrowings primarily from male poets and dramatists, not female.[11]

As an editor and annotator, I have not been completely on the wrong side of history. In 2005, with E. Derek Taylor, I edited *Letters Concerning the Love of God*, by John Norris and Mary Astell, published by Ashgate in its The Early Modern Englishwoman, 1500–1750 series under the fine editorship of Betty S. Travitsky. I was pleased with the space allowed for an elaborate introduction, collation, annotation, and appendices, enabling us to produce an edition for scholarly use. I would have liked for this edition to revive interest in Norris, to whom I will return, but it appears to have furthered interest only in Astell.[12]

The texts we elect to edit, how we edit them, *and* how we receive and make use of them—all these decisions underlie the health of humanistic endeavor, from the classroom to the scholar's study. I have touched on both textual and annotative matters, but annotation appears today far more critical to the survival of literary studies given the last half century of creating rather than seeking the meaning of a work of literature. I am not so critically naïve as to suggest a sharply defined difference between these two approaches, but I do grow cross when critics abandon themselves totally to creativity, as in this instance of an erstwhile postmodernist exclaiming, testily enough, that the Florida annotations to *Tristram Shandy* "re-position Sterne in a grid of borrowings, quotations and allusions that considerably restricts the freedom to read beyond the annotated pale. . . . I think it is a pity to strip initiatives from readers in this way."[13] While the sort of reading practiced by Lamb has already had its moment and faded,[14] the Florida annotations remain (until the next scholarly edition) to plague future critics, threatening their freedom to say whatever comes to mind—literary criticism as a Rorschach test.[15]

The already mentioned John Norris of Bemerton (1657–1711) offers a useful illustration of critical obsession, undeterred by new information. For at least seventy-five years prior to the Florida edition, John Locke had been a central figure in discussions of *Tristram Shandy*, and rightfully so, since he is directly quoted on several occasions and alluded to on others. Darrell Jones offers a most useful survey of this tradition, with one particular insight worth repeating: Sterne's critics are too often abysmally ignorant of Locke's actual writings and their context.[16] The commentary on Locke and Sterne has consisted mainly of topics raised by Walter Shandy within the fiction, the train of ideas, our sense of relative time (duration), clear and distinct (determinate) ideas. As I wrote in my introduction to the annotations: "Without doubt, the influence of Locke's

Essay Concerning Human Understanding (1690) is the intertextual problem that has most engaged modern readers.... We have approached this influence most cautiously in our annotations, limiting ourselves almost solely to definite verbal echoes... to most of which Sterne himself calls attention.... [W]hatever the significance finally assigned to Locke ... Sterne rather consistently dwells upon a few very famous and often-quoted passages" (*Notes* to *TS*, 3:16). This cautious approach surely gave scholars ample room to pursue their notions, although we went on to provide a hint that Locke did need to be contextualized: if the entire discussion of duration appears verbatim in Chambers's *Cyclopædia* (3:17), is it safe to assume that Sterne was an astute rather than casual student of Locke?

The notes to *Tristram* strive to quote extensively as well as cite the relevant text. While excess is not always the road to wisdom, in the case of annotation a generous helping of what has been uncovered will often be more helpful than a thin gruel of documentary citation. And almost as important as amplitude is digression. For example, a useful springboard for further analysis of the Locke question might be found in the annotation of clear and distinct ideas, where some twenty-six lines from Locke's *Essay*, II.29.3, 6 are quoted (*Notes* to *TS*, 3:130–31).[17] But when, in the middle of the discussion, Tristram opines that by means of Dolly's sealing wax everything can be made plain enough for her to understand mental impressions "as well as *Malbranch*,"[18] annotation is again called for. A possible allusion to *De la recherche de la vérité* (1674–75), translated by T. Taylor in 1694 as *Father Malebranche's treatise concerning the search after truth*, is suggested, along with a mention of Locke's posthumous response to Malebranche (*Notes* to *TS*, 3:131–32).

We went no further than this in annotating the passage, because we were moving too far afield from what seemed apropos to Sterne's Dolly; also, at the time, we did not realize the importance of John Norris to Sterne; he is not once cited in the annotations to *Tristram*. Norris had been mentioned, however, in a study of Sterne's sermons as one of his sources, and is quoted at length by Gardner D. Stout in his scholarly edition of *Sentimental Journey*.[19] While editing Sterne's *Sermons* in the 1990s, I had to retrace Hammond's work and discovered several additional borrowings, including a verbatim borrowing from Norris in volume 7 of *Tristram*, the observation concerning Pythagoras and *"getting out of the body, in order to think well."* After quoting Norris, Sterne ends the paragraph with a sentence that reflects not only on the Smelfungus passage in *A Sentimental Journey*, but indeed on Sterne's entire canon: "REASON, is half of it, SENSE; and the measure of heaven itself is but the measure of our present appetites and concoctions" (*TS*, VII.13; 2:593).[20]

This is not the place to explore the importance of Norris to Sterne, but simply to suggest that the connection was recovered by the work of annotation, and that scholars who continue to write about Locke and Sterne without paying attention to Sterne's interest in Norris will fail to situate his invocation of Locke within a valid eighteenth-century context.[21] Had we been more alert, Malebranche might have opened us to this context, because it was Norris who pitted the French philosopher most directly against Locke's *Essay*, and who was the first to publish against it in an often reprinted pamphlet; Locke wrote a response to Norris, and a longer response to Malebranche, considering both as challengers to be confronted.[22] It is possible, of course, to read Sterne without consulting Locke, Malebranche, or Norris, but when one does revisit the beaten path of the Locke-Sterne nexus, the annotations now available make it a serious scholarly lapse not to confront Norris's presence in Sterne's panoply of important sources.[23]

The recovery of Norris is rather an exception in the process of annotation because an annotator will often have no idea how the details offered to elucidate a text could or should influence subsequent scholarship. Because of Tristram's unfortunate encounter with the window sash, Walter is led to consult Albertus Rubenius for advice on putting Tristram into breeches. There is some validity to the citation as explained in *Notes* to *TS*, 3:418–19, but Sterne also gathered material from Addison's *Dialogues upon the Usefulness of Ancient Medals* (1726) and texts more accessible than the Latin of Rubenius; we suggested one such source, a textbook manual, Lefèvre de Morsan's *The Manners and Customs of the Romans. Translated from the French* (1740), and offered in evidence long passages of closely aligned prose. As with so much annotation, however, we had no determinate idea how this information is relevant to understanding *Tristram Shandy*, except that it reinforces what we already knew, that Sterne's cited sources cannot always be trusted. It is precisely this unknowingness that best characterizes the work of annotation, because once we begin we must annotate all elements of the text with similar intensity.[24] Perhaps the sole value of this effort at fullness is to deny scholars their counterfactual readings of the text, for example, that Rubenius is Sterne's sole source. But if the critic decides these four pages of Scriblerus-like parody of learned discourse and its sources mean nothing and rides this opinion "peaceably and quietly along the King's high-way" what have "either you or I to do with it?" (*TS*, I.7; 1:12).

A crucial task for Sterne's annotators is confronting the ambiguities of his bawdry, but I have discussed this elsewhere,[25] and prefer here to engage a more difficult subject, Sterne's long career as an Anglican minister. While I am certain that new scholarly editions will be forthcoming within the twenty-first century for his fictions and his correspondence, his sermons may not as readily find a new editor. To be sure, when I edited them in the early 1990s, the tide was still running against religion as a topic of interest to eighteenth-century scholars, while today there is greater awareness, thanks to many fine studies, that we cannot understand eighteenth-century Britain without paying attention to the tenacious continuation of Christian belief throughout the period.[26] Moreover, as more and more relevant texts are made digitally available, a new edition of *Sermons* may come to be propitious—the possibility of finding additional sources without having to read hundreds of sermons is a compelling inducement.

Annotating sermons is not often attempted and was undertaken in Sterne's case solely because of his other writings. Whether Tillotson, Samuel Clarke, Joseph Butler, or Thomas Secker would be rewarded by a scholarly edition is a question worth contemplating, but we may be certain that Valentine Nalson (1683–1723) will not be. Yet his *Twenty Sermons . . . Most of them Preached in the Cathedral of York* (1737) is quoted six times in my annotations, because, as explained on the first occasion, he was unknown, was a Cambridge graduate, preached at York Minster, and tended a rural Yorkshire congregation (Ripon), a career parallel to Sterne's, though a generation earlier (*Sermons*, 5:60). I would never insist, even at my testiest, that scholars should read Nalson in order to write on Sterne, but I would suggest that reading them side by side helps correct common generalizations about Sterne's "unique" sermon style and clerical indifference.

The opening sermon in the first volume of *Sermons of Mr. Yorick* (1760) bears the title "Inquiry after Happiness," which might suggest to readers of *Tristram* and *Sentimental Journey* a light-hearted, hedonistic discourse on pursuing a satisfying life. To the contrary, it is a traditional "vanity of human wishes" sermon, relying on the likes of Tillotson and Clarke, but also of Nalson, and a substantial quotation from him in my headnote usefully summarizes it. The passage concludes: "in the midst of Plenty they have been in Want; still pursuing what they have not, and tired of what they have; still inventing and projecting Schemes for a Succession of new Pleasures, to supply the Place of the old ones that are worn out."[27] It is this traditional context that fully informs Sterne's observation that "I believe this is no uncommon picture of the disappointments of human life—and the manner our pleasures and enjoyments slip from under us in every stage of our life" (*Sermons*, 4:10). Thus, when we read in the final volume of *Tristram* (9.15; 2:767) that "The fifteenth chapter is come at last; and brings nothing with it but a sad signature of 'How our pleasures slip from under us in this world,'" surely we are better informed than otherwise as to the context of what is, on the one hand, an obvious cliché, but on the other, a Christian's reflection on death, Sterne's subject from the burial of Yorick in volume 1 to this final volume.

Nalson is again quoted to elucidate a passage in sermon 5 ("The Case of Elijah and the Widow of Zerephath") of much interest to readers of Sterne's fictions. This charity sermon was Sterne's first (of only two) separately published sermons (1747) and one of his most polished. It is often cited to argue Sterne's uniquely sentimental pulpit oratory, but annotative analogues from Bishop Joseph Hall's dramatic narrational retelling of biblical stories (*Contemplations upon the Principal Passages in the Holy Story* [1612–26]) and from a traditional charity sermon by Isaac Maddox (1743) suggest otherwise. A heartfelt appeal to (and endorsement of) the goodness of one's congregation is a tried method for inducing charitable giving. In this, Sterne's "charity" sermons are no different from those of other Anglican preachers, despite his also being the author of *A Sentimental Journey*.[28]

Sterne asserts a strong connection between good health and good deeds (body and soul), beginning with Epicurus: even a sensualist admits that happiness is promoted by charity toward others, and the "very *mechanical motions* which maintain life" are best performed by "a great and good soul . . . engaged in charity" (*Sermons*, 4:49). The temptation has been to read such passages (central to Sterne's thinking) as an endorsement of mechanistic thinking, whether from science or philosophy, and hence evidence of Sterne's diluted Christianity. Nalson, neither an Epicurean nor mechanist, is thus useful in letting us know that Sterne is likely embracing a pulpit commonplace: in Nalson's words, "a Soul that is oppressed with a Load of Guilt . . . is no more capable of enjoying any Happiness, than a Man that is racked and tortured with the Gout or Stone . . . is capable of relishing a fine Concert of Musick" (*Twenty Sermons*, 417–18; quoted in *Sermons*, 5:105). Sterne concludes his own similar passage with a quotation from *Merchant of Venice*, V.1.85–88, that a man without compassion was "*fit for treasons, stratagems, and spoils . . . / Let no such man be trusted.*" He omits the two previous lines, 83–84, "The man that hath no music in himself, / Nor is not moved with concord of sweet sounds." An annotator might be justified to offer only the four lines Sterne actually quotes, or only the citation if brevity is a paramount consideration; I provided all six lines in my note, although I did suppress the urge to claim that Nalson had triggered Sterne's recall of Shakespeare's "sweet sounds."

One of the pleasures of annotating Sterne's *Sermons* was the opportunity to call attention to Lansing Hammond's work thirty-five years earlier; every borrowing that he uncovered is carefully credited to him; as indeed are James A. Work's annotations to *Tristram*, Gardner D. Stout's to *Sentimental Journey*, and Lewis Perry Curtis's to Sterne's correspondence.[29] Where critical commentary is often intent on blazing new paths where no one has ventured before, the annotator constantly relies on the work of predecessors, not only those who prepared antecedent scholarly editions but as well on all the notes, essays, and monographs published in the interval between scholarly editions. There are many annotative contributions in such commentary that demand notice in new editions, and crediting their authors is again a pleasurable necessity. In a brief essay in 1972, for example, Françoise Pellan pointed out for the first time Sterne's debt to Pierre Charron's *Of Wisdom* (1612; 1630) for both Walter's homuncular theory in the opening chapter of *Tristram Shandy* and his diatribe against procreation in its final chapter—one of the most valuable recoveries of Sterne's sources in the past fifty years.[30] Yet, to my knowledge, few have pursued these borrowings, with their indication that Sterne might have considered the symmetry of returning to Charron an effective answer to the question of whether or not he considered volume 9 the conclusion of *Tristram Shandy*. More to the point, however, is Charron's relationship to Montaigne and the astuteness of an early admirer, Rev. Robert Brown (1728–1777), who wrote in July 1760 that Sterne must have read Montaigne as much as the Book of Common Prayer—a perception Sterne endorsed: "As for my conning Montaigne as much as my pray'r book—there you are right again."[31] As with so many of Sterne's major sources, Rabelais, Cervantes, Robert Burton, Scripture, and now Montaigne (and Charron), the annotator is faced with large, multifaceted books that must be read many times before one has caught Sterne's many borrowings—and even then, as with John Norris, it is doubtful that these multiple readings will catch every borrowing or analogue. Rereadings will always be rewarded by further discoveries; one pass through, one set of eyes, is never enough to discover the full extent of one author's involvement with another, and especially with favorite sources. Scholarly annotation opens rather than closes paths, indicating to attentive readers the rich veins of valuable ore worthy of further exploration. To write on Sterne without reading (and rereading) the works posited as primary sources and analogues, usually

The Angry Annotator Annotated | 153

those most often cited, is to misconceive the purpose of a scholarly edition—and literary interpretation.

Pellan did, in fact, fail to spot a borrowing that illuminates one of Sterne's most characteristic passages in *A Sentimental Journey*. Observing that he has gained his passport at the expense of taking on the role of jester, Yorick exclaims: "But there is nothing unmixt in this world; and some of the gravest of our divines have carried it so far as to affirm, that enjoyment itself was attended even with a sigh—and that the greatest *they knew of,* terminated *in a general way,* in little better than a convulsion" (*ASJ*, 116). The combination of profundity and bawdiness bears Sterne's signature, and previous editors of *Journey* probably passed over the passage for that reason. But Charron had written: "Good things, delights and pleasures cannot be enioyed without some mixture of euil and discommodity. *Medio de fonte leporum surgit amari aliquid, quod in ipsis floribut angat: Euen from amidst the fountains of delights do arise always some bitternesse, which euen in the height of pleasure doe annoy. The highest pleasure that is, hath a sigh and a complaint to accompany it; and being come to perfection is but debility, a deiection of the minde, languishment.*"[32] Charron leads us to Montaigne, who in his essay "That we taste nothing pure" expresses the same notion: "Of the Pleasure and Goods that we enjoy, there is not one exempt from some mixture of ill and inconvenience." Quoting the same Latin tag (from Lucretius, book 4.1133–34), he adds, "Our extreamest Pleasure has some Air of groaning and complaining in't. Would you not say that it is dying of Pain?"[33] Without sliding from elucidation into interpretation, it does seem rather important for readers of Sterne to know that his seemingly characteristic embawdiment of a classical and Christian commonplace has its origin in Montaigne (and Charron); the notion that Sterne's combining of sex and sentiment (body and soul) throughout *Sentimental Journey* is somehow unique to him is unsustainable after one has read Montaigne.

I started this essay with Sterne's debt to Addison's *Cato*, and would like to return to that passage to conclude this *apologia* for annotation and the angry annotator. Toward the end of *Sentimental Journey*, in a chapter titled "The Bourbonnois," Yorick delivers his famous apostrophe to "Dear sensibility," which entails a direct quotation from the opening of act 5 of *Cato*, in which the hero contemplates suicide: "*my soul shrinks back upon herself, and startles at destruction*" (*ASJ*, 155). Most critical attention to Yorick's words at this point has been focused on "Sensorium," which follows shortly thereafter,[34] and scant attention to the opportune borrowing from one of the most popular plays of the century—and even less consideration to the "mere pomp of words" with which Yorick seems to dismiss Cato's sentence. While that phrase may be commonplace, it does occur within an interesting context in Rowe's *The Fair Penitent* (1703):

> Hast thou e'er dared to meditate on death?
> . . . .
> Say, hast thou coolly thought?
> 'Tis not the stoic's lessons got by rote,
> The pomp of words, and pedant dissertations
> That can sustain thee in that hour of terror.[35]

Considered within the context of Cato's speech, it seems possible that the entire passage reflects Sterne's own impending death and reminds us that *A Sentimental Journey* was written under severe illness during the last year of his life.

Cato's argument is that fear of death is the source of belief in God and eternity (immortality). Sterne is arguing, instead, that our sensibility, our capacity for loving and caring for others, creates that belief. Interpretation is called on to weigh not only the invocation of the "sensorium," but the presence of two of midcentury's most popular plays as part of the discussion—and the sentence that follows it: "I feel some generous joys and generous cares beyond myself—all comes from thee, great—great SENSORIUM of the world! Which vibrates, if a hair of our heads but falls upon the ground, in the remotest desert of thy creation" (*ASJ*, 155). Annotators of eighteenth-century authors sometimes serve best by simply noting what was true for authors and readers of that time (but not ours), that the Bible was at their fingertips. Sterne alludes here to Scripture's fundamental providential assertion, Matthew 10:29–31 (quoted by the Florida editors, rather than merely cited, along with several Old Testament precursors of the idea). The annotations for this passage also include a generous quotation from Sterne's sermon "Trust in God" (borrowed from another obscure cleric, Walter Leightonhouse),[36] another generous passage from Adam Smith's *Theory of Moral Sentiments* (1759), and several citations of critical commentary, including portions of Stout's annotation (*ASJ*, 371–76). In short, the passage is so packed with an allusive structure that good annotation, whether in scholarly editions or scholarly articles, will almost always construct paths rather than walls. What matters to the annotator, I would suggest, is not the meaning of the passage, but what it might mean, given the context in which its particular diction is embedded.

In any work of literature there are individual items, words, names, titles, places, and the like, for which the annotator supplies definitions and identifications that may or may not already be known to readers (who range from the greatly learned to the unlearned). Objecting to this sort of annotation is simply nonsense, as is objecting to the identification of a verbatim borrowing. The most important work of annotation, however, comes when confronting a passage as complicated as the "Bourbonnois" chapter of *Sentimental Journey*, a chapter that, prior to one's editing, has already drawn much critical attention. Here the annotator negotiates the boundary separating elucidation and interpretation, first by sifting through the opinions of those who have emerged as pertinent commentators, then by bringing to bear on the passage nonverbatim texts that are invoked or seem to be invoked. The annotator of this passage, for example, must be able to bring Sterne's life and canon to bear on it. "The Bourbonnois" comes just before a "feast of love" (*ASJ*, 158) and a chapter titled "Grace" (159), it is written by a dying cleric who has entered into an impossible love fantasy with a married woman half his age (who is now sailing back to India), and it praises sensibility as a reflection of God's providential care. Surely, each of these elements, separately, would suggest to an annotator (and to an informed critic) the need to bring Sterne's sermons to bear on the chapter; to read it without knowing something of what Sterne preached from the pulpit seems counterintuitive, if not simply counterfactual.

The most satisfying aspect of annotation, and most particularly of annotating passages rich for interpretation, is that I rarely felt called on to inflate my material into a twenty- or thirty-page-essay, much less into a monograph. Even the most extensive notes are but a few pages in length before one moves on to the next problem. Literary critics are invested in the creation of extensive arguments able to confront and dismiss alternative readings as part of justifying their own reading of a particularly knotty passage. I have written many such essays over a long career, alternating the hats of editor and critic, even wearing a postmodern disguise in my more abandoned moments, so I do recognize from experience how very different the roles are.[37] But I also know, because of these critical essays, just how important a good annotated edition has been to my understanding of an author, and so I do occasionally waste a drop of spleen, disturbing the tranquility of irenic reviewers.

156 | Notes on Footnotes

Let me simplify: three common critical practices draw my ire: first, when I read criticism that, without ample explanation or justification, is counterfactual to what annotation has offered; second, when critical commentary fails to take into account the paths opened to it by the annotator and speaks instead of being walled in; and third, my most special testiness is directed toward those who never consult the scholarly edition but instead use the paperback text they used in college in order to write, *ab ovo*, a brilliantly imaginative discourse on Sterne and satire, or sources, or sentimentalism, or sex, all subjects this erstwhile scholar is convinced have never once been touched on in the last 250 years. Still, as my colleagues at the University of Florida long ago discovered, I have always been a curmudgeon.

NOTES

1. W. B. Carnochan, review of Laurence Sterne, *The Miscellaneous Writings and Sterne's Subscribers: An Identification List*, ed. Melvyn New and W. B. Gerard (Gainesville: University Press of Florida, 2014), *Scriblerian* 47–48 (Spring–Autumn, 2015): 73–75. Alternative descriptors for testiness were "acidly," "grumpy," and "grumpier." Sadly, Bliss Carnochan died while this collection was in production. I believe he would have received my essay with what his obituary notice in the *San Francisco Chronicle* describes as his "deep, rich, contagious laughter."

2. Stanford University may not have the same ambience as the University of Florida, where I spent my career, which may account for Carnochan's cheerfulness.

3. Melvyn New, "'The Unknown World': The Poem Laurence Sterne Did Not Write," *Huntington Library Quarterly* 74, no. 1 (2011): 85–98. The author was Hubert Stogdon (1692–1728), who sent a copy to Elizabeth Singer Rowe; a version appears in the second volume of her posthumous *Miscellaneous Works in Prose and Verse* (1739).

4. See *A Sentimental Journey*, ed. Melvyn New and W. G. Day, The Florida Edition of the Works of Sterne (Gainesville: University Press of Florida, 2002), 6:372–76 (hereafter *ASJ*). Critical readings of the passage have always been divided, but both sides might now be better informed in their commentary, which will need to account for Addison's presence.

5. At least this contextualizes the edition; the review by Norma Clarke (*London Review of Books* 41, no. 4 [February 21, 2019]) summarizes the life of Goldsmith she offered in *Brothers of the Quill* (2016), without commenting at all on the new edition.

6. *Eighteenth-Century Studies* 52, no. 2 (2019): 263–70.

7. Amory's review (*Papers of the Bibliographical Society of America* 79, no. 4 [1985]: 602–11) objected primarily to a perceived mischaracterization of Fredson Bowers's theory of copy text. My response to his review was not anger but a letter of appreciation because he had spent time and care over my work. The result was a rewarding correspondence for almost two decades, and a treasured acknowledgment in his edition of Fielding's *Miscellanies*, vol. 3: "[His] suggestions helped me rethink the purpose and function of the apparatus, and to recast it in a more useful and intelligible form" (The Wesleyan Edition of the Complete Works of Henry Fielding [Oxford: Clarendon Press, 1997], xii).

8. See Melvyn New, "Thoughts on Reviewing Textbook Editions and Student Companions," *Scriblerian* 52, no. 1 (Autumn 2019): 77–82.

9. Sarah C. E. Ross and Paul Salzman, eds., *Editing Early Modern Women* (Cambridge: Cambridge University Press, 2016).

10. For details supporting these assertions, see my review in *Scriblerian* 48, no. 2 / 49, no. 1 (2016): 155–58.

11. See my "In Quotes: Annotating Maria Edgeworth's *Belinda*," in *1650–1850* 26 (2021): 112–30. After this essay was accepted for publication in Spring 2019, Linda Bree published a second Oxford edition of *Belinda* in 2020; it is interesting to compare her annotations to the suggestions in my essay.

12. Astell entries in the MLA Bibliography outnumber Norris entries by roughly ten to one; and many of his are solely because of his connection to her.

13. Jonathan Lamb, *Sterne's Fiction and the Double Principle* (Cambridge: Cambridge University Press, 1989), 2–3.

14. See my review of Lamb's monograph, *Scriblerian* 23, no. 2 (1991): 228–31. Apropos annotation, this observation is telling: "Lamb quotes Tristram on the 'double rotation of the earth'" and informs us that the image is Dryden's, and that Sterne's allusion is "designed to recall his approval of tragicomedy" (Lamb, 23). In the Florida *Notes*, ed. Melvyn New, Richard A. Davies, and W. G. Day (Gainesville: University Press of Florida, 1984), 3:117–18, the passage is paralleled to both Swift (*Tale of a Tub*) and Dryden. Lamb rejects annotation because allusions are not decipherable messages but moments of "unannotatable ambiguity"; nonetheless, here (and elsewhere) he draws on the Florida notes, selects the parallel that he likes, and then *deciphers* ambiguity by telling us what Sterne's allusion is "designed" to do. For an extended response to "indeterminateness" as the "key" to *Tristram Shandy*, see my "Sterne and the Narrative of Determinateness," *Eighteenth-Century Fiction* 4 (1992): 315–29.

15. Being threatened by annotation seems to me much the same as being threatened by a therapist's interrupting to suggest that every inkblot is not a vagina; the attempt to cure a reader's critical hobby-horses by a reengagement with the text is the worthy aspiration of both physician and annotator.

16. Darrell Jones, "Locke and Sterne: The History of a Critical Hobby-Horse," *Shandean* 27 (November 2016): 83–111. A year after this essay appeared, perhaps an insufficient time to ward off further uninformed discussion, Andrew Hadfield (the same scholar who located Toby at Waterloo) edited a collection dedicated to Sterne and philosophy. He found the "divine watchmaker" a Lockean theory ("Sterne Amongst the Philosophers," *Textual Practice* 31, no. 2 [2017]: 225–32 [online]).

17. The general editors of the Cambridge Works of Samuel Richardson have labeled this generosity "the Florida style," by way of arguing their own notion of conciseness and uniformity of annotation; the *Grandison* edition, which I coedited, was cut to conform to their word count; see below, Elizabeth Kraft's essay, for one example. Years ago, reviewing the excellent John Brooke edition of Walpole's *Memoirs of King George II* (New Haven: Yale University Press, 1985), I suggested that a note to Walpole's observation that the citadel "surrendered and the garrison were made prisoners," namely, "For the number of prisoners, see Add. MS 32903, ff. 37–9," merely sends us to the British Library (*Eighteenth Century: A Current Bibliography*, n.s., 11 [1985]: 676–77). As an annotator I have tried to render such journeys unnecessary.

18. *Tristram Shandy*, ed. Melvyn New and Joan New, The Florida Edition of the Works of Laurence Sterne (Gainesville: University Press of Florida, 1978), II.2; 1:99 (hereafter *TS*).

19. Lansing Van der Heyden Hammond, *Laurence Sterne's Sermons of Mr. Yorick* (New Haven: Yale University Press, 1948), 142–44; Hammond's study is basically an exercise in

annotation, providing side-by-side entries from the sermons and their sources. Stout was annotating the Smelfungus passage in his edition (Berkeley: University of California Press, 1967), appendix E, note to 120.54–64; see *ASJ*, 6:38, 273–75).

20. In every volume of the Sterne edition I have made the point that annotation is always going to be incomplete, awaiting not only correction and amplification, but also new recoveries and further questions. I was fortunate that Roy Wolper, long-time doyen of the *Scriblerian*, was willing to include a "Scholia to the Sterne edition" in each issue, open to additions and corrections; the Autumn 1994 issue (27.1, 94–95) contains this particular discovery. To date we have published more than fifty-two items, the first thirty-seven gathered together in "Scholia to the Florida Edition of the Works of Sterne from the *Scriblerian*, 1987–2005," *Shandean* 15 (2004): 135–64; and another fifteen in the *Shandean* 30 (2019): 73–87.

21. See Melvyn New, "The Odd Couple: Laurence Sterne and John Norris of Bemerton," *Philological Quarterly* 75, no. 3 (1996): 361–85. Several scholars have now paid attention to Norris when discussing Sterne, including Tim Parnell, "A Story Painted to the Heart? *Tristram Shandy* and Sentimentalism Reconsidered," *Shandean* 9 (1997): 122–35, and Geoff Newton, "Laurence Sterne and his Church," *Shandean* 19 (2008): 71–89. Or, as Tom Keymer wrote in his introduction to the *Cambridge Companion to Laurence Sterne*: "Even Tristram's famous declaration that 'we live amongst riddles and mysteries' (*TS*, IV.17; 1:350) has now been recuperated as a more or less verbatim quotation by Sterne from a Restoration sermon of unimpeachable Pauline credentials" (Cambridge: Cambridge University Press, 2009, 3). He means John Norris of Bemerton. Since Sterne's sermons are often diminished as mere "discourses," it is worth observing that all four volumes of Norris's profoundly serious sermons were published as "*Practical Discourses*." For a discussion of "riddles and mysteries," see *Sermons*, 5:218–20; the term should never again be invoked to suggest Sterne is a non-Christian postmodern existentially indeterminate deconstructionist.

22. See Norris, *Cursory Reflection Upon a Book Call'd, An Essay Concerning Human Understanding* (1690); and "Odd Couple," 381n5. Norris's major philosophical work, *An Essay Towards the Theory of the Ideal or Intelligible World*, 2 vols. (1701–4), is a response to Locke in many of its arguments. A useful introduction to Norris's thought is W. J. Mander, *The Philosophy of John Norris* (Oxford: Oxford University Press, 2008).

23. One might even suggest that rather than Locke's epistemology underwriting the eighteenth-century novel, it is Norris's ontological response to Locke that provides its organizing principle; see, e.g., E. Derek Taylor, *Reason and Religion in "Clarissa": Samuel Richardson and "The Famous Mr. Norris, of Bemerton"* (Burlington, VT: Ashgate, 2009). See also Sandra Macpherson's *Harm's Way: Tragic Responsibility and the Novel Form* (Baltimore: Johns Hopkins University Press, 2010); Macpherson's reconsideration of the "rise of the novel" is very fine but would have been finer had she read Norris.

24. For example, having defined the various pieces of clothing from the sources we consulted, it was necessary to note (*TS*, 3:423) that we had not found "calceus incises" (cutwork shoe) in any of them.

25. "'At the backside of the door of purgatory': A Note on Annotating *Tristram Shandy*," in *Tristram Shandy: Riddles and Mysteries* (London: Vision Press, 1984), 15–23; and "Sterne's Bawdry: A Cautionary Tale," *Review of English Studies* 62 (2011): 80–89.

26. The literature is multiplying rapidly, so I will cite only a few outstanding examples, one early and two recent: Richard E. Brantley, *Locke, Wesley, and the Method of English Romanticism* (Gainesville: University of Florida Press, 1984); William J. Bulman, *Anglican Enlightenment: Orientalism, Religion and Politics in England and Its Empire, 1648–1715* (Cambridge: Cambridge University Press, 2015); and Robert G. Ingram, *Reformation Without End: Religion,*

The Angry Annotator Annotated | 159

Politics and the Past in Post-Revolutionary England (Manchester: Manchester University Press, 2018). See also *Theology and Literature in the Age of Johnson: Resisting Secularism*, ed. Melvyn New and Gerard Reedy, S.J. (Newark: University of Delaware Press, 2012).

27. Valentine Nalson, *Twenty Sermons . . . Most of them Preached in the Cathedral of York* (1737), 37–38 (quoted from *Sermons*, 5:60). It is worth noting that Nalson writes a very fine prose sentence and that his sermons were published one year before Sterne joined the Yorkshire clerical establishment as an assistant curate (Arthur H. Cash, *Laurence Sterne: The Early and Middle Years* [London: Methuen, 1975], 65).

28. See *Sermons*, 5:94–111, esp. 94–98).

29. Work's textbook edition (New York: Odyssey Press, 1940) was for many years the quoted text for scholars working on Sterne and is indeed an exemplary effort; Lewis Perry Curtis's edition of Sterne's *Letters* (Oxford: Oxford University Press, 1935) served several generations of scholars before being superseded by the Florida *Letters* in 2009.

30. Françoise Pellan, "Laurence Sterne's Indebtedness to Charron," *Modern Language Review* 67 (1972): 752–55.

31. Laurence Sterne, *Letters*, ed. Melvyn New and Peter de Voogd (Gainesville: University Press of Florida, 2009), 8:691–93; 7:168).

32. See *ASJ*, 347; I first pointed out this borrowing from Charron in "Some Sterne Borrowings from Four Renaissance Authors," *Philological Quarterly* 71 (1992): 301–2.

33. *Essays*, trans. Charles Cotton (London, 1686), 2:547 (the translation Sterne used); quoted from New, "Borrowings," 302.

34. Stout's edition, for example, devotes two pages to his elucidation (353–54).

35. Act 5, ll. 77, 79–82; ed. Malcolm Goldstein (Lincoln: University of Nebraska Press, 1969), 63; quoted from *ASJ*, 373. Stout annotates "mere pomp of words" with Johnson's statement that *Cato* communicates "no vibration to the heart" (278); the Florida edition provides context for that sentence, indicating Johnson's divided opinion: on the one hand, the "innumerable beauties which enamour us of its author" and the play's "just and noble sentiments," on the other, the absence of "human sentiments or human actions" and its "artificial and fictional manners." In short, Johnson is not as dismissive of the play as Stout's note suggests (see *ASJ*, 371–76).

36. From *Twelve Sermons* (1697); so obscure is Leightonhouse that until August 2020, all I discovered about him was that he received his BA from Magdalen College, Cambridge, his MA from Lincoln College, Oxford, in 1679, and was a prebendary of Lincoln Cathedral; Robert Walker, challenged by my ignorance, uncovered his death date, 1701, and that he was "a celebrated preacher" (Charles Henry Cooper, *Memorials of Cambridge*, 1861, 175); Sterne's extensive borrowing from him has been known since 1798; see *Sermons*, 5:353.

37. It is another source of irritation when it is assumed that editors cannot possibly be as sophisticated as contemporary literary critics, an attitude behind the indifference to such premodern virtues as citing the correct text, quoting it accurately, paying attention to bibliographical matters, and using the *OED* to find definitions for words one does not understand. I will therefore direct attention to Melvyn New, "Proust's Influence on Sterne: A Remembrance of Things to Come," in *MLN* 103 (1988): 1031–55, an essay avoided, as too theoretical, I testily assume, by most innovative thinkers writing about *Sentimental Journey*.

CHAPTER 10

🙷 Annotating the Yale Edition of the Works of Samuel Johnson

Robert DeMaria Jr.

The Yale Edition of the Works of Samuel Johnson was first proposed by Allen T. Hazen in a letter to interested parties on December 10, 1951: "The edition is planned . . . in 12 volumes . . . the apparatus is to be minimal. The text printed is to be sound as the first requisite, with enough apparatus to enable users to follow the textual problems. . . . Explanatory annotation is to be helpful and adequate, but never discursive or all-inclusive. . . . [T]he edition ought to be ready to print within about two years."[1] As this inaugural statement indicates, the emphasis in the Yale edition was to be on the text rather than on commentary. Presentation of a text merely "sound" was less than what a scholar of Hazen's bibliographical sophistication could offer, but it was still more, in its sphere, than was a commentary merely "helpful and adequate," at a time when heavily annotated editions such as the Lewis-Yale edition of Walpole's Letters, the Yale edition of Milton's *Complete Prose Works*, and the Twickenham Pope were in progress. Hazen had come to Columbia after serving as the head librarian at the University of Chicago and before that as a cataloguer in the Yale University Library. He held a joint appointment at Columbia between the English Department and the School of Library Service. As the first general editor of the Yale Johnson, Hazen set the project on a course that favored relatively scientific (but not overly scrupulous) attention to the text and a much more casual approach to commentary.[2]

Despite Hazen's emphasis on the text, his Yale edition did not at first please other bibliographers. Fredson T. Bowers unleashed a torrent of criticism on the texts of volumes 1 (*Diaries, Prayers, and Annals*) and 2 (*The Idler and The Adventurer*). A few years later J. David Fleeman weighed in with such a scathing condemnation of the text in the *Rambler* volume that it tested his friendship with Hazen. Hazen defended the textual approach of the Yale edition to the end, which sadly came prematurely for him because of heart troubles. The editorial protocols shifted somewhat under Hazen's successor to the general editorship of the edition, his former assistant John H. Middendorf, and some individual editors—notably Gwin J. Kolb—departed altogether from some of its protocols. Nevertheless, many aspects of Hazen's approach to the text survived throughout the twenty-three volumes of the edition, which reached completion in 2018.

As the treatment of the text in the Yale volumes evolved over time without changing completely, so did its attention to scholarly annotation. The key statement in the beginning was the Yale editorial committee's resolution on "Explanatory Annotation" (September 28, 1956; revised May 20, 1957), which "incorporates discussions at meetings in May and September 1955, and March and September 1956." It is worth quoting at length. because it explains a great deal about commentary in the edition:

> Before writing footnotes, try to imagine a user who starts to read SJ, perhaps in Australia, fifty years hence. Then plan the notes.
> Notes to [be] held down to
>
> (1) correction of actual errors
> (2) cross-references within the canon
> (3) identification of puzzling allusions, sources, classical mottoes
> (4) helpful explanations of SJ's meaning, reading, or way of working
>
> This will mean:
>
> (1) no notes to identify line numbers of Hamlet's soliloquy if reference in text is clear
> (2) no notes when a reference is clear to an obvious work
> (3) a note to identify vague reference to a classical author or to a contemporary not now generally or widely known
> (4) a note when a reference to Voltaire is to some fusion of passages or to an unfamiliar essay

Note will point out a change of theory between the *Plan* and the *Preface to Dictionary*. But the fact that other dictionaries before or after agreed with him belongs in a monograph.

Notes will not summarize all modern scholarship on each work, although most modern explication will be drawn upon if helpful. This means that a source, a meaning, a misunderstanding will be cited in the note, with mention of pertinent studies if necessary to explain or correct; but the note will not become a bibliography of all publication on the subject up to a fixed date preceding publication. Try to plan notes that will not be obsolete even when an important new monograph is published. But the notes should equip a student to use the text readily in conjunction with any previous or subsequent monographs.

Notes should not become merely exclamatory, laudatory, or discursive; no monographs on matters mentioned incidentally in the text. For example, Hill's notes on the first page of his edition of SJ's *Annals* (in *Miscellanies [I.129]*) are interesting in themselves, certainly to Hill and doubtless to many readers, but they do not elucidate SJ's autobiography:

> Franklin's letter to his wife concerning change in calendar
> Smith's tabulation of wheat prices
> [on man-midwife] accoucheur is not in SJ's Dictionary, and citation
>   from Tristram Shandy
> the baptism of SJ's father

Biographical notes

Not encyclopedic as in Yale Walpole. No note at all for casual references to people of 18th-century (or earlier) distinction; in practice, no note for a person in DNB unless his identification is immediately useful in comprehending the allusion. Thus, no notes for a reference to Pope or Spenser. Index will give dates of people. No note to identify Boswell or Warburton, and no note when SJ writes that Dyer studied at Westminster School under Dr. Freind. But a note is needed for Ford, to identify him as Parson Ford because of his association with SJ; and Hill's identification of George Hector (first page of SJ's *Annals*) is needed.

Cross-references within the canon

Remember that references to any other edition will seem peculiar once the present edition is completed. . . .

The index, by what is called "common-noun indexing," will collect the important critical dicta at a major point, with sparing use of references to this passage.

Example:

Entry in index only when SJ writes merely of the "disgust which blank verse . . . superadds to an unpleasing subject" in *Dyer*.

The purpose of the edition will be to present a sound and readable text. . . . Explanatory notes, it is hoped, will not run much above an average of some dozen lines to a page.[3]

How were these directions interpreted by the various editors of individual volumes? To what extent were they followed in the execution of the edition over the ensuing sixty years? Now that the edition is complete, these are the questions to which we can sketch answers. Two points are easy to make, given how events transpired. Most cross-references to other volumes in the edition were not possible as the print edition proceeded because progress was so slow; many were only instituted in the digital edition. Second, the general index presumed in the instructions above was never compiled. The labor and the cost did not seem worthwhile, especially once the digital edition was assembled. The keyword searches made possible by insertion of the metadata takes the place of the "common-noun indexing" referred to in the instructions.

If one looks at other aspects of the instructions, it becomes clear that many of the statements are cautionary rather than prescriptive: they suggest curbs on excess rather than rules for proceeding. Do not be "merely exclamatory, laudatory, or discursive. No monographs." That is broad advice at best, and it only gets a bit finer when the document says, do not be like the Yale Walpole and do not be like G. B. Hill. The Yale Walpole was a well-oiled machine run under the direction of Wilmarth Lewis, and the editors followed his guidelines religiously. He assembled a library of reference works and created chronologies so that all editors had a common fund of knowledge on which to draw. (One volume, for example, tracked Walpole's whereabouts on virtually every day of his adult life so all editors could agree on biographical facts.) The commentary reflects and may even be said to expound this common fund of knowledge. The Yale Johnson is much more the work of individual editors who interpreted the general guidelines in individual ways, but the negative injunction about the Yale Walpole is not so much a prescription for individuality as it is a warning not to create a work of reference. As the guidelines elsewhere suggested the

164 | Notes on Footnotes

Yale Johnson was a book for "informed literate readers" rather than researchers. G. B. Hill, the other model to be avoided, represents an extreme of individual effort that verges on the idiosyncratic: it is full of what has been called "Victorian clutter." The examples from Hill in the directions read almost as parody, but they are direct quotations. Like two Yale editors of the *Lives* (Hilles and Middendorf), Hill died before his work was done. His edition was completed by his nephew, but the notes of idiosyncrasy and clutter remain in his *Lives* as they do in his *Annals*, the Hill edition cited in the Yale guidelines.[4]

Theoretically, the notes in the Yale edition would only identify relatively obscure allusions: the imagined readers are familiar with everyone in the *Dictionary of National Biography*, so no need to gloss any of their names. These readers also recognize allusions to all the major works of Voltaire, though a composite reference might trip them up. There can be notes on Johnson's meaning and practice, but not on anyone else's: no digression into intellectual history. In addition, although classical mottoes need identification, there is no mention of translation. The edition's ideal readers would not need these, presumably, and there are few translations (none of modern languages and only a few of Latin) in the early volumes. These are very high standards for readers, which would seem to be contradicted by the injunction to imagine a reader in Australia (i.e., the hinterlands, for this group of sophisticated New Yorkers) fifty years from now (when the world would surely be worse than it was in 1958). In the face of such confusing advice, what did the editors of the various volumes actually do?

All the volumes in the Yale Johnson differ from one another, but volume 1, *Diaries, Prayers, and Annals*, is truly anomalous. It provides the only text drawn mainly from manuscripts (although most of the "Annals" comes from an early printed version), and instead of individual footnotes, it has a running commentary at the foot of the page. To recall the Guidelines' scathing condemnation of Hill's *Annals*, there is in Yale an explanation of New Style dating, but no reference to "Dr. Franklin" and no list of baptisms, stretching back in Hill's edition to 1579, and including Michael Johnson's siblings. Hill's edition reads more like Allen Lyell Reade's amazing compilation of documents, *Johnsonian Gleanings* (11 vols., 1909–52), and less like a modern commentary on a text. The Yale edition, however, is not without its excesses. On page 11, for example, Johnson mentions "lessons in Aesop . . . not those in Helvicus." The Yale editors appropriately identify *Aesop* as Charles Hoole's edition and Helvicus as Christopher Helwig (1581–1617). Given that Johnson said "not . . . Helvicus," however, the rest of the note seems excessive:

[His] *Familiaria Colloquia Auctoritate Superiorum Selecta et Adornata*, 1613, now very rare, went through at least eight German editions in the seventeenth century and reached an "editio novissima" at Nuremberg in 1715 (copy at University of Illinois). Soon after the first edition it was, according to the title page of the 1715 edition, "with the consent of the author turned into German," which was printed facing the Latin text. Of the fifty dialogues, thirty-three are from Erasmus's Colloquies, originally written for Erasmus's pupils at Paris in 1496, twelve from Juan Luis Vives, and five from Hermannus Schottennius, author of *Instructio Prima Puerum*, 1527. A London printing described as the eleventh edition appeared in 1673 (copy in the Bodleian). It is in Latin only and contains no vocabulary.

I love this bibliographical information, and it is linked to the text, as Benjamin Franklin in Hill's note is not, but its inclusion nevertheless seems contrary to the spirit of the Yale Guidelines. Some of the information is irrelevant; the note takes up more than the statutory twelve lines; Helvicus gets dates, but Vives does not (not even in the index), nor does Schottennius, who also does not, like Helvicus, get his birth name. Providing the location of copies of the largely irrelevant titles qualifies as Hillean excess.

One could go on about the annotation in Yale 1, but that volume is sui generis. Yale 2–5 present problems that are the opposite, in many ways, but generally more characteristic of the edition. In the introduction to volume 2, the editors say, "Explanatory notes have been kept as lean in style as the editors could conscientiously make them" (Yale, 2:xxvi) and in volume 3, "the annotation . . . has been as lean in style as we could conscientiously make it" (Yale, 3:xxx–xxxi). Claude Rawson seized on the word "conscientiously" in his review for *Essays in Criticism*.[5] He calls the word "uppish, though this hauteur may seem slightly unfocused. Is it of the gentleman who won't shirk his duty, but also won't impose garrulous pedantries on the civilized reader, or disfigure a handsome book with ink-horn glosses? or is it of the no-nonsense professional, who gives it clean and straight, without the messy informativeness of a Birkbeck Hill? Doubtless a bit of both" (304). Rawson goes on to record very numerous failures both on the side of the professional who is not willing enough (as Hill was perhaps too willing) to pursue the cultural context of many of Johnson's references, such as his allusion to the "blind man, who after long enquiry into the nature of the scarlet colour, found that it represented nothing so much as the clangor of a trumpet" (Yale, 4:139), and of the professional who fails to

166 | Notes on Footnotes

refer to the best scholarly editions of other writers or take advantage of the annotation in recent work on Johnson. By now the "lean" quality of the annotation in the *Rambler*—perhaps Johnson's most richly allusive work—is the stuff of legend. I can personally recall editors of other volumes in the Yale edition repeating the word "lean" with scorn.

To be fair, rich annotation of the *Rambler* would have taken a great deal of time, and the Yale edition was originally projected to be completed in two years. More than ten years elapsed between the publication of volume 1 and the publication of the *Rambler* (vols. 3–5), even with lean annotation. On the other hand, all of Rawson's suggestions are persuasive and many would not have taken much time to add. It would have been easy, as he says, to add a reference to Claudian's "Old Man of Verona" in no. 38 (Yale, 3:205). But it is unclear where such a note could end. Should the editor mention that Johnson cites this poem in his draft of *Irene*? that he had a copy of Claudian's poems, edited by Heinsius, in his Pembroke College library? that the book is now in the Hyde Collection? that in his draft of *Irene*, right next to his reference to Claudian's "Veronese," he cites Martial's epigram 10.47, which Heinsius uses to gloss Claudian's "Veronese," and which recurs in *Rambler* 203 (Yale, 3:293)?[6] Is it adequate to make a bare mention of Claudian's poem (*Carm. Min. Corp.*, XX [LII], 11) or in Loeb (*Shorter Poems*, trans. M. Platnauer [Cambridge, MA: Harvard University Press, 1922]), 194–97? Perhaps one should at least cite the particular lines to which Johnson refers ("frugibus alternis, non consule computat annum:/ autumnum pomis, ver sibi flore notat," ll. 11–12), with the translation: "For him the recurring seasons, not the consuls, mark the year: he knows autumn by his fruits and spring by her flowers." These are hard questions to answer.

To track just one more of the *lucunae scholiasticarum* cited by Rawson, he notes the absence of any commentary on the dream vision in no. 67 in which Johnson imagines "the gate of Reason," from which "there was a way to the throne of Hope, by a craggy, slippery, and winding path" (Yale, 2:357). Rawson rightly suggests there may be a memory of Donne's Third Satire (ll. 79ff.) and "more particularly of the 'versified version' by Thomas Parnell" (310). The relevant lines are 79–80 in Parnell's poem,[7] and they are nearly the same as those in Donne's poem. Interestingly, Johnson quoted them under *cragged* in the *Dictionary* but attributed them to Crashaw. Johnson's whole allegory in *Rambler* 67, however, is reminiscent of his "Vision of Theodore: The Hermit of Teneriffe." That vision is itself much like the traditional *Tabula of Cebes*, which, like "The Vision of Theodore," appears in the last chapter of *The*

Preceptor, 2 vols. (London: R. Dodsley, 1747). The new variorum edition of Donne's *Satires* (Bloomington: Indiana University Press, 2016) includes the suggestion of Charles Mosely in 1989 that Donne's imagery recalls the *Tabula of Cebes*.[8] Of course Johnson might have thought of Donne (or Crashaw), Parnell, and Cebes. The question for the commentator is where to draw the line. It can easily feel as though there is no medium between leanness and supernumerary annotation or between spare identification and adscititious intellectual history. As Johnson said in his Preface to *Shakespeare*, "It is impossible for an expositor not to write too little for some, and too much for others. He can only judge what is necessary by his own experience; and how long soever he may deliberate, will at last explain many lines which the learned will think impossible to be mistaken, and omit many for which the ignorant will want his help" (Yale, 7:103).[9]

After the publication of the Yale *Rambler* and the harsh criticism of its leanness, a change in Yale's style of annotation began, but it began slowly. The lightly annotated *Poems* (1964) and slightly better *Johnson on Shakespeare* (1968) were followed by somewhat more richly annotated editions of *A Journey to the Western Islands of Scotland* and *Sermons* (1978). The real turning points, however, were Donald Greene's *Political Writings* (1977) and Gwin Kolb's *Rasselas* (1990). Greene was against leanness, and his volume shows this in its richer annotation and in its much more extensive introductions. Arguably, his commentary too often goes beyond explanation to tendentious interpretation. Greene had a powerful vision of Johnson's political life, and that colors many of his footnotes and introductions. Nevertheless, his volume set a new standard for the Yale edition, and this standard was not only observed but exceeded by Gwin Kolb's *Rasselas*. Even Claude Rawson was pleased; he said of Kolb's volume: "The new edition of *Rasselas* is the fullest to-date, long awaited and worth waiting for."[10]

Kolb's *Rasselas* was very long in the making. An earlier version was his doctoral dissertation, written at the University of Chicago under the direction of Ronald S. Crane (1948). Kolb's introduction and commentary display Crane's influence in their emphasis on genre, generic antecedents, and, in general, the attempt to place the composition of the work in its most immediate context. The edition is rich in parallels to Johnson's earlier writings because he would obviously have drawn on these in composing *Rasselas*. It is also rich in references to works by those whom Johnson probably (or possibly) drew from in writing *Rasselas*. In this assemblage of references, generic considerations and chronology usually trump considerations of intellectual history or the history of ideas. For example, in chapter 6, "A Dissertation on the Art of Flying," Kolb glances at the "ancient tradition, as old as Icarus, of the ambitious aeronaut," brings it roughly up-to-date with mention of Richard Owen Cambridge's *Scribleriad*, and cites Louis Landa's article on the contemporary intellectual background. Thereafter, however, Kolb focuses almost exclusively on John Wilkins's *Mathematical Magick: or the Wonders that may be Perform'd by Mechanical Geometry* (1648). He had given his reasons for seeing this work as Johnson's principal source for *Rasselas*, chapter 6, in an article published in 1959. He refers readers to that article but goes on in his notes to "detail the chief resemblances between passages in *Mathematical Magick* and SJ's 'Dissertation'" (Yale, 16:22n1). Eighteen of the thirty footnotes—and all the longish ones—to this chapter concern Johnson's indebtedness to Wilkins, and they describe it very thoroughly. Kolb is trying to reveal, as closely as he can, Johnson's "procedure" in composing *Rasselas*. In this chapter and throughout his edition, he attempts to put readers at Johnson's side and show which books were open on his desk (or at least his mental desktop) as he wrote.

The volume of Kolb's annotation in Yale 16 goes far beyond that in earlier volumes, and he is more methodical than earlier Yale editors. The full force of Kolb's method came home to me when I coedited with him Yale 18, *Johnson on the English Language* (2005). After due consideration, Gwin asked me largely to scrap the long introduction I had written on the intellectual history of dictionaries. He asked me instead to focus on generic antecedents to the Preface, Plan, Grammar, and History of the English Language—the specific parts of the *Dictionary* included in our volume. Instead of reading dictionaries, I read proposals for dictionaries and other large works of reference. I had read prefaces to dictionaries before, but I gave them more prominence in my account of the Latin, Continental, and British lexicographical antecedents to Johnson's work. This adjustment is registered in the footnotes as well. In annotating Johnson's "Grammar of the English Tongue," for example, I focused attention on Lily's Latin grammar and John Wallis's *Grammatica Lingua Anglicana*, laboriously determining that Johnson used the fourth edition (1674) of Wallis's work. I counted the references to other authors and listed them in the introduction. In the footnotes, I showed precisely where Johnson adhered to Wallis—translating or paraphrasing his *Grammatica*, particularly in the section on "derivation" (Yale, 18:328–46). Other grammarians come in, and Johnson certainly looked at Ben Jonson and James Greenwood, but Wallis must have been open on his desk most of the time. The footnotes try to show him turning the pages of his source as he wrote.

The last several volumes of the Yale edition are annotated in the Greene or Kolb way, though none is as methodical or as rich as *Rasselas*. The notes to the three volumes of the Parliamentary Debates, largely provided by Thomas Kaminski, resemble those in Greene's *Political Writings* in richness, but avoid their tendentiousness. The two volumes on which I worked with O M Brack are very much in the Kolb tradition. With the master no longer on the scene, I will admit that the notes are somewhat less methodical than those in Gwin's *Rasselas*, but his lessons were not lost on me or Brack.

Inevitably, I must conclude with *Lives of the Poets*. The difference between Middendorf's annotation in the Yale edition (3 vols., 2010) and the much fuller annotation in the Oxford edition (4 vols., 2006) is not simply one of bulk. When he was still a member of the Yale editorial committee, Lonsdale wrote that he could not follow the dictum that Yale would be "an edition of Johnson and not of the authors he wrote about." Let me give just one example of what this means in practice. Early in the first of the *Lives*, "Cowley," one finds the oft-quoted remark "The true genius is a mind of large general powers, accidentally determined to some particular direction." Middendorf comments, "Cf. Papilius's letter to the *Rambler* (No. 141): 'Whoever shall review his life will generally find, that the whole tenor of his conduct has been determined by some accident of no particular moment . . .'" (Yale, 21:6n6). He also cross-references a passage in "Pope." Lonsdale, on the other hand, begins by quoting Johnson on "genius" in his *Dictionary* and follows it with quotations from Pope's *Essay on Criticism*, *Rambler* 25, *Rambler* 141, *Idler* 61, and several reports of Johnson's conversation on the subject in Boswell's *Life* and other sources. In addition (and this is where he really begins to deviate from the Yale style), he quotes Alexander Gerard's *An Essay on Genius* (1774) for an opposing view. Still not finished, he quotes Gibbon on Reynolds's view of genius and pursues the sources of Gibbon's belief in Reynolds's own statements about his finding his inspiration as a painter in Jonathan Richardson's essays on painting (Lonsdale, 1:309–10). This is the kind of annotation the original editors of Yale wanted to curtail; they might have compared it to Hill's, though it is much better organized. Lonsdale is writing intellectual history, whereas Middendorf is mainly trying to reveal what Johnson had in mind, and perhaps on his desk, as he composed this Life.

Despite their differences in approach, the respective commentaries of Middendorf and Lonsdale generally assume the same professional tone. The old-fashioned "hauteur" of the Yale edition, as Rawson called it, is absent in Middendorf's *Lives* and most of the other late volumes of the edition. The project that began in the 1950s under the auspices of book collectors and librarians gradually fell under the influence of professional, scholarly editors with PhDs in English. Although these editors changed their tone, they never entirely drowned out the more gentlemanly voices of those who first announced the edition.

NOTES

1. Houghton Library MS Hyde 98 (827).

2. For more on the text and on the founders of the Yale edition, see Robert DeMaria Jr., "The Yale Edition of the Works of Samuel Johnson 1958–2018," *Book Collector* 69, no. 3 (Autumn 2020): 487–97. Although the present article has a different emphasis, it draws on some of the same material as the one already published.

3. I have taken these excerpts directly from the materials distributed to the Yale Johnson editorial committee and now in our archives. They are discussed by Donald Greene in "No Dull Duty: The Yale Edition of the Works of Samuel Johnson," in *Editing Eighteenth-Century Texts: Papers Given at the Editorial Conference, University of Toronto, October 1967*, ed. D. I. B. Smith (Toronto: University of Toronto Press, 1968), 92–123.

4. Cf. Robert G. Walker's more indulgent attitude toward Hill's Victorian "clutter" below, "Annotation and Scholarly Conversation: The Musings of a Non-Editor Annotator."

5. *Essays in Criticism* 22, no. 3 (1972): 303–12.

6. Draft of *Irene* in *Poems*, ed. David Nichol Smith and Edward L. McAdam, 2nd ed., rev. J. D. Fleeman (Oxford: Oxford University Press, 1974), 383; cf. Yale, 6:176n. Claudian Claudianus, *Cl. Claudiani quae exstant*, ed. Nicolaas Heinsius, 2 vols. (Amsterdam: Elsevir Press, 1665), 2:865. Cf. Robert DeMaria Jr., *Samuel Johnson and the Life of Reading* (Baltimore: Johns Hopkins University Press, 1997), 82–83 and n. 29.

7. *The Collected Poems of Thomas Parnell*, ed. Claude Rawson and F. P. Lock (Newark: University of Delaware Press, 1989), 316.

8. Donne, *The Variorum Edition of the Poetry of John Donne, Volume 3: The Satyres* (Bloomington: Indiana University Press, 2016), 754; Charles Mosley, *A Century of Emblems: An Introductory Anthology* (Aldershot, Scolar Press, 1989), 24.

9. For a present-day effort to provide a richer edition of *The Rambler*, see Anthony W. Lee's essay "Annotating *The Rambler* / *The Annotated Rambler*," this volume.

10. "Samuel Johnson Goes Abroad," *London Review of Books* 13, no. 16 (August 29, 1991): 15–17.

CHAPTER 11

❧ Annotating *The Rambler* / *The Annotated Rambler*

Anthony W. Lee

The twentieth century witnessed a golden age of eighteenth-century scholarly editing.[1] The California Dryden, the Wesleyan Fielding, the Florida Sterne, and the Yale Boswell are but a few of the many editions that could be cited. Amid the bustle of these activities, Samuel Johnson has received prominent attention. His letters have been admirably edited by Bruce Redford, as have the *Lives of the Poets* and the *Journey to the Western Islands*, by Roger Lonsdale and J. D. Fleeman, respectively. Thomas M. Curley completed an excellent edition of Johnson's collaboration with Sir Robert Chambers, *A Course of Lectures on the English Law, 1767–1773*. The centerpiece of all this activity is, of course, the Yale Edition of the Works of Samuel Johnson. Curiously, however, the work that stakes a claim to being his finest prose accomplishment, *The Rambler*—Johnson once said of it, "My other works are wine and water; but my *Rambler* is pure wine"[2]—has been ill served. The 1969 Yale Works version, edited by W. J. Bate and Albrecht B. Strauss, constitutes one of the most defective contributions to the series.[3] Other twentieth-century redactions include *Samuel Johnson: The Rambler*, edited by Sir Sidney Roberts (New York: J. M. Dent and Sons, 1953), and *Samuel Johnson: Selected Essays*, edited by David Womersley (New York: Penguin, 2003); while the last is serviceable for the classroom or the general reader, neither constitutes a truly rigorous scholarly engagement.[4] Furthermore, both are currently out of print. This chapter

172 | Notes on Footnotes

examines the Yale *Rambler*'s annotation and textual practices, particularly with respect to Johnson's own practice and methodology as an editor, and concludes with a comparative account of a version I have been working on for more than fifteen years, *The Annotated Rambler*.[5]

JOHNSON THE ANNOTATOR

Johnson famously remarked of annotation: "Particular passages are cleared by notes, but the general effect of the work is weakened. The mind is refrigerated by interruption; the thoughts are diverted from the principal subject; the reader is weary, he suspects not why; and at last throws away the book, which he has too diligently studied." Against this dismissive appraisal, however, we have Johnson's active practice: the copious annotation found, for example, in his Shakespeare edition, prefaced by his positive yet ambivalent proclamation that "Notes are often necessary, but they are necessary evils."[6]

Exemplary annotation of his own works includes *London* and the *Lives of the Poets*. The former's 1748 revision contains six notes written to assist in clarifying references potentially obscure to a later generation of readers;[7] in the *Lives of the Poets*, he included notes when referring, for example, to a manuscript of Joseph Spence's *Anecdotes* in the "Life of Pope" (and elsewhere). His most considerable annotation of the work of others is found in his massive eight-volume Shakespeare edition—a scholarly encounter that, in the words of distinguished Johnson critic Bertrand H. Bronson, possesses "a value that continues even today" (YW, 7:xxxv) and served as the springboard to the later Shakespeare Variorum editions. We find additional annotative activity in his translation of Crousaz's *Commentaire sur la traduction en vers de M. Abbé, de l'Essai de M. Pope sur l'homme* and his 1756 edition of Sir Thomas Browne's *Christian Morals*. It is this last title that I examine in some detail as exemplifying Johnson's approach to writing scholarly notes.

Johnson deploys four types of annotation:[8] (1) glosses of unfamiliar words, (2) explanatory notes, (3) identification of allusions and sources,[9] and (4) elucidation of obscure passages. The following canvass provides examples of each.

1. Dealing with a writer who deployed a deeply involuted style and frequently arcane diction—characteristics in fact often marking Johnson's own writings[10]—Johnson as *editor* felt compelled to define difficult or "hard" words. His labors on the recently completed *Dictionary of the English Language* (1755) preeminently prepared him for this task. An exemplary specimen of such an

Annotating *The Rambler* / *The Annotated Rambler* | 173

interface may be found in the first sentence of Browne's work, part of which reads, "Tread softly and circumspectly in this funambulatory track and narrow path of goodness." In his edition, Johnson defines "funambulatory" as "Narrow, like the walk of a rope-dancer."[11] The Yale Works editors observe that the word does not appear in Johnson's *Dictionary*; however, under the entry for "ropedancer," Johnson cites an illustrative passage from John Wilkins's *Mathematical Magick*, where, in the same paragraph, Wilkins writes: "It is a usuall practise in these times, for our Funambulones, or Dancers on the Rope, to attempt somewhat like to flying."[12] Johnson most likely got his definition from this source. Numerous other instances of word glosses appear; see, for example, "pinax," "flaws," "grain'd," among others (Browne, *CM*, 8, 15; YW, 19:342, 343, 345). The permanent value of Johnson's observations is reinforced by the frequent inclusion of many of them in the most recent edition of Browne's writings.[13] The insistently larger point is this: Johnson as editor was attentive to the capacities, needs, and expectations of his readers. He was aware that few people possessed Browne's—or his own, for that matter—extensive and often obscure vocabulary, and, fresh on the heels of the publication of his *Dictionary*, he was just the person to provide such assistance.[14]

2. Johnson at times offers explanatory notes designed more precisely to clarify Browne's intended meaning. In section 33, Browne writes, "Since thou hast an alarum in thy breast, which tells thee thou hast a living spirit in thee above two thousand times in an hour." This provokes Johnson to conjecture about the number, "The motion of the heart, which beats about sixty times in a minute; or, perhaps, the motion of respiration, which is nearer the number mentioned" (Browne, *CM*, 46; YW, 19:353). Johnson was fascinated by mathematical calculations, and here was unable to resist the temptation that Browne offers.[15] Yet his conjecture certainly elucidates the "alarum" and its "telling," or counting, for the common reader's comprehension.[16]

Earlier in *Christian Morals*, Browne had used a metaphor to render an admonishment about the virtuous life: "Think not that you are sailing from Lima to Manillia, when you may fasten up the rudder, and sleep before the wind" (Browne, *CM*, 8; YW, 19:343). Johnson, also interested in geography,[17] chooses to explore the metaphor's vehicle, and adds, "Over the pacifick ocean, in the course of the ship which now sails from Acapulco to Manilla, perhaps formerly from Lima, or more properly from Callao, Lima not being a sea-port" (Browne, *CM*, 8; YW, 19:343).[18] Both examples demonstrate Johnson's mastery of Browne's context as well as text and his ability to share this knowledge to assist the less learned reader's comprehension. That Browne's modern editor

Kevin Killeen uses both notes in his annotative apparatus testifies to their enduring value.

3. While many of the notes Johnson added to *Christian Morals* are word glosses, the overwhelming number of them are identifications of allusion. We see in the wealth of these and other similar offerings Johnson's erudition—an erudition matching that of the learned Browne. For example, the latter wrote, "There is no Damocles like unto self-opinion, nor any siren to our own fawning conceptions." Many readers would probably think of the famous sword of Damocles and deduce that the sword corresponds to the imminence of divine judgment. However, Johnson notes, "Damocles was a flatterer of Dionysius" (Browne, *CM*, 32; YW, 19:349). This is indeed the same Damocles that sat uneasily beneath the sword, but Johnson's note crucially goes beyond the obvious and specious to divulge the lesser-known point of Browne's allusion, the indulgence of flattery. Elsewhere, seeking to inculcate generosity, Browne urges, "for since he who hath pity on the poor lendeth unto the Almighty rewarder, who observes no ides but every day for his payments." Remarking on the allusion to "ides," Johnson observes:

The ides was the time when money lent out at interest was commonly repaid.

> ———Fœnerator Alphius
> Suam relegit Idibus pecuniam,
> Quaerit calendis ponere. Hor. (Browne, *CM*, 13–14; YW, 19:345)

Most common readers would associate the Roman "ides" with the assassination of Julius Caesar and nothing else, but again Johnson's knowledge of classical culture and literature renders him a fit annotator of his subject and directs him to make the pecuniary association that Browne intends. This knowledge further allows him to invoke an allusion to one of his own favorite authors.[19] We find, then, an intricate literary structure embedded in the apparatus—an annotation of an allusion that fosters an additional allusion, thus further clarifying Browne. And again, Killeen makes room for both of Johnson's annotations in his own edition—offering silent approval to the clarifying intricacy of Johnson's note.

4. As in his Shakespeare edition, Johnson at times pauses to untangle obscure passages[20]—and Browne's labyrinthine prose affords God's plenty. For example, in section 4 Browne writes, "ends of penitent publick sufferers,

who go with healthful prayers unto the last scene of their lives, and in the integrity of their faculties return their spirit unto God that gave it." Johnson, sensing the possible confusion of "integrity of their faculties," adds "with their faculties unimpaired" (Browne, *CM*, 12; YW, 19:344), a restating of the original phrase for clarification. He did the same thing on the previous page, where Browne's "Make the quarrelling Lapithytes sleep, and Centaurs within lie quiet" leads to this explication: "That is, 'thy turbulent and irascible passions'" (Browne, *CM*, 10; YW, 19:343). Killeen includes the first in his edition, but not the second.

Despite his theoretical protestations against the evils of annotation, then, Johnson, in his edition of Browne's *Christian Morals*, provides a textbook example of a carefully considered and judiciously executed practice of the scholarly footnote: as he remarks in the Preface to *Shakespeare*, "I have confined my imagination to the margin" (YW, 7:108). In the following section, I examine how his successors in the Yale Works edition of the *Rambler* failed to exert a similar marginal imagination in their editing practice.

JOHNSON ANNOTATED I: THE YALE *RAMBLER*

In a May 28, 1750, letter to Elizabeth Carter, Catherine Talbot wrote, "The author of the Rambler . . . ought to be cautioned . . . not to use over many hard words. In yesterday's paper (a very pretty one indeed) we had *equi-ponderant*, and another so hard I cannot remember it, both in one sentence."[21] Talbot's letter to Carter—a good friend of Johnson who herself penned two *Ramblers* (44 and 100)—refers to *Rambler* 20, published May 26, 1750, which contains the following sentence: "If we therefore compare the value of the praise obtained by fictitious excellence, even while the cheat is yet undiscovered, with that kindness which every man may suit by his virtue, and that esteem to which most men may rise by common understanding steadily and honestly applied, we shall find that when from the adscititious happiness all the deductions are made by fear and casualty, there will remain nothing equiponderant to the security of truth."[22] The forgotten word that Talbot pairs with "equiponderant" is "adscititious." Johnson defines the former in his *Dictionary*, "Being of the same weight"; the latter, "That which is taken in to complete something else, though originally extrinsick; supplemental; additional." Johnson had already used "equiponderant" in *Rambler* 1; "adscititious" will appear again in *Rambler* 49, 123, 155, and 179. W. K. Wimsatt Jr. has articulated the importance of this

176 | Notes on Footnotes

adjective to Johnson's style: "The meaning of a word like 'adscititious' depended on a form of the Latin verb *adscicsere* [*sic*], which in turn was an inceptive form of the verb *scire*, whose meaning was one of the most basic and simple of our ideas. Such a word as 'adscititious' may itself not have been current in any science, but it might have been or ought to have been. . . . 'Adscititious' was a word which few might understand, but which all should understand—all who knew the roots of the language and could put two and two together."[23] Wimsatt's reflection would be accurate only in a culture where the intended audience knew Latin; most present-day readers of the *Rambler* do not. When Johnson again uses "adscititious" in the *Voyage to Abyssinia*, the Yale editor annotates it with the *Dictionary* definition (YW, 15:212). Given the contemporary as well as later reception of these "hard words," to say nothing of ministering to the needs of the common reader, the sentence from *Rambler* 20 surely also requires annotation. Yet, the editors of the Yale *Rambler* refrained from annotating either of the two "hard words"—nor many others clustered throughout the three volumes.

Explanatory notes of the kind Johnson employed in his edition of Browne are largely absent in Yale. Let one example suffice. In *Rambler* 2, after discussing the human tendency to always project a hopeful future, Johnson returns to his motto's warning that too much preparation can also be destructive: "Yet as few maxims are widely received or long retained but for some conformity with truth and nature, it must be confessed, that this caution against keeping our view too intent upon remote advantages is not without its propriety or usefulness, though it may have been recited with too much levity, or enforced with too little distinction" (*AR*; YW, 3:11). Johnson here uses the term "nature" for the first time in the *Rambler*, roughly rendering it equivalent to "truth." In the eighteenth century, "nature" was a complex word, one fraught with a genealogy of possible meanings. The modern reader is most likely to associate it with the natural world of trees, clouds, and animals. Or perhaps, as in "human nature," expressing the essence of a thing, a human being. However, in Johnson's age, numerous additional meanings were available—many quite different from the two primary modern ones familiar to us. In the present instance, for example, the word is used in a way proximate to Johnson's *Dictionary* definition 5: "The regular course of things." "Nature" often conjured for denizens of the eighteenth century a harmonious providential world order that embraced the entire universe, physical, social, and moral (*AR*; YW, 3:115).[24]

Annotating *The Rambler* / *The Annotated Rambler* | 177

There is yet another important sense in which Johnson uses the word. See, for example, the end of *Rambler* 37, where he concludes his discussion of the pastoral form:

> The facility of treating actions or events in the pastoral stile, has incited many writers, from whom more judgment might have been expected, to put the sorrow or the joy which the occasion required into the mouth of Daphne or of Thyrsis, and as one absurdity must naturally be expected to make way for another, they have written with an utter disregard both of life and *nature*, and filled their productions with mythological allusions, with incredible fictions, and with sentiments which neither passion nor reason could have dictated, since the change which religion has made in the whole system of the world. (*AR*; see also YW, 3:204; my italics)

In a paper devoted to literary criticism, Johnson now uses the word in an aesthetic or critical sense. In his 1756 *Dissertation on the Epitaphs Written by Pope* (appended to his "Life of Pope"; YW, 23:82), he expounds on the particular meaning arising from this context: "What is commonly called *nature* by the criticks, [is] a just representation of things really existing, and actions really performed." Under the definition of *nature*, 7, in the 1773 fourth edition of the *Dictionary*—"The constitution and appearance of things"—Johnson quotes a passage from the final paragraph of Sir Joshua Reynolds's *Discourses* no. 4 (a work Johnson helped Reynolds correct and possibly compose):[25] "The works, whether of poets, painters, moralists, or historians, which are built upon general nature, live forever; while those which depend for their existence on particular customs and habits, a partial view of nature, or the fluctuations of fashion, can only be coeval with that which first raised them from obscurity."[26] Thus, the word "nature," when used as a term in literary theory or criticism, is roughly approximate to the modern "realistic," or "realism." Again, the Yale edition is silent on this matter in *Rambler* 37—and elsewhere.

Bate sometimes does a better job at annotation when tracking allusions, but at other times he is either wrong, misleading, or curiously silent. For an example of the former, in *Rambler* 140, Johnson writes: "It is common among the tragick poets to introduce their persons alluding to events or opinions, of which they could not possibly have any knowledge. The barbarians of remote or newly discovered regions often display their skill in *European* learning. The god of love is mentioned in *Tamerlane* with all the familiarity of a

Roman epigrammatist" (*AR*; YW, 3:11). Bate identifies "*Tamerlane*" as Marlowe's *Tamburlaine the Great* (1590; pt. 2: II.iv.84–87). Closer scrutiny, however, reveals that Johnson more likely refers to Nicholas Rowe's *Tamerlane*, III.ii (1701):

> The idle God of Love supinely dreams,
> Amidst inglorious Shades and purling Streams
> In rosie Fetters, and fantastick Chains,
> He binds deluded Maids and simple Swains.

Elsewhere, a statement in Johnson's "Life of Rowe" supports this reading: "In *Tamerlane* there is some ridiculous mention of the God of Love" (YW, 22:582). And according to the *General Advertiser* (April 10, 1751), Rowe's *Tamerlane* was performed on Thursday, April 11, 1751, at the Theatre Royal, Covent Garden, five weeks before this *Rambler* was published; hence the play would perhaps have been fresh in Johnson's mind, whether he saw it, read about it, or talked about it with others.[27]

For an example of an inappropriately silent editor, we need only return to *Rambler* 37 and its thematic companion, *Rambler* 36, which constitute Johnson's most serious reflections on the pastoral, a genre he notably marginalized through much of his life. Here is a critical passage from *Rambler* 37:

> If we search the writings of Virgil, for the true definition of a pastoral, it will be found *a poem in which any action or passion is represented by its effects upon a country life*. Whatsoever therefore may, according to the common course of things, happen in the country, may afford a subject for a pastoral poet.
>
> In this definition, it will immediately occur to those who are versed in the writings of the "modern criticks," that there is no mention of the golden age. (*AR*; YW, 3:201).

Lying behind this association of the pastoral form with the golden age is a literary war dating from the 1710s, when Pope and Ambrose Philips each published distinctly different versions of pastoral poems. Philips sought to follow Edmund Spenser's example and produce rough-speaking rustics. Pope, on the other hand, sought to produce a more polished and refined pastoral, one he saw as sanctioned by the ancients and Virgil in particular: "If we would copy nature, it may be useful to take this idea along with us, that pastoral is an image of the golden age. So that we are not to describe our shepherds as shepherds at this day really are, but as they may be conceived then to have been; when the best of men followed the employment."[28] Pope's ideas on the pastoral golden age are borrowed from René Rapin's *Dissertatio de carmine pastorali* (1659), translated by Thomas Creech in 1684 and prefixed to his translation of Theocritus. Those of Philips are generally seen to stem from the other great French neoclassical theorist of the pastoral, Bernard de Fontenelle, found in his *Discours sur la nature de l'églogue* (1688), translated into English by Peter Motteux in 1695.[29] In this debate, Johnson retrospectively came down on the side of Virgil and Pope: see *Rambler* 37 §3.

Historicizing Pope's theory of pastoral and the debate between the Scriblerians, who supported Pope, and Addison's Kit-Cat members, who supported Philips, reveals circumstances crucial to understanding Johnson's discussion of the pastoral. Yet, the Yale Edition is sadly silent on the issue. Examples like these—and I have discovered many more from my study of the *Rambler* for more than fifteen years—demand a new edition.

JOHNSON ANNOTATED 2: *THE ANNOTATED RAMBLER*

And this is precisely what motivates *The Annotated Rambler*, which will seek to remedy the deficiencies noted above by providing a textually reliable, orthographically accurate, old-spelling,[30] abundantly annotated edition. Here briefly are some important differences between the Yale *Rambler* and my edition.

The Yale edition makes significant—and unfortunate—adjustments to type and orthography. It changes many of the upper-case initial letters to lower case. And it frequently converts italic type to Roman.[31] Both of these procedures render the text unreliable. In the eighteenth century, personification, a widely used literary trope, was often signaled by upper-case letters; the decision to convert to lower case thus may obliterate this significant authorial intent. Likewise, in the eighteenth century, italic font would signal either emphasis or, equally possible, a quotation or literary allusion; hence uniform romanization will mask authorial stress or indication of a conscious borrowing. The Yale editors do not indicate specifically where and why these changes are made. This combination of abnegation of editorial responsibility and global tinkering with the text renders the Yale edition suspect and untrustworthy to serious scholars. *The Annotated Rambler*, on the other hand, avoids these missteps and provides a faithful text of the 1756 fourth duodecimo edition—the last one Johnson edited, the one where he made considerable stylistic and semantic alterations—collated against the first folio edition.

Another significant point of difference between the Bate-Strauss edition and my own is annotation—indeed, it is the primary premise of my edition. As we saw above, in the Preface to *Shakespeare*, Johnson wrote, "Notes are often necessary, but they are necessary evils." *The Annotated Rambler* contains an exuberance of annotation versus Yale's sparseness—perhaps an evil but, in my opinion, following Johnson, a necessary one. The pages of the text itself are clean, having been prepared with a minimum of notational distraction: following the example of Roger Lonsdale's magnificent edition of *Lives of the Poets*, the annotation is cued to each title, motto, paragraph, and signature, and presented as endnotes following the conclusion of each *Rambler* essay. Those who prefer to read the essays and skip or use sparingly the annotation will thus be free to do so. For those who choose to avail themselves of the annotation, I have devised a system of cross-referencing among the notes that will allow an expansive exploration of Johnson's main themes and repeated allusions—not only among *The Rambler* essays but throughout his oeuvre, the capaciousness of his mind itself as found in conversations and contemporary accounts, as well as among selected eighteenth-century authors (and some earlier ones) that I have found useful or illuminating to include.

The Yale edition, on the other hand, makes this comment: "the annotation of the periodical essays has been as lean in style as we could conscientiously make it,"[32] which one takes to mean moderate. But as an early reviewer, Clarence Tracy—himself an editor of Johnson—noted: "Professor Bate's explanatory notes are more than lean; they are emaciated. The common reader will need fuller explanations and the scholar will usually welcome them." Tracy then goes on to offer a handful of particularly egregious examples, such as the failure to list all variants in accidentals.[33] *The Annotated Rambler*'s annotation is by contrast "fat"—though I prefer the adjectives "fertile" and "full"—rather than emaciated.

In addition to providing word glosses, the notes in my edition perform a variety of other functions. They identify names, events, and literary and historical allusions that are probably unfamiliar to most twenty-first-century readers. Other notes provide more extensive background and interpretive annotation. These are designed: (1) to flesh out the dense allusiveness of Johnson's style, by offering quotations of works he invokes, (2) to provide helpful commentary that situates Johnson's writing in its historical and cultural milieu,

(3) to offer interpretive hints for a fuller understanding of Johnson's complex literary achievement. Allusion, the direct or indirect reference to a previous literary work, historical event or personage, or cultural image, was one of the major literary techniques of poets such as Dryden, Pope, and Swift.[34] Johnson frequently employs the same mode of allusion in his prose, not only to ornament and illustrate, but to shape, direct, and amplify meaning. In the *Rambler* this is especially true; as Boswell noticed: "Every page of the Rambler shows a mind teeming with classical allusion and poetical imagery: illustrations from other writers are, upon all occasions, so ready, and mingle so easily in his periods, that the whole appears to be of one uniform vivid texture" (*Boswell's Life*, 1:217).

Johnson had a photographic memory, and his reading was immense. Adam Smith, no slack reader himself, once remarked: "Johnson knew more books than any man alive" (*Boswell's Life*, 1:71). He carried an encyclopedic knowledge in his head, and this trove informs his writing at nearly every point. Tracing his allusions and quotations is a humbling experience: the reach of his literary range is at once vast and intricate, and following him carries the reader into literary recesses long forgotten in today's world (and often obscure even in his).[35] My edition, whenever feasible and advisable, offers translations of the classical passages Johnson alludes to from the versions that would likely be familiar to him, both for convenience—many are to be found only in rare book collections—and as an aid to interpretation. For example, in the sixth paragraph of *Rambler* 1, Johnson refers to Thucydides's *History of the Peloponnesian War*: "They [authors], perhaps, believed that when, like Thucydides, they bequeathed to mankind κτῆμα ἐς ἀεί, 'an estate for ever,' it was an additional favor to inform them of its value." My note would refer to Hobbes's translation: "And it [the *History*] is compiled rather for an EVERLASTING POSSESSION, than to be rehearsed for a prize."[36] (Incidentally, Johnson here obliquely announces to the world that he is writing not just to his contemporaries, but with a view toward posterity, such that the *Rambler*, like Milton's poetry, was "so written to aftertimes, as they should not willingly let it die.")[37] Of course, the bulk of Johnson's classical quotations would have been known to him in the original Greek or Latin, but by supplying contemporary translations I hope to give a sense of how Johnson's own age digested the classics into English. When this has not been possible, or when the translation seemed too obscure for ready readerly apprehension, I have had recourse to the Loeb Classical Library.

On April 6, 1775, Johnson remarked, "The greatest part of a writer's time is spent in reading, in order to write: a man will turn over half a library to

182 | Notes on Footnotes

make one book."[38] The annotation to the present edition will, I hope, help readers to apprehend the rich literary, historical, and cultural context of the *Rambler* without having to turn over a library.

NOTES

1. Cf. John H. Middendorf, "Eighteenth-Century Literature," in *Scholarly Editing: A Guide to Research*, ed. D. C. Greetham (New York: MLA, 1995), 283: "It is no depreciation of the enormous contributions made to eighteenth-century literary studies by biographers, bibliographers, and critics to say that future generations will think of editions as among the most valuable and lasting contributions of twentieth-century scholars."

2. *Boswell's Life of Samuel Johnson*, ed. G. B. Hill, rev. L. F. Powell, 6 vols. (Oxford, 1934–64), 1:210n1. Johnson here perhaps refers to the ancient Greek practice of watering down strong wine with water to make it a more sociably moderate drink; alternatively, he might also be glancing at the issue from a religious angle, given debates between High Church and Low Church Anglicans over the mixed chalice versus use of pure wine.

3. For negative responses, see J. D. Fleeman, "Review of *The Rambler*, vols. 3–5," *Review of English Studies* 22, no. 87 (1971): 348–52; and Clarence Tracy "On Editing Johnson," *Eighteenth-Century Studies* 4, no. 2 (1970–71): 231–35.

4. Other texts intended for classroom use containing *Rambler* essays include *Samuel Johnson: Selected Poetry and Prose*, ed. Frank Brady and W. K. Wimsatt (Berkeley: University of California Press, 1977); *Samuel Johnson: The Major Works*, ed. Donald Greene (Oxford: Oxford University Press, 2008); and *Samuel Johnson: Selected Writings*, ed. David Womersley (Oxford: Oxford University Press, 2020), in part a reprint of the essays found in his 2003 Penguin edition. The most recent—and, I think, the finest—contribution is *Samuel Johnson: Selected Works*, ed. Robert DeMaria Jr., Stephen Fix, and Howard D. Weinbrot (New Haven: Yale University Press, 2021).

5. When quoting from the text of the *Rambler*, I use my edition but also refer to the Yale Works for the reader's convenience (hereafter YW).

6. Preface to *Shakespeare*, YW, 7:111. On April 3, 1773, he remarked, "all works which describe manners require notes in sixty or seventy years, or less" (*Boswell's Life*, 2:212); see also "Life of Butler" (YW, 21:221); letter to William Strahan, March 7, 1774 (*Letters of Samuel Johnson*, ed. Bruce Redford, 5 vols. [Princeton: Princeton University Press, 1992], 2:131).

7. See *Samuel Johnson: The Complete English Poems*, ed. J. D. Fleeman (New Haven: Yale University Press, 1971), 196.

8. This taxonomy is my own, which includes the typical intentions of eighteenth-century annotators. For a slightly different construct, geared toward modern editors, see Michael Edson, introduction to *Annotation in Eighteenth-Century Poetry*, ed. Michael Edson (Bethlehem: Lehigh University Press, 2017), xiv.

9. The Yale editors of the "Life of Browne" account for most of Johnson's sources: see YW, 19:304–5.

10. For the effect of Browne's style on Johnson's and "Anglo-Latin diction," see *Boswell's Life*, 1:221–22, 308. In the "Life of Browne," Johnson writes, "[Browne] must . . . be confessed to have augmented our philosophical diction; and in defence of his uncommon words and

Annotating *The Rambler* / *The Annotated Rambler* | 183

expressions, we must consider, that he had uncommon sentiments, and was not content to express in many words that idea for which any language could supply a single term" (YW, 19:338). See also W. K. Wimsatt, *The Prose Style of Samuel Johnson* (New Haven: Yale University Press, 1941), 117–20.

11. Sir Thomas Browne, *Christian Morals*, 2nd ed., ed. Samuel Johnson (London, 1756), 7 (hereafter Browne, *CM*); YW, 19:342.

12. John Wilkins, *Mathematical Magick. Or, The Wonders that May be Performed by Mechanicall Geometry. In Two Books* (London: Samuel Gellibrand, 1648), 207.

13. See *Thomas Browne: Selected Writings*, ed. Kevin Killeen (Oxford: Oxford University Press, 2018), 931. Like the Shakespeare annotations, Johnson's notes to *Christian Morals* retain "a value that continues even today." This value extends to other authors, such as John Gay, one that Gay's Oxford editors unfortunately failed to grasp: see, e.g., Anthony W. Lee, "Dryden, Pope, and Milton in Gay's *Rural Sports* and Johnson's *Dictionary*," *Notes and Queries* 65, no. 2 (June 2018): 241–43.

14. Johnson quotes frequently from Browne in the *Dictionary*: 1,962 times in the first and fourth editions, according to one tally (see YW, 19:302n3); for a partial list, see *A Dictionary of the English Language: A Digital Edition of the 1755 Classic by Samuel Johnson*.

15. In 1628, William Harvey published *Exercitatio anatomica de motu cordis et sanguinis in animalibus* (An Anatomical Exercise Concerning the Motion of the Heart and Blood in Animals), which estimated that the heart beats approximately two thousand times per hour. Johnson was familiar with this (see *Rambler* 140, YW, 4:377); however, he most likely came up with his own, admittedly low but yet more realistic, figure by personal experimentation: see *Boswell's Life*, 3:207, and W. Jackson Bate, *Samuel Johnson* (New York: Harcourt Brace Jovanovich, 1977), 72, 106, 415.

16. The phrase "common reader" was a favorite one of Johnson's: see "Life of Gray," in *The Lives of the English Poets*, edited by Roger Lonsdale, 4 vols. (Oxford: Clarendon Press, 2006), 4: 184 and 500n51. Virginia Woolf was also taken with the phrase: see *The Common Reader, First Series*, ed. Andrew McNeillie (Orlando: Harcourt, 1984), 1.

17. See Introduction to *The Preceptor*, section 3 (YW, 20:179–80); *Vanity of Human Wishes*, ll. 1–2.

18. For Johnson's knowledge of the geography of this area, see "Life of Sir Francis Drake" (YW, 19:151).

19. "Horace's Odes were the compositions in which he took the most delight" (*Boswell's Life*, 1:70); he translated a good number of Horace's poems into English, at least nine of which survive: see Yale Works, 6: index, "Horace" (420).

20. Cf. Johnson's comment in the 1756 Proposals for *Shakespeare*: "The business of him that republishes an ancient book is, to correct what is corrupt, and to explain what is obscure" (YW, 7:51).

21. Montagu Pennington, *A Series of Letters Between Mrs. Elizabeth Carter and Miss Catherine Talbot, From the Year 1741 to 1770*, 4 vols. (London, 1809), 1:349.

22. *Annotated Rambler* (hereafter *AR*); YW, 3:115.

23. *The Prose Style of Samuel Johnson* (New Haven: Yale University Press, 1941), 112; see also Wimsatt, *Philosophic Words: A Study of Style and Meaning in the Rambler and Dictionary of Samuel Johnson* (New Haven: Yale University Press, 1941; reprinted Archon Books, 1968), 112.

24. For the seminal study of the evolution of the word "nature," see Basil Willey, *The Eighteenth-Century Background: Studies on the Idea of Nature in the Thought of the Period* (New York: Columbia University Press, 1950), especially chap. 3, "Cosmic Toryism."

184 | Notes on Footnotes

25. See Frederick H. Hilles, *Literary Career of Sir Joshua Reynolds* (Cambridge: Cambridge University Press, 1936), chap. 8, "The Making of the *Discourses*."

26. *Discourses on Art*, ed. Robert R. Wark (New Haven: Yale University Press, 1997), 73 (December 10, 1771). For similar sentiments cf. *Rasselas*, chap. 10 (YW, 16:43–44).

27. For a more thorough consideration, see Anthony W. Lee, "Nicholas Rowe, Samuel Johnson, and *Rambler* 140," *Scriblerian* 51 (Autumn 2018): 41–45.

28. "Discourse on Pastoral Poetry" (1717) (Alexander Pope, *Pastoral Poetry and The Essay on Criticism*, ed. E. Audra and Aubrey Williams, The Twickenham Edition of the Poems of Alexander Pope (New Haven: Yale University Press, 1961), 1:25. Johnson possibly may be alluding to John Hughes, who wrote in his 1715 edition of *Works of Mr. Edmund Spenser* (1:cii–ciii): "But in the first Ages of the World it was otherwise; that Persons of Rank and Dignity honour'd this Employment; that Shepherds were the Owners of their own Flocks; and that *David* was once a Shepherd, who became afterwards a King, and was himself too the most sublime of Poets." But Pope is more likely, given the congruence of diction. For a good recent discussion of the debate, see David Fairer, "Pastoral and Georgic Poetry," in *The Cambridge History of English Literature, 1660–1780*, ed. John Richetti (Cambridge: Cambridge University Press, 2005), 259–86.

29. See J. E. Congleton, *Theories of Pastoral Poetry in England, 1684–1717* (Chapel Hill: University of North Carolina Press, 1944), 2–10. See also Paul Alpers's excellent study, *What Is Pastoral?* (Chicago: University of Chicago Press, 1996).

30. See, e.g., Fleeman, *Samuel Johnson: The Complete English Poems*, 14.

31. In this, the *Rambler* editors follow editorial policy set forth for the Yale edition as a whole: see "Style Sheet for the Yale Edition of Johnson": "Reduce caps and italics to modern usage" (revised version, December 1962, p. 1). My thanks to Robert DeMaria Jr. for generously sharing his copy of this instrument. For a more detailed history of the editorial policy and its impact on the early Yale editions—including *The Rambler*—see DeMaria's essay above, "Annotating the Yale Edition of the Works of Samuel Johnson."

32. YW, 3:xxx–xxxi. This is a restatement of the protocol of the previous volume of periodical essays: see YW, 2:xxvi.

33. Tracy, "On Editing Johnson," 232, 235.

34. For the classic statement of this phenomenon, see Rueben Brower, *The Poetry of Allusion* (Oxford: Clarendon Press, 1959), which, however, focuses primarily on Pope. See also Christopher Ricks, *Allusion to the Poets* (New York: Oxford University Press, 2004), and *The Force of Poetry* (Oxford: Clarendon Press, 1984), especially chap. 4, "Samuel Johnson: Dead Metaphors and 'impending death.'"

35. See the Macrobius reference he made at Oxford while still a youth, in *Boswell's Life*, 1:59.

36. *Hobbes's Thucydides*, ed. Richard Schlater (New Brunswick: Rutgers University Press, 1975) 41.

37. John Milton, *The Reason of Church Government*, in *Complete Poems and Major Prose*, ed. Merritt Y. Hughes (Indianapolis: Odyssey Press, 1957), 668. The remarks on Thucydides are taken from the note to the passage in *AR*.

38. *Boswell's Life*, 2:344. Cf. also the description of him by Boswell's uncle, "A robust genius, born to grapple with whole libraries" (ibid., 3:7). And also Roberto Bolaña's *2666*: "There's nothing inside the man who sits there writing. Nothing of himself, I mean. How much better off the poor man would be if he devoted himself to reading" (2004; London: Picador, 2008), 786.

CHAPTER 12

🙋 Annotation and Scholarly Conversation
The Musings of a Non-Editor Annotator

Robert G. Walker

With one very minor recent exception I have never edited a text; yet my work has, on reflection, consisted almost entirely of annotations of text, and here I consider that fact and its relevance to broader scholarly activity. As an annotator without portfolio, I have benefited greatly from the monumental work produced by modern scholars of eighteenth-century literature and have tried to make useful contributions in the same vein in articles, notes, and reviews. My method here is to use as starting points several of those contributions before moving in each case to implications for what it is we do or should be doing.

ON THE SHOULDERS OF GIANTS

A decade ago, I read for the first time the edition of James Boswell's periodic essays, *The Hypochondriack* (1777–83), published in two volumes by Stanford University Press (1928) and edited by Margery Bailey. Here much more than in his *Life of Johnson* Boswell was heavily allusive, and Bailey responded to the challenge, to such an extent that one of her reviewers, R. S. Crane, wrote, "if one has any fault to find, it is that in her zeal to leave nothing undone she has done too much. We could certainly spare some of her notes." R. W. Chapman observed the "formidable mass of annotation," which may frighten off those new to the essays, but he concluded his review with an implicit endorsement of Bailey's method: a list of twenty addenda and corrigenda, all worthy today of submission to *Notes and Queries (N&Q)* or *ANQ*.[1]

Assuming that any activity good enough for R. W. Chapman was good enough for me, and equipped with technology not even dreamed of in 1928, I set out to update his list. The resulting thirty-three items included a few corrections to Bailey, but most were entirely new identifications. Eager to continue the conversation about Boswell's texts begun by Bailey and continued by Chapman, I sent the list, along with an introduction for those not familiar with Bailey's edition or Boswell's essays, to a distinguished journal of historical criticism, where it was summarily rejected. Rejections do not surprise me—I have had my share. What was surprising was the reader's report, shared by the journal's editor: "It doesn't seem appropriate for *SP*: it isn't an article. . . . It's fine, it's informative, but it feels idle, & in any case out of place." There are, as they say, horses for courses, and my horse found its proper course: *English Studies* published the piece without alteration.[2] Occasionally the reader's reason for rejection is not the only cause; the editor noted his two-and-a-half-year backlog. Still, it seems odd that almost pure annotation can strike some in the profession as inappropriate to scholarship. The displacement in our journals of fact-based essays by theoretical approaches has been noted before, but this provides an especially vivid example.

Another important takeaway is the direction of Chapman's review. Clearly, he saw his task as not just making a pronouncement on the worth of the edition but also advancing the state of information about the text edited. He was continuing the conversation about Boswell's essays that Bailey had begun. Indeed, Bailey does digress in her notes, but I find it almost always worth the candle to follow her. For example: Boswell's essay "On Quotations" (about which more later) defends their use against charges of pedantry—exactly what we would expect from the allusive Boswell. Near the end he turns toward "a species of Quotation which is very frequently used with great success, which is citing other persons' sayings to themselves, or in their presence with respectful approbation, in the way of flattery" (1:271). After two passages from *Boswell's Life* somewhat pertinent, Bailey concludes with an anecdote that is peripheral but too good not to include:

> Gibbon could not "hear without emotion the personal compliment" which Sheridan paid him "in the presence of the British nation" at Warren Hastings's trial . . . though Samuel Rogers shows how profound a compliment

it was, in his *Table-Talk*. . . . "During one of these days, Sheridan, having observed Gibbon among the audience, took occasion to mention 'the luminous author of *The Decline and Fall*.' After he had finished, one of his friends reproached him with flattering Gibbon. 'Why, what did I say of him?' asked Sheridan. 'You called him the luminous author, &c.' 'Luminous! oh, I meant voluminous!'" (1:271n20)

Gibbon's annotations famously occupy a full one-quarter of his text, so both adjectives are appropriate. Bailey thus comes by her bent honestly, and with the pattern of extensive annotation close to hand in G. B. Hill's great edition of an eighteenth-century classic, *Boswell's Life of Johnson*, which would soon be made even greater by L. F. Powell.

The work of the Victorian Hill (1887), revised by the twentieth-century scholar Powell (1934–64), provides us with a still irreplaceable resource and a pattern of scholarly activity that serves us well in the twenty-first century. Hill's extensive commentary—his notes are always voluminous, if not always luminous—is typical of Victorian editing, a style reflected in the variorum editions of Shakespeare (Furness) and, later, of Spenser (Greenlaw). Their pattern, in turn, lay in previous centuries' editions of the classics.

Unlike many prefaces, Powell's preface to his new edition makes interesting reading. His decision to maintain the pagination of Hill's edition—due to its prevalence as the standard text—awkwardly necessitated numerous appendices; his view "that Dr. Hill's commentary should be retained but, if necessary, amended and supplemented [because] the chief glory of Dr. Hill's edition is the commentary"[3] is more to our point. Overlaying his annotations, thus making it possible easily to distinguish them from Hill's, not only preserved the integrity of both editors' work but also highlighted the critical conversation, always springing from the literary text itself, proceeding over decades and now centuries, a conversation that is frequently apparent today (or should be) in annotations in subsequent texts as well as in distinct scholarly efforts, whether notes, essays, or monographs. Twenty-first-century editors of scholarly texts might be well served to follow Powell's pattern, at least in spirit, by quoting verbatim previous editors' notes when possible, even when emended with new or additional facts.

Powell's interest lay primarily in annotation. After he finished his collaborative work on the *New English Dictionary*, his publications at first consisted entirely of items in *N&Q*, a dozen from 1920 to 1923, before he began to sprinkle short pieces into the *Times Literary Supplement* and *Review of English Studies*.[4]

188 | Notes on Footnotes

He did, in addition, revise the text of *Boswell's Life*, but modern textual bibliography was still in its early days. Recently Gordon Turnbull has suggested that the completion in 2019 of the four-volume Yale Boswell project's manuscript edition of the *Life* means "it is time for the Hill-Powell edition to be re-done."[5] Even if undertaken immediately and completed expeditiously, the projected edition would have trouble reducing Hill-Powell's useful life to only a century. It is a time frame annotators understand. An article from a recent issue of *N&Q* concludes with this sentence: "This note belatedly addresses certain of the queries posed [in this journal] on 16 May 1868."[6]

LENGTH MATTERS

Annotators, then, understand that *ars longa, vita brevis*. And length, it turns out, is also important to annotators because it seems to be increasingly important to journal editors and publishers. My first publication in *N&Q* appeared in 1977. At that time there were a number of journals that welcomed short pieces, either exclusively or as part of their overall design. Three other places where I published in those early days, *Studies in Short Fiction*, *Notes on Contemporary Literature*, and *Ball State University Forum*, have gone the way of all flesh, and others have ceased to welcome notes. For example, *Philological Quarterly*, where I had published a note on Johnson in 1982, no longer accepts submissions of that length. *TLS*, in a marked difference from Powell's era, may publish at most one or two scholarly notes a year, and the *Scriblerian* may include a note on occasion, but the vast majority of short pieces on eighteenth-century literature now appear in only three journals, all reflective, perhaps, of their individual editors' tenacity and commitment to scholarship: the *Johnsonian Newsletter*, the *Eighteenth-Century Intelligencer*, and the *Shandean*. Of course, *N&Q*, like the earth, abides forever. And *ANQ*, formerly *American Notes and Queries*, after experiencing several major interruptions over the past fifty years, seems back on track as a viable outlet for notes and short articles.

Given this shrinking number of outlets for annotations, and being unwilling to burden a few journals with repeated submissions, I experimented with two approaches to give vent to my annotative urge. The first was pure honesty, to which even an addicted annotator must resort at times. I queried an editor about the acceptable length for a submission, mentioning what I had to offer. He responded by quoting Lincoln about the proper length of a person's legs, and shortly thereafter "Notes on *Boswell Laird of Auchinleck, 1778–1782*" appeared in the annual *Age of Johnson*.[7] In eight pages I provided sources for four previously unidentified Boswellean allusions, and in addition corrected my mistake made two years earlier in *English Studies*, a misidentification of "a curious gentleman" from one of the *Hypochondriack* essays. The frequency with which annotators are able (and willing) to add to and correct past annotations, including their own, is a telling indication of the purpose of annotation: the establishment of accurate and useful elucidations of the text. The best literary critics engage previous interpretations, including their own, in a like manner, but recently this has taken the form of an initial footnote citing two dozen works on the same subject, which are then ignored for the rest of the essay or chapter. As for correcting one's own interpretation, I realize this could be construed as talking to oneself, thus reducing the scholarly conversation I have been advocating to a monologue.

My second approach to length solved nothing. I wished to discuss several passages in *Boswell in Search of a Wife* that had not been treated satisfactorily by the editors of the Yale edition. I had been struck as well by how little attention, despite the valuable Yale editions, Boswell's journals have received (excepting, of course, the *London Journal*, with its first meeting between Boswell and Johnson) and thought I could meaningfully link the current disfavor of Boswell's personal writings to present-day cultural biases. My gentle argument was that Boswell's alleged misogyny did not destroy the pleasure of reading him, which I demonstrated by the elucidation of passages devoted primarily to courtship and marriage. Acceptance by *SEL* was made contingent not on correcting errors in my annotative materials but rather on removing the word "charming" to describe poor Boswell. The essay was subsequently placed in *1650–1850*, where it appeared without further revision as "Fugitive Allusions in *Boswell in Search of a Wife*, or The Charming Mr. Boswell." Clearly, the innocent identifying of allusions could not protect me from offending some journal referees, and I contemplated again retreating to the safety of the short note while leaving to braver souls the charms of interpretation.[8]

The length of our publications is, of course, an issue not just for annotators who find themselves coming up short, so to speak, but for all scholars. In the 1970s, a story circulated about a university English department instituting a system whereby books, articles, and notes could be quantified for tenure and promotion: thus, an article equaled five notes, five articles a book. The advantage to chairs and deans was obvious, it being less time-consuming to count than to read. Perhaps the story is apocryphal, but the current trend toward the homogenization of submission length is certainly real, including in collections of essays such as this one. The economics of academic publishing has never been more pressing than it is today, and both ends of the spectrum, notes and long essays, are the first (but not the last) victims.

To be sure, vehicles and savvy editors still exist. Melvyn New and I had completed a manuscript of sixteen thousand words, a reconsideration of Thomas Cumming the Quaker, friend of Samuel Johnson. We decided to query journal editors before wasting their time and ours with a submission, since every appropriate journal we looked at had a desired range of seven thousand to ten thousand words. *Eighteenth-Century Studies* seemed, otherwise, a logical place for this interdisciplinary study, but the response was cool: if we cut 25 percent before submission, they would reluctantly look at it, since it would still be larger than they wanted. Fortunately, *Modern Philology* was willing to read the article as it was, publishing it in 2019 without a single excision. Neither my coauthor nor I is subject to tenure or promotion consideration, but it is tempting to consider whether, because of its length, this recent publication should be counted as two articles.

THE IMPERFECT ANNOTATOR

Annotators soon learn how imperfect their activity is, in at least two senses. I have already mentioned correcting a previous error in "Notes on *Boswell Laird of Auchinleck, 1778–1782*." More typical is a correction by another scholar, an excellent example of which I found in two notes on Dryden that appeared in nearly consecutive issues of *N&Q*. The crux discussed is the identity of one of the Panther's fellow Anglicans, the subject of this couplet from "The Hind and the Panther": "'Twas well alluded by a son of mine, / (I hope to quote him is not to purloin)." The Panther has just offered a lodestone analogy, basically our only clue to the identity of this "son of mine." Paul Hammond offered John Smith (*d.* 1652), based on the presence of the same lodestone metaphor in his writings and what Hammond believed to be a "private allusion" to Smith's village being near Dryden's own birthplace.[9] In reviewing the note for the *Scriblerian*, I concluded that the identification "should be, for the present at least, accepted."[10]

The present was just after the old year was out "and time to begin a new." Earlier, I cited an entry in *N&Q* that answered a query from 151 years ago. Here the ink was hardly dry on Hammond's note—and my review not yet in print—when Steven Zwicker advanced a better candidate by far, Edward

Stillingfleet (1655–1699), who also had employed the lodestone metaphor just before Dryden's poem appeared and whom Dryden had accused of "purloining" in a pamphlet exchange. Zwicker writes, "now the charge is renewed not by Dryden (as it were) but by the Panther, that emblem of Stillingfleet's own Anglican faith, as if the Anglican Church itself were providing this needling reminder of the accusations of plagiary and purloining that Dryden had made against Stillingfleet."[11] Zwicker refers to his proper identification of the "son of mine" as "a minor point." Hardly. I would argue that his work is an excellent example of how the conversation about literature should continue and of how the identification of allusions—now a growth industry in the Age of Google—if done well can reveal many intricacies and subtleties previously overlooked in even frequently examined literature because of the absence of necessary details. At times the conclusions reached will be incorrect, but anyone who practices annotation knows it shares much with the inconclusiveness of art (and life), and only rarely rises (or falls) to the certainty usually attributed to science.

Publishing corrections to the work of others creates temptation for the annotator, even more so in a world, both inside and out of academe, where a "gotcha" mentality seems dominant. Inside, however, this temptation is rarely acted on, because few scholars want to be labeled impolite or worse in a profession still adhering to notions of noblesse oblige, and even fewer want to take the time to do the necessary collation and fact-checking required to discover errors. The noble example of R. S. Crane talking truth to the power of print, imitated today by the likes of Robert Hume and James E. May, is not often followed; only the bravest will risk alienating the sixty or more specialized "experts" thanked in the acknowledgments, as the dear friends who have contributed to the work in one's hand.

But a second sense of the "imperfections of annotating" should give us pause. When Johnson titled chapter 49 of *Rasselas* "A Conclusion in Which Nothing Is Concluded," he drew our attention to the paradox implicit in the repeated word, where the narrative is con-cluded, or *completely shut*, while—to be trite where Johnson was not—life goes on. The conflict between one's infinite aspirations and finite means of accomplishment dominates *Rasselas* and culminates with the author's implicit association of himself (as author) with his aspiring characters and the need, sooner or later, to conclude one's efforts. Just so the word "imperfection" sums up the view that no matter how diligent an annotator is, more will be left for others to do, if only because of the passage of time and the discovery of new information.

All annotators face this issue, but none more so than those engaged in producing scholarly texts. Yet discussions of this issue by editors are relatively rare. Here is an exception, from the introduction to the third volume of the Florida Edition of the Works of Sterne: after quoting George Steiner ("*In practice*, the homework of elucidation may be unending. No individual talent or life-span, no collective industry, can complete the task"), Melvyn New continues, "Steiner concentrates on the elusiveness of answers, but just as problematic are the questions one asks of a text, which are not stable but constantly changing. The infinitude of annotation, that is, lies not only in the inexhaustibility of context but as well in the infinite variety of possible readers, both what they will and will not bring to the text."[12] At the outset I mentioned my minuscule firsthand experience at editing. To compare great things with small, I produced a transcription, with introduction and annotations, to the last will and testament of Thomas Cumming, subsequently published in the *Johnsonian Newsletter*.[13] I came across the document in my work on Cumming, and was distressed not by its lack of availability—for a small fee it can be downloaded from PRO—but by the difficulty of reading the script-text. Thus, my primary aim was the production of a legible text.

The will also helped identify or confirm people I had encountered elsewhere in piecing together Cumming's life, and this biographical work became the major task of my annotations. Other notes speak to peripheral (but "noteworthy") issues like the relationship of Quakers to other religious sects at the time. For instance, I was pleased to discover and make available to scholars the fact that even so conspicuous a Quaker as Cumming trusted as his executors men of a variety of faiths, suggesting that borders between diverse nontraditional Protestant sects in Britain during the century were more porous than might otherwise be assumed, with Methodists, Quakers, and Moravians forming close personal relationships. Of course, Cumming's reciprocal friendships with deist Benjamin Franklin and Anglican Samuel Johnson again tell us of a budding ecumenical spirit during midcentury.

Without the experience of preparing this most modest of texts, I could not fully appreciate New's phrase "the infinitude of annotation." My work took but a few months. I can only begin to imagine the years of work required by large editions of collected works, coupled with the knowledge that the editors must certainly come to if not start with, that the task is infinite, their means finite, and the result inevitably imperfect. Or as New has said elsewhere several times, once an edition is "completed," it is time for someone to begin again.[14]

ENDNOTES AND FOOTNOTES: A DIGRESSIVE EDITORIAL

If you are a regular reader of the *Times Literary Supplement*, chances are you turn first to the "letters to the editor." You are often rewarded with a witty response or correction to a previous review, a response at times worthy of publication in a scholarly environment. The conversation may extend over several issues, as the reviewer or the reviewed author replies to the first correspondent, and then a second, third, even fourth correspondent gets involved. In a recent such exchange, a reviewer defended his review against the author's charge that it contained a factual error, namely that the author had failed to annotate something when he could point to the "unmissable footnote" that did so. The reviewer's riposte: "it is not quite true to say it concerns something as unmissable as 'a footnote': it is an endnote, a rather different beast. I said that [the author] didn't mention Gorey's illustrations for Beckett . . . and in fact he does; they are tucked away amid sixty-odd pages of largely source notes like a body in a back garden" (*TLS*, April 5, 2019). Setting aside this specific dispute, I would like to focus instead on two significant annotation issues it raises. First, exactly what should be in notes, whether at the foot of the page or the end of the chapter or book? Second, is it good that endnotes have become so popular with presses and journals at the expense of their older sibling?

For scholarly texts everyone will agree that notes should be luminous, and I would accept voluminous if the editor deems it appropriate. The presumption is that the edition will be used over a long stretch of years for various purposes and by varying audiences. My attitude is different, however, when it comes to notes for critical books and articles. I am sure I am still influenced by the advice of Aubrey Williams, echoed by many an editor and stylist, that if a note is not documentary—one of the "source notes" mentioned above—it should be tested thus: does it say something important? If yes, move it to the text. If not, omit it.

Pierre Bayle has been considered the father of the modern footnote, and his capacious annotation in the *Dictionnaire* (1697) dwarfs even Gibbon's, although it displays an interesting distinction. His marginal notes are source notes, while his famous *Remarques* "can perhaps be most aptly described as 'essayistic footnotes.'" Both initially appear on the main page of the text, but the *Remarques* often go on for many pages. A modern scholar has said of them, "it is here that Bayle weights opinions, corrects the errors of other historians, and engages in discussion with commentators across the centuries."[15] Bayle differentiates between his two types of notes both spatially and typographically, and gives the *Remarques* primacy of length if not of placement in his text. Anyone who has consulted the work will realize that his accommodation for these extended commentaries was not a long-term solution, given its diminution of primary text and commentaries extending well beyond the passage commented on. The maddening unreadability because of reduced type size is, of course, also a problem.

Does this mean that all notes, documentary or otherwise, are best printed as backnotes? I suggest not. Years ago, publishers explained that this would reduce printing costs, but that was before texts could be positioned with a keystroke or two. In fact, endnotes buried in the back garden frequently turn into valueless lists of everything even slightly related to the subject at hand. In a Gresham's Law of Annotation, such bad notes drive good notes out of circulation, or at least impede their discovery by the reader (witness the poor *TLS* reviewer). If documentary notes were footnotes on the bottom of the page where the callout is, and if publishers would universally accept internal citations rather than insisting on repetitive notes for the same source (even when quoted a dozen times within two paragraphs), there would be far fewer such notes overall, and the addition of discursive footnotes would be more possible, desirable, and readable. Instead we have books with a multitude of documentary endnotes, reminiscent of the first chapters of dissertations, where the motive of demonstrating a beginning scholar's familiarity with the territory has at least some relevance. Whether discursive backnotes could then also be footnotes is a more difficult question, as one weighs convenience for the reader versus the appearance and readability of the primary text, but certainly it would help if the documentary notes were substantially reduced by internal citation. My own preference would be that editions use backnotes, as rich and full as they need to be, while monographs and journals use footnotes as more convenient for following the argument of the scholar's text.

JAMES BOSWELL, ANNOTATOR

It may be surprising to label as an annotator arguably the greatest of all English biographers. Indeed, the notes to his *Life of Johnson* are functional but usually unexceptional. Johnson was certainly the more prominent annotator in view of his edition of Shakespeare (1765) and *Lives of the Poets* (1779–81). But Boswell seemed continually to be interested in annotation and the concomitant topic of literary allusion. One example of that interest I documented when explaining a reference that had thwarted the editors of *Boswell: The Great Biographer*, the final installment of the trade edition of Boswell's journals. Boswell twice wrote "vexing thoughts" within quotation marks (in September 1793 and January 1794), forcing the editors to admit the source was still unidentified. I discovered that Boswell quotes Johnson using the same phrase on March 29, 1776, in a passage that first appeared in the *Life* in 1791, without being otherwise remarked. But in the second edition of the *Life* (July 1793) Boswell annotated the passage:

> The phrase "vexing thoughts," is, I think, very expressive. It has been familiar to me from my childhood; for it is to be found in the "Psalm in Metre," used in the churches (I believe I should say *kirks*) of Scotland, Psal. xliii.v.5:
>
> > Why art thou then cast down, my soul?
> > What should discourage thee?
> > And why with *vexing thoughts* art thou
> > Disquieted in me?[16]

In annotating the second edition of his *Life of Johnson*, Boswell provided the missing annotation for his personal journal, published two centuries later.

Even before the *Life*, we find him trying his wings, so to speak, by practicing the craft of the annotator in the second of two linked *Hypochondriack* essays. In June and July 1779, Boswell wrote two essays (21 and 22), entitled by Margery Bailey "On Quotations" and "On Similarity Among Authors." In addition to illustrating Boswell's kitchen-sink approach to periodical composition, the essays also reveal his, and the period's, interest in annotation and the related topics of quotation, pedantry, imitation, coincidence, and plagiarism. Boswell begins the first essay with Johnson's *Dictionary* definition of quotation as "a passage adduced out of an author as evidence or illustration," then immediately suggests the word "has been in effect extended to many other meanings" (1:261). To readers who would "be apt to consider Quotation as downright pedantry"— and if to quote another was to be a pedant, how much worse to annotate the quotation!—Boswell follows the approach taken by Johnson in his exchange with Wilkes, subsequently documented in *Life of Johnson*: "The subject of quotation being introduced, Mr. Wilkes censured it as pedantry. JOHNSON. 'No, Sir, it is a good thing; there is community of mind in it. Classical quotation is the *parole* of literary men all over the world.'"[17] Quotation, whether written or spoken, is, Boswell maintains, far from the display of intellectual pride that

196 | Notes on Footnotes

a charge of pedantry would imply. Rather, "it is a pretty certain evidence of that humility of mind, which extensive thinking and knowledge can scarcely fail to produce." In an outrageous example of question-begging that must be deliberate, Boswell extends his point with a classical quotation: "An opinion which one distinguished genius hazarded, becomes more secure, when adopted by another, like Fame in Virgil, '*Vires acquirit eundo*—It gathers strength in its progress'" (1:262).

Boswell continues in this playful way, lightly commenting on whether extensive use of quotation might be a sign of "indolence and habitual want of thought," what type of quotation may justly be considered "evidence," how quotation can vivify certain types of communication (the Methodist Whitefield is cited here), the successful flattery of quoting people in their presence (termed "this complimentary species of Quotation"), and even referring to a moribund literary genre, the cento, or work composed entirely of quotations from other writers (1:262–72). He then ends rather than concludes his essay, one suspects because he had reached its required length.

This suspicion is confirmed when *Hypochondriack* 22 begins, "the subject of this paper appears to me to be a very proper sequel to my last, in which I treated of *Quotation*." Boswell had material remaining on the topic that he now intends to use: "before proceeding . . . I shall avail myself of that liberty which is the peculiar privilege of such a species of writing as a periodical paper like this, and shall give my readers something supplementary to my last number." Although he still can recall no other writer who has "considered" his topic, he now remembers a few who have "mentioned" it, and comments briefly on them. Most important is Francis Osborn[e], who in *Advice to a Son* (1656) "confounds *Quotation* with *Plagiarism*. Most assuredly a writer who means to make what has been written by another pass as a part of his own work, which is at best but a theftuous trick, the only merit he can have is, being a dexterous thief. But I flatter myself I have shewn in my last number that quotations from other writers may contribute both to utility and amusement" (1:273–74).

Boswell completes the first third of his new essay by reprinting, in full, a handbill he came upon in the Newcastle Fly going to London: "for who could expect to find both the tragedy of Hamlet and the Bible, quoted in an advertisement for the sale of salt beef and pork?" (1:275). From this, perhaps the lowest or laziest point of all the *Hypochondriack* essays if not of all periodic essays in the century, Boswell recovers when he returns to his first topic, "some thoughts upon that sameness or similarity which we frequently find between passages in different authors without quotation. This may be one of three things[:] either what is called *Plagiarism*, or *Imitation*, or *Coincidence*" (1:273).[18] From the seeming certainty of this regime Boswell quickly retreats to the subjective standard of length:

> I must candidly acknowledge, that . . . the sameness or similarity which we frequently find between passages in different authors cannot be with absolute certainty ascribed to its proper origin unless where there is a passage of considerable length in one author, which we can discover in the very same words in another author; and then we may without hesitation pronounce that it is *Plagiarism*. A passage of considerable length, somewhat varied, may be *Imitation*; or it may be *Coincidence* to a certain degree both in thought and expression. A very short passage in one author may be precisely the same with one in another, from pure coincidence, or from ascribing that to instantaneous invention which is truly the effect of memory. (1:276)

Boswell's struggle to construct objective criteria, perhaps motivated by the well-known literary frauds of the century, is somewhat obscured by his occasionally imprecise use of "quotation." The most contentious discussions arise, of course, when authors eschew the common signs of quotation, either italics or quotation marks, thus opening the possibility that they are attempting to pass off another's work as their own.

Boswell was not alone in attempting such definitions; he now mentions Richard Hurd's anonymously published *Letter to Mr. Mason on the Marks of Imitation* (1757): "I never saw this performance, but by extracts from it in the Monthly Review it appears to be learned and ingenious. The author of it traces many fine passages in English writers to a classical original, and some he shews to have been taken from other English writers" (1:277–78). Hurd's letter is, if anything, overly ingenious. He attempts to isolate signposts of imitation, but they are so numerous that the way is lost. It is, however, a disinterested tract, with the word "plagiarism" appearing only twice. The writer in the *Monthly Review* compliments Hurd for his nonvituperative approach: "How delightful, how amiable, are literary pursuits, when men of learning and genius thus exert their talents in candid and friendly criticisms. How different is this polite and learned intercourse from those invidious and sarcastic contests, which have disgraced some of our best Writers."[19]

Hurd helps Boswell get to the main purpose of his essay, to offer examples of his own discoveries of similarities between the words, phrases, and sentiments of various authors. He writes, "I shall give a few instances of similarity which I have remarked," and when he starts with what he sees as an allusion to Osborne's *Advice to a Son*, we can be relatively certain this attribution was his intention from the beginning. Linking Osborne to Vanbrugh's *Provoked Wife* (1697) is among the most convincing of the several instances of borrowing that Boswell offers, and one that I do not believe has been observed by modern critics and editors. Heartfree is quoted: "I always consider a woman not as the taylor, the shoemaker, the tire-woman, the sempstress; but I consider her as pure nature has contrived her." Boswell points out that Osborne had written, "If you consider beauty alone, quite discharged from such debentures, as she owes to the arts of tire-women, taylors, shoemakers, and perhaps painters, you will find she remains so inconsiderable as scarce to deserve your present thoughts, much less to be made the price of your perpetual slavery" (1:278). As Bailey remarks, "The warnings against women are to many the most interesting passages in Osborne's *Advice*" (1:278n11). Osborne's work was well known, so perhaps Boswell expected his readers, once the possible echo was pointed out, to speculate on Heartfree's employing it: Vanbrugh's character certainly evinces cynicism toward marriage, as does the entire play, yet he finally marries; moreover, Heartfree modifies the quotation, taking away much of its sting. Boswell is silent on these points, and Bailey's comments are limited to the single sentence just quoted. But a critic, different from an editor, might find here the kernel for an argument that Heartfree's modification indicates a softer view of marriage than he otherwise reflects, or at least that Boswell, in comparing Osborne with Vanbrugh, is advancing a softer, mid-eighteenth-century view of himself, if not of the play.

Boswell's next instance is equally convincing and was subsequently noted again in periodicals at the end of the century, where one writer characterized it as "too palpable a plagiary." Boswell uses a different word: "In *The Spleen*, a poem, which is in general truly original, a lively image struck me, where he [Matthew Green] represents *Scandal* telling that a lady and gentleman were seen in a coach together 'Like Will and Mary on the coin.' But this is probably an *imitation* [my emphasis] of Hudibras: 'Still amorous, and fond, and billing, / Like Philip and Mary on a shilling'" (1:278).[20] Boswell then moves on to several fairly convincing allusions he finds to the poetry of Edward Young. (I pass over two of Boswell's "finds" that I think strained and not credible.)

At least to the end of the eighteenth century, Young's lines would be recognized in the way we might now recognize lines from Yeats or Eliot. It is

Boswell's way of treating the references, however, that is of interest. One of our best contemporary annotators, Roger Lonsdale, gives a very complete picture of the following allusion, much more complete than Boswell, who writes, "In Goldsmith's beautiful little poem, *The Hermit*, there is a delicate philosophical sentiment: 'Man wants but little here below, / Nor wants that little long.' Which is certainly borrowed from Dr. Young's Night Thoughts. 'Man wants but little, nor that little long.' Goldsmith, I suppose, had got the line by heart, and it had afterward remained unperceived amongst his own store of poetical thoughts" (1:279–80). Information in Lonsdale's detailed headnote to the poem allows us to speculate with some confidence about Boswell's stance here. First, he was probably aware that Goldsmith's poem had created a controversy on its appearance. In the *St. James's Chronicle* (July 18–20, 1767) "a letter signed 'Detector' (usually identified as William Kenrick) . . . accused G[oldsmith] of having virtually plagiarized" the poem, not from Young but from Thomas Percy.[21] Goldsmith and Percy both subsequently weighed in on the topic. Boswell trod softly ("Goldsmith, I suppose, had got the line by heart") and may have done so because he remembered the poem from its appearance in *The Vicar of Wakefield* (1766), where quotation marks "round these two lines were abandoned, perhaps by mistake" (Lonsdale, 600). Those quotation marks are present in versions of the poem published as "Edwin and Angelina," which appeared in 1765 and 1767. Lonsdale adds, "During the nineteenth century the poem was often entitled *The Hermit*, which seems first to have been used in 1777" (598). That is the title Boswell uses two years later, so he may have been aware of the 1777 publication, which also fails to identify the lines as a quotation, or he may have simply been repeating what had become a commonly used title at the time. Lonsdale, then, in annotating Goldsmith, allows us to recover much of the context of Boswell's "annotation."

Boswell demonstrates the ubiquity of reference to Young among prose as well as poetry writers with his next example: "In Soame Jenyns's lively and agreeable defence of Christianity, I read with pleasure the following conclusive and at the same time witty remark, that he who believes that the undoubted history of the Gospel happened without supernatural assistance, 'must be possessed of much more faith than is necessary to make him a Christian, and remain *an unbeliever from mere credulity*.' But this is either taken from Dr. Young's Night Thoughts, or is a clear coincidence with this:—'How strange / To disbelieve thro' mere credulity!'" Boswell refers to this and to the Goldsmith allusion as "two instances of borrowing, or imitation, or coincidence with Dr. Young" (1:280), using all related terms except plagiarism.

To conclude with a final example of a borrowing from Young, Boswell calls attention to the echo of a couplet from *Universal Passion*—"Pure gurgling rills the lonely desert trace, / And waste their musick on the savage race"—in Gray's *Elegy*—"Full many a flower is born to blush unseen, / And waste its sweetness on the desert air." Ever scrupulous, Boswell credits this discovery to a Scottish acquaintance and fellow advocate, George Wallace, in a note in a law book Wallace wrote, evidence that allusion-hunting was a widespread intellectual occupation at the time. Gray's unacknowledged borrowing is now part of the established critical heritage, but it arrived there only with Lonsdale's scholarly edition. Before then, despite the recognition of the borrowing by Wallace and Boswell, then two years later by a correspondent in the *Gentleman's Magazine*, and by others at the time, items would appear every few decades with the breaking news that Gray's famous lines owed much to Young's.[22] "Many sources for this famous image have been suggested," writes Lonsdale at the beginning of his extensive note, in which he mentions W. Chamberlayne, Ambrose Philips, Pope, Young, Thomson, Racine, J. Armstrong, and Celio Magno (127). Lonsdale does not presume to have written the last word on the subject, of course, but scholars who refer to his text will save themselves from publishing already discovered "discoveries," surely a major benefit that a properly annotated text offers to us all. I have not met Lonsdale but have been told that he is extremely unassuming. His work on Gray, Collins, and Goldsmith, however, not to mention his more recent monumental edition of Johnson's *Lives of the Poets* (2006), numbers him with those giants among scholarly editors on whose shoulders we all stand. Boswell, on the other hand, was not a giant among annotators, but his tentative gestures—"some thoughts upon that sameness or similarity which we frequently find between passages in different authors without quotation"— may now be seen as embryonic moves toward the modern annotator, especially in view of his locating his source suggestions among English authors, rather than the classical sources so many had previously traced.

NOTES

1. James Boswell, *The Hypochondriack*, ed. Margery Bailey, 2 vols. (Stanford: Stanford University Press, 1928); hereafter cited by vol. and page number. R. S. Crane, review of *The*

Hypochondriack, Modern Philology 26 (February 1929): 375–76. R. W. Chapman, review of *The Hypochondriack, Modern Language Notes* 44 (February 1929): 109–13.

2. Robert G. Walker, "Addenda and Corrigenda to the Annotations of the Bailey Edition of Boswell's *Hypochondriack*," *English Studies* 91 (May 2010): 274–88. *SP* is, of course, *Studies in Philology*.

3. *Boswell's Life of Johnson*, ed. G. B. Hill, rev. L. F. Powell, 6 vols. (Oxford: Clarendon Press, 1934–64), 1:v, vii (hereafter Hill-Powell).

4. A festschrift in Powell's honor, *Johnson, Boswell, and Their Circle* (Oxford: Clarendon Press, 1965), includes a list of his publications, 320–28.

5. *Johnsonian Newsletter* 70 (March 2019): 46–47.

6. Peter J. Tyldesley, "A Jacobite Standard 1715," *N&Q* 66 (March 2019): 96.

7. Robert G. Walker, "Notes on *Boswell Laird of Auchinleck, 1778–1782*," *Age of Johnson* 22 (2012): 123–30.

8. Robert G. Walker, "Fugitive Allusions in *Boswell in Search of a Wife*, or The Charming Mr. Boswell," *1650–1850* 22 (2015): 93–111.

9. Paul Hammond, "A Source for the Image of the Loadstones in Dryden's 'The Hind and the Panther,'" *N&Q* 64 (2017): 457–58.

10. *Scriblerian* 51 (2019): 124.

11. Steven N. Zwicker, "That Alluding 'Son of Mine' in Dryden's 'The Hind and the Panther,'" *N&Q* 65 (2018): 223–25.

12. *The Life and Opinions of Tristram Shandy, Gentleman*, vol. 3, *The Notes*, ed. Melvyn New, Richard A. Davies, and W. G. Day (Gainesville: University Press of Florida, 1984), 3:3.

13. Robert G. Walker, "'Curious Particulars': The Will of Thomas Cumming, the Fighting Quaker," *Johnsonian Newsletter* 70 (September 2019), 18–27.

14. A year after writing this, I had an inquiry from a relation, seven generations removed, of Cumming's primary heir and executor, John Samuel, identified in the will as his "nephew." Over the course of several fascinating exchanges, we have now written a jointly authored annotation to Cumming's life that offers tentative yet persuasive evidence that John Samuel was not his nephew but his illegitimate son. Endless is the search for truth.

15. Mara Van Der Lugt, *Bayle, Jurieu, and the "Dictionnaire Historique et Critique"* (Oxford: Oxford University Press, 2016), 19, 23.

16. See Marlies K. Danziger and Frank Brady, eds., *Boswell: The Great Biographer, 1789–1795* (New York: McGraw-Hill, 1989), 237, 274; James Boswell, *The Life of Samuel Johnson, L.L.D.*, 2nd ed. (London, 1793), 2:367; Robert G. Walker, "Boswell's 'Vexing' Self-Quotation," *Johnsonian Newsletter* 63 (September 2012): 49–50.

17. Hill-Powell, 4:102; this passage is noted by Bailey.

18. Cf. Johnson's three categories in his periodic essay on this topic, *Rambler* 143: "As not every instance of similitude can be considered as a proof of imitation, so not every imitation ought to be stigmatized as plagiarism" (*The Rambler*, ed. W. J. Bate and Albrecht B. Strauss [New Haven: Yale University Press, 1969], in Yale Works 4:401). This is the closest verbal parallel I find between Boswell's essay and Johnson's, which is much more focused.

19. *Monthly Review* 18 (1758): 114–25; 125.

20. Bailey points out that Boswell was working from memory and slightly mistakes the dramatic situation in Green's poem. The charge of plagiarism appears in a letter to the editor of *The Monthly Mirror* 9 (January 1800): 11–12, where W. P. Taylor mistakenly identifies the lines from *Hudibras* as from Matthew Prior. A close reading of the two passages by Stephen Dowell (1835–1898) calls attention to the different postures involved, at least on the respective

coins, with Will and Mary side by side and Philip and Mary vis-à-vis (*Thoughts and Words*, 2 vols. [London: Spottiswoode, 1891], 2:49).

21. Roger Lonsdale, ed., *The Poems of Thomas Gray, William Collins, Oliver Goldsmith* (1969; 1st paperback ed., New York: Longman, 1976), 596 (hereafter Lonsdale).

22. See "Strictures on Gray Discussed," *GM* 52 (1782), 20; the letters from "Atticus" in *GM* 91 (September 1821): 229; and F. C. Birkbeck Terry in *N&Q*, 8th ser. (October 6, 1894): 271.

CHAPTER 13

❧ Annotation and Editorial Practice
Twenty-Five Years (and Counting)

Elizabeth Kraft

In a 1795 review of John Aikin's edition of John Armstrong's *The Art of Preserving Health*, the *British Critic* expressed regret that Aikin confined his remarks to a prefatory critical essay: "we could have wished that he had undertaken the task for which he was so eminently qualified, of giving critical notes upon particular passages of the poem, and had thus more effectually contributed to the improvement of the general taste."[1] The point of the edition itself was to make available an elegant presentation of a popular and esteemed poem at a price affordable to "common purchasers," who, it is presumed, might aspire to taste, but who do not necessarily feel confident that they have it (295). Some guidance as to what is worthy in the work at hand, the critic feels, would be most welcome and most beneficial to the general good. Further, as a doctor of medicine, as well as a poet himself, John Aikin can bring expertise to bear on the poem's specific recommendations—or he could have done so, had the project's specification allowed. He was asked only to write an introduction.

My own work as an editor of eighteenth-century texts began with a project that had no such constraints. Had I been an expert, I could have wielded my expertise at will. However, I undertook my first editorial enterprise as a complete novice, both as to editing and the topic at hand: John Aikin's sister, the poet Anna Letitia Barbauld. It is true that I had authored a biographical essay on her for the *Dictionary of Literary Biography of Eighteenth-Century Poets*, edited by John Sitter, and in the process of doing so had come to feel her poetry should be more widely read. I particularly responded to her poem "Washing-Day," which begins with a mock-epic invocation of washerwomen as muses and ends with the image of children blowing soap bubbles that somehow transform into hot-air balloons. It is a charming poem with very specific referents to a host of details that, at the time, did not have a place in my mental lexicon. When I discovered the identity of Guatimozin and Montgolfier, I loved the poem even more for its capacious cultural sweep.

Shortly after conceiving of a vague plan to prepare an edition of Barbauld's poems, I found that William McCarthy was setting about similar work; so we teamed up to collaborate on the project that was published by the University of Georgia Press as *The Poems of Anna Letitia Barbauld* in 1994. This volume served as the standard edition of her increasingly popular poetry until it was replaced in 2019 by the first volume of the Oxford University Press edition of Barbauld's complete works, titled *The Poems, Revised*. While I have responsibility for volume 3 of this edition (centered on Barbauld's literary criticism), volume 1 is edited by McCarthy alone. It is gratifying to see that most of the 1994 annotations have been retained in substance and, often, in phrasing and style.

McCarthy continued his interest in Barbauld and ultimately published an award-winning biography.[2] His depth of engagement, on a par with mine at the beginning, has become much more profound. He is the world's leading authority on the writer—one reason it *is* so gratifying to see many of the annotations we wrote in the early days still standing. *Poems, Revised* does offer one important change to the annotations of "Washing Day," attributable to McCarthy's biographical work. Where in 1994 we glossed Barbauld's reference to her grandmother toward the end of the poem with the identities of both maternal and paternal relatives, she is now identified as Barbauld's paternal grandmother, who lived with the family for a period of time. Still, most of the other detailed references remain secure—not only in their obvious status as fact but also in what we made of the fact. Guatimozin is still identified as likely known to Barbauld from William Robertson's *History of America* (1777). The Montgolfier note is still, basically, the note I wrote in 1994, based, as it was, on research I completed for an article on the poem: "Anna Letitia Barbauld's 'Washing Day' and the Montgolfier Balloon," published shortly after *Poems* appeared.[3] Of course, that may not be surprising. After all, Guatimozin is Guatimozin and Montgolfier is Montgolfier. But my note on the latter in 1994 was a compilation of a research process I well remember, combing through microfilmed eighteenth-century magazines for articles about balloons. The annotation is certainly pared down from the essay, but it bears traces of that essay's argument, namely, that the poem celebrates the way the imagination, both scientific and poetic, finds nurturance in the details of domestic life. I was especially fascinated, in both my essay and my annotation, with Joseph Priestley's experiments with "dephlogisticated air" or oxygen and the connection of that interest to developments in air travel. That particular detail did not, as it turns out, make it into McCarthy's revision of *Poems*, being extraneous to the poem itself, but my inclusion of it in the Georgia edition is an efficient indication of the way annotation bears traces of the annotator's critical or scholarly preoccupations.

Indeed, other notes in that edition send clear signals that one of us (that is, Bill) is working on the biography of Barbauld—for example, the mournful admission that "we are unable to identify the mother to whose unborn child" the poem "To a Little Invisible Being Who Is Expected Soon to Become Visible" is addressed. I remember McCarthy's fondness for this poem, akin to mine for "Washing Day." In fact, in the course of our work together he and I both presented Barbauld's poems as gifts to family and friend ("Washing Day" to my mother, "To a Little Invisible Being" to a pregnant friend of McCarthy and his wife). There was obviously a certain level of emotional investment that I can clearly recall both from these memories and from reading the annotations themselves. And I was pleased to see, on publication of *Anna Letitia Barbauld: Voice of the Enlightenment*, that McCarthy had found the identity of the expectant mother of the soon-to-be visible little being: Barbauld's "Hampstead friend, Frances Carr" (*VOE*, 390).

The annotation process for *Poems* (1994) was collaborative in that I had a coeditor with whom to consult. For the annotations themselves, we relied mostly on print resources—encyclopedias, dictionaries, and works to which the library card catalogue directed us. McCarthy, having begun his biographical research, also brought manuscripts into play. In addition, we "networked," as one did in the days prior to what we now know as the "net"—we cultivated (at our universities, at conferences, and through the mail) acquaintance with others working on similar projects or possessed of expertise in fields of which we had more limited knowledge than did Barbauld. Our annotations, therefore, reveal a good deal of engagement with scholars in the burgeoning field of recovery work—that is, recovery of women's writing neglected for two hundred (or more) years. In our acknowledgments, we thanked Roger Lonsdale, Paula Feldman, Mitzi Myers, Paula Backscheider, Margaret Doody, Marilyn Butler,

Stuart Curran, Isobel Grundy, Nancy Grayson, and Katherine Rogers, all of whom were essential to scholarship on eighteenth-century women writers at the time of the volume's publication. But we did not stop there! In our enthusiasm, McCarthy and I pay tribute to the advice of thirty-eight colleagues, friends, and student assistants by name, and each of us thanks a graduate seminar by course number and semester.

Of these names, even at this distance in time, I remember a few specific discussions (with Bill Free about "The First Fire" and "The Ice House" and with Phyllis Gussler about "To Mrs. P[riestley]") but I do not see reference to them in the annotations. On the other hand, names left out of the inclusive list (Elissa Henken and Alyssa Ward) appear in annotations I do not remember writing, but must have written, since these were colleagues of mine whose expertise in Welsh literature and classics I obviously consulted in Park Hall, the University of Georgia campus building where we all labored as assistant professors in the 1990s. It is pleasantly nostalgic to read these tributes today, more than twenty-five years after the publication of *Poems*. I am also keenly aware that the habit of long thank-you lists in academic books is a kind of self-praise, and I now view all of my long lists with mild chagrin, to be sure. (I did not stop this habit until persuaded to do so by one of my coeditors [the curmudgeonly one, see above, p. 144] of the Cambridge edition of *Sir Charles Grandison*.) However, in the case of Barbauld, the extravagant number of names that McCarthy and I invoke in such acknowledgment was intended not only or even most importantly to signal gratitude; it was meant—and I think I can speak for McCarthy as well as myself here—to serve as evidence of a community dedicated to acknowledging the worth of a wrongly neglected literary talent. Putting this author "on the radar" of those I consulted was truly an "agenda" of mine at the time. My intent was to vitalize the study of Barbauld's poetry; the annotations and headnotes were, to my mind, not just tools to enhance the reading experience, but hints as to the richness and depth of the author's cultural, literary, and historical knowledge, and aids for the sophisticated critical analyses I felt her poems deserved. And while that "community" might have been something of a fiction when we wrote the acknowledgments and annotations, it soon became a fact, and our work provided exactly the kind of stimulus I had envisioned.

Susan Rosenbaum, for example, elaborates on the annotation to "An Inventory of the Furniture in Dr. Priestley's Study," in which we identify allusions to *The Dunciad*. While we had mentioned the words "embryo," "mass," and "chaos" in Barbauld's lines as echoes of *The Dunciad* 1:55ff., Rosenbaum extends the hint to fuel her meditation on the female poet's admonishment of masculine "isolation and melancholy" and Barbauld's own negotiation of significance in the literary marketplace.[4] Julia Saunders likewise builds part of her argument that "Barbauld equates science with intellectual liberty" on our annotation to the Duke of Bridgewater's canal, mentioned in "The Invitation."[5] More recently, Daniel P. Watkins has included a long note engaging our annotation of Barbauld's reference to Tasso's *Jerusalem Delivered* in "To Mrs. Priestley with Some Drawings of Birds and Insects" to further his argument that Barbauld both celebrates and warns against "the powers of the poetic imagination."[6] Taking her title from Barbauld's rich poem, E. J. Clery's *Eighteen Hundred and Eleven: Poetry, Protest, and Economic Crisis* (2017) explored its significance far beyond the annotations we offered, but citations of our glosses reveal a thorough engagement with our work, and Clery's dedication to McCarthy signals her appreciation for his ongoing commitment to Barbauld studies.[7] The work of all these scholars (and others) in expanding critical and intellectual engagement with Barbauld is highly gratifying as well as instructive and illuminating.

With Charlotte Smith's *The Young Philosopher* (1798), I continued my work in the field of recovery as well as my association with Nancy Grayson, who, as commissioning editor at the University of Georgia Press, had presided over the publication of *Poems*. In 1993, Grayson became the editor-in-chief at the University Press of Kentucky, and one of her first projects was the launching of a series, Eighteenth-Century Novels by Women, under the general editorship of Isobel Grundy. Asked if I had an interest in editing any particular novel (preferably one with American scenes), I proposed Smith's narrative centered on the travails of a mother and daughter, Laura and Medora Glenmorris. I had long been interested in Smith's own travails—her struggles with her marriage, her devotion to her children, and her complicated legal battles to secure their future. This project would be an opportunity, I thought, to develop that interest and, again, to bring attention to the writings of a neglected woman author. I probably should have chosen *The Old Manor House* (1793) as my text, since it contains episodes set in America, while America in *The Young Philosopher* is not so much a setting as an idea.[8] *The Old Manor House*, as well, is the Smith novel that appears in Barbauld's fifty-volume edition of *The British Novelists*, published in 1810, so that choosing it would have provided some continuity between projects. But, at the time, there was an excellent student edition of *The Old Manor House* edited by Anne Henry Ehrenpreis originally for the Oxford English Novels series and republished with an introduction by Judith

Phillips Stanton for the Oxford World's Classics series. *The Young Philosopher*, meanwhile, languished on library shelves in a four-volume Garland facsimile edition. I thought (perhaps wrongly) that Charlotte Smith would be better served by my choice of the less familiar, more ambitious novel inspired by the French Revolution, the philosophy of William Godwin, the feminism of Mary Wollstonecraft—a novel, moreover, published in the year of the Irish Rebellion.

As I began work on this project, the advent of the internet began to transform the process of annotation. The eighteenth-century listserv, managed by Kevin Berland, and the database LION or Literature Online were tools that I used (or asked others to use for me) in tracking down quotations and in getting help with translations for inclusion in the annotations to this novel. In fact, C18-L provided me the opportunity to engage in the activity that would become known as "crowdsourcing," though it was not called that at the time—and, indeed, I thought of the activity as "collaboration" and "marked" it as such in my string of acknowledgments.[9] As in the Barbauld project, however, I also relied on friends, colleagues, acquaintances, and others working in the field of eighteenth-century women's literature. I came to know the premier Smith scholars, Judith Phillips Stanton and Loraine Fletcher, whose aid and advice were immensely helpful.

To this point, I have emphasized the conditions that gave rise to the projects with which I was involved in the 1990s; now I want to turn more specifically to the way those conditions governed (and continue to govern) my approach to annotation. I focus on the Smith project as I was the sole editor in that case; however, my observations apply as well to both the Georgia edition of Barbauld's *Poems* (1994) and the 2001 Broadview Press edition of Barbauld's selected poetry and prose (coedited, again, with McCarthy). There are three aims that guided my annotations in each case: identification, contextualization, and explanation (which often amounted to affirmation or resistance).

First, and most obvious, is the identification of references and allusions for a student readership. While the 1994 *Poems* was not, in the end, a classroom text, my personal mission all along was to introduce Barbauld to students, a mission later accomplished by the Broadview edition. The Kentucky novel series was intended for classroom adoption—a goal facilitated by immediate publication in paperback. Given the nature of the novels themselves, I assumed a readership of advanced undergraduate and graduate student populations. My primary challenge with what I will call annotations of identification had to do with Smith's use of epigraphs. Each chapter began with a quotation that had to be tracked down, and there are many that I did not manage to find and a few tentative misidentifications as well. The use of epigraphs begins on the title page, with a quotation that I identify as from William Mason's "Elegy II. Written in the Garden of a Friend."[10] The lines are indeed drawn from that work, but they are significantly altered (something Smith does quite often), although I did not note this in my annotation despite being aware of it.[11] The differences between Smith's epigraph and her source seem worthy of comment to me today.

> SMITH: Of Man, when warm'd by Reason's purest ray,
> No slave of Avarice, no tool of Pride;
> When no vain Science led his mind astray,
> But Nature was his law, and God his guide.
> MASON: Of Man, while warm'd with reason's purer ray,
> No tool of policy, no dupe to pride
> Before vain Science led his taste astray;
> When conscience was his law, and God his guide.[12]

I cannot say today why I did not annotate the alteration. Indeed, I would now be inclined to go a bit further and comment on the significance of the change of "tool" to "slave," "policy" to "Avarice," and "conscience" to "Nature." Certainly, Smith could have been quoting from memory, but the valences of her substitutions speak to the novel's major themes. But, for some reason, I simply gave the source, though for more minor alterations, I often noted the changes. For example, I mention that Smith's quotation of Shakespeare's "Oh! coz, coz, coz, my pretty little coz, that thou didst know how many fathoms deep I am in love," is slightly altered in the epigraph to chapter 5 of volume 1.[13] However, even here, I did not comment on what seems to be the purposive alteration; Smith adds a "*but*" in italics between "didst" and "know," the emphasis calling attention to her emendation.

In identifying the sources of these quotations, I did not mention the obvious intertextuality between epigraphs and text, nor did I comment on what Harriet Kramer Linkin has referred to as the "citational networks" indicated by Smith's epigraphs. It was not, I believed, an annotator's responsibility to elaborate such interpretive connections. But, as Linkin points out, invoking Gerard Genette, "the habitual use of epigraphs to mark each chapter of a prose narrative begins with the gothic novels of the 1790s," and, given Smith's participation in this newly defined "habit," it now seems to me that it would have been useful to note the significance of her efforts in the interest of future elaboration. The "gothic" valence (given the events of volume 2) is pertinent, but even more telling is the way Smith employs epigraphs as, in Linkin's words, "opportunities . . . to signal [her] place in a cultural tradition, to acknowledge or choose [her] peers and predecessors, and to proleptically instantiate [her] consecration in a particular literary pantheon."[14] And, though I do not explicitly call attention to the fact, my annotations identifying the sources of Smith's epigraphs (and occasional internal quotations) provide ample evidence of the company in which she wished to be considered, the tradition in which she was staking her claim. Interestingly, in the Pickering and Chatto edition of *The Young Philosopher*, edited by A. A. Markley for *The Works of Charlotte Smith*, many of the epigraphs I could not identify receive attributions that affirm the novel's "citational network." Passages from Godwin's *Enquiry Concerning Political Justice*, Voltaire's *Dialogues*, Madame Roland's *Memoirs*, Thomas Pennant's *Tour of Scotland*, and works by Bolingbroke, Metastasio, Rousseau, Gaffigny, and Bruyère confirm the novel's general interest in political philosophy, sentiment, nature, and Scotland.

The second type of annotation was, to me, the most enjoyable. The annotation of contextualization provided opportunity for scholarly discovery as I searched for answers to questions the text made me ask about the world reflected and created in the pages of the novel. Interesting and little-known facts, I thought, had the potential to deepen student engagement not only with the novel but with the historical moment in which it was written. For example, I took great pleasure in discovering and reporting the difference between a curricle and a post chaise, the meaning of "turnpike roads," and the exact dates of the beginnings of legal "hunting seasons"—for grouse (April 12), for pheasant (October 1). For the second volume's scenes in Scotland, I combed (as did Smith) the accounts of Johnson and Boswell, along with Thomas Pennant, all of whom are echoed by Smith and noted in my annotations. The seriousness of Smith's political commentary in the novel was signaled by her own annotation to the passage in which she describes Delmont's acquisition of a "more general and correct knowledge of history than is usually obtained" (30). Smith indicates her notion of "correct" by the examples she gives of "the follies and enormities of the rulers of the earth," from Louis XI and Charles IX of France to Henry VIII, Mary I, James I, and Charles I of England (359–60n50). Her text goes on to counter this catalogue with the examples of Lucius Junius Brutus, Cato, and Marcus Brutus, whom I glossed, and Tiberius and Caius Gracchus, whom she herself annotated. Other references to more recent history required brushing up on details of the French Revolution—the speech of Mirabeau at the National Assembly in June 1789, the period known as "the Great Fear," the revolutionary thought of the *philosophes*, and the ideological opposition of Burke. A reference to George Delmont's cropped hair (volume 1, chapter 8) drew my attention and resulted in the following annotation: "George Delmont's hair is cut short, as we are told in chapter 2, 'like that of the farmer or the peasant.' Here, however, the term 'cropped' suggests that the fashion adopted by George may have a more overt political significance, for the Irish rebels of 1798 wore their hair in this fashion to signify sympathy and affiliation with the French Revolution. One who affected such a style was called a 'croppy'" (362–63n97). This detail proved so intriguing to me that I continued research toward an essay eventually published as "Encyclopedic Libertinism and 1798: Charlotte Smith's *The Young Philosopher*."[15]

Some of my contextualizing notes were aimed toward elaborating Smith's connection with other women writers of the period. Smith admiringly invoked Jane Collier, Wollstonecraft, and Burney, but she parodied the "bluestockings" in the character of Mrs. Grinsted. My annotation includes a quotation from a letter Smith wrote to Mary Hays in which she reports attending a colloquium at "Mrs. [Elizabeth] Montague[']s" where she "found the greatest difficulty . . . to resist a violent inclination to yawn" (378n52). Certainly, this disdain is an inconvenient attitude for a novelist in the Eighteenth-Century Novels by Women series, but I felt it necessary as an annotator to comment on Mrs. Grinsted's significance as well as to reveal Smith's stated indifference to Montagu and other bluestockings.

The third type of annotation—the annotation that seeks to explain, justify, or resist—perhaps seems intrusive and unnecessary, but I have found among editors of "recovered" works a sense of responsibility not only to the author and the text but to current readers who, after all, might not have heard of the book—or even the author—but for the effort to bring them (back) to light. To me, there needed to be an indication of the worth of the material beyond historical recovery. With Barbauld, I have described my initial response to her poetry as an aesthetic pleasure to which I felt others should have access. With Smith's novel, I appreciated its moral purpose, its philosophical bent, and its reflection of Smith's progressive intellectual interest in the natural world as a site of reflection, wisdom, and mutual obligation. My favorite scene of the novel occurs in volume 2. In it, Laura Glenmorris hides in a Highland cave and, despite her abject sense of isolation and fear, reflects on the plants she sees outside the cave—the "holly," the "common bramble," the "houseleak," "the pellitory, the fescue grass, and the poa," the "stonecrop," and the "mountain crane's bill," "rock lichen," "tessellated lichen," "silver bryum," "spleenwort" and "wall hawkweed" (127–28). I did not annotate these plants; Smith did so herself—but not with explanatory descriptions. Rather she provided the Latin names for the plants: "Rubus preticasus" for the common bramble, for example, and "Hieracium murorum" for the wall hawkweed (371, nn. 97, 106). Like many late eighteenth-century women, Smith was a serious botanizer—and I thought it best to allow her glosses to stand without interference from me. After all, as Loraine Fletcher notes, the interplay between the character Laura and the author Smith is significant here: "the Latin names . . . give Laura's perceptions the stamp of authority for the reader" and emphasize her inner strength in a time of duress.[16]

Impressed with Smith's botanical knowledge, I did wonder if her interest in and expertise about the natural world extended to animals. Did she know what she was talking about when, in volume 4, she describes Delmont's approach to a farmhouse as being noted by "wild-ducks and other water-foul [sic] from the river and lake, whose keen sense of smell informed them that a stranger had intruded among their reedy recesses and willowed haunts" (288)? I suspected she did not, having never thought about birds of any kind having a sense of smell, but decided to investigate further by calling the veterinary school at the University of Georgia, where I was put in touch with a wildlife specialist, Dr. Todd Cornish, who confirmed that waterfowl do indeed have a "keen sense of smell" (388n72). Happily, I was able to vindicate Smith with an annotation that could inform other skeptics whose lack of knowledge might cause them to doubt Smith's careful attentiveness to the small details of her somewhat sprawling narrative.

Having learned to trust Smith, I was able (with help) to resolve other seeming inconsistencies. Jeannie and Donald, Laura's Highland rescuers, for example, were said to be unable to write at one point but later portrayed as able to read. Isobel Grundy was the one who informed me that "the poor were often taught reading but not penmanship if their trade did not demand the keeping of accounts" (372n112). And while I could not reconcile another inconsistency, I was able to explain it to Smith's advantage. In volume 3, Laura Glenmorris is said to have scheduled a morning meeting with a solicitor, but two paragraphs later we are told that she sets out at 2 p.m. to keep the appointment. In my annotation, I note the contradiction, but take the opportunity to mention that Smith had lost her proofreader, William Hayley, somewhere in the midst of volume 3 (378–79n65)—a comment that allowed me to remind readers of Smith's circle of friends sympathetic to the French Revolution and to hint at the pressures under which she usually wrote as she struggled to support herself and her children. As someone who had voluntarily sought the opportunity to bring this work from obscurity into (I hoped) some degree of light, I felt it my duty to seek the best possible explanation for shortcomings. I could not, however, go so far as to exonerate a blatantly anti-Semitic slur; nor could I ignore it. And, therefore, in one annotation, I am not Smith's advocate. I label "shocking" the fact that in the same passage in which we find "sympathetic reference to the plight of the slave" we read "a cruel reflection on the English Jews that, in effect, denies them participation in the common humanity shared by all other populations in England and the English colonies" (381n111). The blind spot in Smith's enlightened worldview is not unique to her, I go on to imply, by noting contemporary parallels in Sheridan's *School for Scandal*, Burney's *Cecilia*, and Edgeworth's *Castle Rackrent*.

I had my own blind spots in preparing this edition. It bothered Isobel Grundy, for example, that I was content to celebrate the ending of the novel rather than question its social conservatism; given the extraordinary wrongs the narrative had exposed in terms of abusive patriarchal power and the considerable strengths attributed to the women at the center of the text (both Laura and Medora), it seemed to Professor Grundy that the ending—with Laura broken and silent and everyone looking forward to life in America, which has yet to be described!—was much bleaker than I cared to admit. Were I to revise the front matter today, I believe I would be less Pollyannish in my reading of the novel's conclusion. Most of the annotations, however, would remain the same, for I think they do the work and its author good service by elaborating elements of the text that profit from identifying, contextualizing, and explaining.

My next annotating project began in or around December 2004 and is, at this date (March 2020), finally moving into production: Cambridge University Press's edition of Samuel Richardson's final novel, *Sir Charles Grandison*, to be published in the Complete Works of Samuel Richardson under the general editorship of Tom Keymer and Peter Sabor. My coeditors on this project are the editor of Sterne, Melvyn New, and Richardsonian scholar E. Derek Taylor. It is a project distinct from my earlier editorial work in several important ways. First, I did not choose the text or the author; I agreed, when approached, to join the editorial team. Of course, this fact speaks to the second significant difference: Richardson is and long has been a canonical novelist, though, as the general editors note in the very first sentence of the preface with which each volume opens, "the Cambridge Edition of the Works of Samuel Richardson is the first fully annotated scholarly edition of Richardson's works." The novels, including *Grandison*, "have appeared since the 1970s" in "trade or textbook formats," but as such they were "limited in scope and ambition" from providing "the extensive commentary and additional material necessary to situate and understand them in their cultural, historical, linguistic, and literary contexts."[17] Jocelyn Harris edited *Grandison* for Oxford in 1972, and since that date her edition has been cited by scholars as the standard one. Many of her annotations provided a starting point for our own work, but the stated aims of the Cambridge project emphasized richer contextualization than the parameters of the Oxford edition allowed. The third major difference from my other projects has to do with the now ubiquitous availability of online resources— ECCO, Google Books, Google itself, EBBO, JSTOR, and the like—a rich vein of information to mine for just the kind of annotations required by the edition at hand.

As we began our work, "team Grandison" (as we called ourselves) agreed on certain likely resources: the *Oxford Dictionary of English Proverbs*, the *OED*, the *Tatler* and *Spectator* essays, Richardson's other works, his letters, Tilley's *Dictionary of Proverbs*, Shakespeare, Pope, Fielding, and some resources specific to *Grandison* itself. My favorite directive, though, came from Melvyn New, who suggested that we be especially alert to echoes of biblical verses. In the end, that attention produced more than 185 references in the annotations, Matthew being the most often cited, with 34 mentions. Proverbs ranks a distant second with 16, while the book of John ties for third place with the Apocryphal book of Ecclesiasticus, each with 11 references. In total, we documented echoes or direct quotations of passages from 37 biblical books, 17 from the Old Testament, 19 from the New Testament, and 1 from the Apocrypha. This kind of comprehensive investigation was possible prior to the searchable databases of the electronic world, and I certainly used biblical concordances for both the Barbauld and Smith projects. But, in the case of Richardson, the ability to enter a phrase in quotation marks along with the word "bible" made the process very easy and, given Google's increasing ability to guess at one's likely meaning, very lucrative. Once we had a hit, we double-checked the Bible, and the information was recorded in our drafts.

Of course, as all readers of this essay will know, internet research can yield false positives and send us down rabbit holes; I know I spent hours pursuing leads that eventually came to nothing—or nothing worth keeping, at any rate. More often, such searches yielded some significant information, but not all was deemed (by me or my coeditors) worthy of inclusion in our final draft. However, some draft annotations were regrettably sacrificed to another end—a limiting of the "scope and ambition" of the edition by the practical concerns of publication. To be blunt, on completion of the final draft of our notes, we were directed to cut 30 percent of the 200,000-word document. There were annotations that benefited from the consequent tightening of language, pruning of sources, editing of summary; but valuable information was also sacrificed in the process. As an example, I offer the following annotation from my draft of notes to volume 3, last modified on August 5, 2015:

> *the Cremonese*: A territory in the north of Italy in the Duchy of Milan; Cremona is its capital. Perhaps significantly, Cremona was the site of a famous battle fought on February 1, 1702 and led by Prince Eugene of Savoy (allied with England and the Duke of Marlborough), in the War of the Spanish Succession. Prince Eugene occupied the town, but a crucial fort was successfully defended by Irish regiments allied with the French. In the end, Eugene had to withdraw from Cremona. The War of the Spanish Succession (1701–1714) was a war about balance of power in Europe. While the specific issues at stake in the actual conflict were not of imminent concern as Richardson penned *Sir Charles Grandison*, the general anxiety about England's place vis-à-vis Europe is certainly still at issue in 1753 as it will continue to be for quite some time. That the War of the Spanish Succession remains a touchstone of English identity in the mid-eighteenth century is evident in Uncle Toby's obsession with that conflict in Laurence Sterne's *Life and Opinions of Tristram Shandy* (1759–1767).

In the now published version, only the first sentence remains.[18] I am not sure which of us decided the information in this note was too extraneous to the text to retain, given the need for rather drastic cuts. The original version, though perhaps in need of fine-tuning, meets the stated aims of the edition as ideally conceived. The new note, while obviously shorter, strikes me as more expendable—indeed, for all it tells us, it could be eliminated (a savings of another eighteen words!).

Lest I seem resentful here, I should also note that many of my annotations survive almost verbatim from my earliest drafts. The following explanation of "trombone" exemplifies the succinct, yet contextually rich annotation that we strove to provide: "trombone, *a kind of blunderbuss*: Baretti, *Dictionary*, s.v. *blunderbuss*: 'Blunderbuss . . . [a wide-mouthed brass gun] *un mochetone, un trombone*.' In *The Mysteries of Udolpho* (1794) III: 301, Radcliffe footnotes her use of *trombone* with the same appositive as Richardson ('A kind of blunderbuss'), but without attribution."[19] Here, the invocation of Baretti and Radcliffe speaks to Richardson's own literary community (his friendship with Baretti and his reliance on his advice for the Italian scenes) and the literary community he helped create (Radcliffe and other readers, many of whom were female and some of whom went on to write their own novels); the annotation fully situates the passage in the pertinent cultural context.

Currently, I am again editing the work of Barbauld, who was herself an editor of Richardson (his *Correspondence* in 1804 and *Clarissa*, and *Grandison*, volumes 1–15 of her fifty-volume edition of *The British Novelists* in 1810). My volume in the Oxford University Press edition of Barbauld's complete works is focused on her literary criticism. It is a fitting project with which to complete my career as an editor because, in a sense, this is exactly where I began. My investment in Barbauld's poetry was first and foremost the investment of a literary critic. To engage in the kind of literary criticism of her work that I thought necessary, however, I needed other readers of Barbauld who would be equally invested in her poetry. An edition was mandated by my need for a critical community. That community now exists in sufficient numbers to mandate, in turn, an authoritative scholarly edition of Barbauld's complete works. Like the Cambridge edition of Richardson, this edition plans to include all known writings—the major works as well as those we have considered minor. Barbauld's literary criticism falls into the latter camp, too often discounted as "work for hire," secondary to the poems and essays she produced without incentive from booksellers. Her cultural authority as one to whom the booksellers turned in their publishing projects has been underappreciated. Though the annotations to the volume I am preparing will be factual and forthright, I will also be making the case for the worth of her contributions in that sphere. The extensive commentary demanded by a scholarly edition will serve implicitly if not explicitly to investigate and celebrate the powers of an approach to literary criticism that rendered Barbauld an authority in her own time—and one who should be trusted in ours. Stay tuned.

NOTES

1. "Poetry. Art. 19," *British Critic* 5 (1795): 295.

2. *Anna Letitia Barbauld: Voice of the Enlightenment* (Baltimore: Johns Hopkins University Press, 2008) won the 2011 Annibel Jenkins Biography prize from the American Society for Eighteenth-Century Studies. Professor McCarthy is, happily, a contributor to this volume; see his essay below, "The Rhetoric, Ethics, and Aesthetics of Annotation: Some Reflections."

3. Elizabeth Kraft, "Anna Letitia Barbauld's 'Washing Day' and the Montgolfier Balloon," *Literature and History* 4 (1995): 25–41.

4. Susan Rosenbaum, "'A Thing Unknown, Without a Name': Anna Laetitia Barbauld and the Illegible Signature," *Studies in Romanticism* 40 (2001): 380.

5. Julia Saunders, "'The Mouse's Petition': Anna Laetitia Barbauld and the Scientific Revolution," *Review of English Studies* 53 (2002): 506.

6. Daniel P. Watkins, *Anna Letitia Barbauld and 18th-Century Visionary Poetics* (Baltimore: Johns Hopkins University Press, 2012): 102, 214n9.

7. See my review of this work in conjunction with Paula R. Feldman and Brian C. Cooney's edition of *The Collected Poetry of Mary Tighe, European Romantic Review* 29, no. 4 (2018): 514–19.

8. As Joseph F. Bartolomeo notes, "The vehemence with which the Glenmorrises prefer America is amply justified by the horrific consequences of their return to England: the kidnapping and attempted seduction of Medora, the cruelties that lead Laura to an insane asylum, and the arrest of Glenmorris for an old debt contracted out of kindness toward a friend. The novel, however, provides virtually no description of their presumably idyllic lives in America" ("No Place Like Home: The Uses of America in 1790s British Fiction," *Yearbook of English Studies* 46 [2016]: 255).

9. *OED* records the first use of "crowdsource" as 2006.

10. The 2006 Pickering and Chatto edition under the general editorship of Stuart Curran prints the correct lines from Mason but identifies the elegy as "Elegy III."

11. As evidenced by my colleague David Gants's email to me, August 4, 1996; he also identifies the elegy as "Elegy III," which is the identification LION still yields (from the 1811 edition of Mason's poems). Eighteenth-century editions have it as "Elegy II Written in the Garden of a Friend."

12. Mason, "Elegy II," in *Elegies by William Mason* (London, 1763), 13.

13. Smith, *The Young Philosopher*, ed. Elizabeth Kraft (Lexington: University Press of Kentucky, 1998): 32. The quotation is from *As You Like It*, IV.i.214–15.

14. Harriet Kramer Linkin, "The Citational Network of Tighe, Porter, Barbauld, Lefanu, Morgan, and Hemans," in *Women's Literary Networks and Romanticism: "A Tribe of Authoresses,"* ed. Andrew O. Winckles and Angela Rehbein (Liverpool: Liverpool University Press, 2017), 197. Melvyn New makes the point that citational networks in eighteenth-century novels by women are often networks populated largely by male authors. His focus is Maria Edgeworth's *Belinda*, but the same could be said of Smith's *The Young Philosopher*. See his "In Quotes: Annotating Maria Edgeworth's *Belinda*," *1650–1850: Ideas, Aesthetics, and Inquiries in the Early Modern Era* 26 (2021): 112–30.

15. Elizabeth Kraft, "Encyclopedic Libertinism and 1798: Charlotte Smith's *The Young Philosopher*," *Eighteenth-Century Novel* 2 (2002): 239–72.

218 | Notes on Footnotes

16. Loraine Fletcher, *Charlotte Smith: A Critical Biography* (London: Macmillan, 1998), 273.

17. Keymer and Sabor, "General Introduction," in *Sir Charles Grandison*, ed. E. Derek Taylor, Melvyn New, and Elizabeth Kraft, The Cambridge Edition of the Works of Samuel Richardson, 8–11 (Cambridge: Cambridge University Press, 2022), 8:x, xi.

18. *Sir Charles Grandison*, ed. E. Derek Taylor, Melvyn New, and Elizabeth Kraft, The Cambridge Edition of the Works of Samuel Richardson (Cambridge: Cambridge University Press, 2022), 1971n19.

19. Ibid.

CHAPTER 14

 The Rhetoric, Ethics, and
Aesthetics of Annotation
Some Reflections

William McCarthy

The barest of barebones statements about annotations to texts is that their purpose is to give information. As soon as one asks *what kind* of information, one walks into a thicket. Annotations are meant to give information their writer presumes the reader will need for understanding the text. Because annotators cannot know exactly who their readers will be or what their readers will know, they address the presumed needs of expected readers. Annotators must guess what their readers are likely to know, or—as usually happens in practice—they address their annotations only to their likeliest readers, whose knowledge they can estimate. Either way, annotators *imagine* an audience and aim to provide what they believe that audience needs. To satisfy the audience they must convince it that their annotations are credible. Thus, annotators engage in rhetorical acts, according to the Aristotelian idea of rhetoric: "the faculty or power of observing in any given case the available means of persuasion. It is the audience ... which determines the means: the kinds of oratory—political or deliberative, forensic or legal, and epideictic or display—are determined by consideration of kinds of audience; the character which will be effective in the speaker depends on the susceptibility of audiences; and questions of rhetorical style and arrangement are in large part questions of appropriateness to the various kinds of oratory."[1]

Scholarly annotations, the kind of "oratory" I am concerned with, mediate between the knowledge or belief embodied or implicit in the text and the knowledge or belief presumed in the reader, on the assumption that text and reader differ. The annotator is thus a go-between, a "messenger," representing the text and its author to the reader. The annotator has obligations on two sides: to the author whose text is being presented, and to the reader of that text today. To speak of "obligation" to an author who may be long dead seems peculiar; should we not speak only of obligation to the living reader? The issue of readers' relations to texts lies miles beyond the scope of this chapter; if, however, only the present needs and present interests of readers were to count, there would seem to be no need for annotation—or for texts that do not mesh with readers' present needs and interests. In that case there would also be no need for historical texts, or indeed for history itself, as readers would live happily in the present state of their knowledge and belief, innocent of anything different.

Clearly, then, the annotator must wish to *change* the reader, to make the reader aware of what the annotator believes to be the dead author's mind—or, in the case of a neglected author (as Anna Letitia Barbauld once was), the dead author's value, or even existence. Thus, the annotator sets out to educate the reader. This effort is rhetorical, but its purpose, to mediate between dead author and living reader for the reader's benefit, is ethical. As general editor of the Collected Works of Anna Letitia Barbauld, editor of volume 1, and coeditor of other volumes in that edition, I have many occasions to ponder what annotations are needed and why, and to explore these issues as they arise in actual or potential annotations. This chapter is not a foray into theory but rather reflections on cases (actual and hypothetical), aspiring only to raise into consciousness what annotators may already know tacitly.

To decide *what* to annotate is itself the most basic rhetorical decision. Can the reader be expected to know the meaning of this word or the identity of that name? It depends on the annotator's expectation of who the reader will be. To identify the name "Milton" in a note ("John Milton, 1608–74, author of *Paradise Lost*") would imply one's expectation that the reader has not heard of Milton. That would be an insult to a fellow scholar or graduate student in English, but not to an undergraduate, not even a beginning English major. Thus, the annotator of an anthology for undergraduate classrooms would identify the name and provide dates. (The fourth edition of *The Norton Anthology of English Literature* not only identifies Milton and gives dates but provides two pages of biography in small print.)[2] The annotator of a text intended for

The Rhetoric, Ethics, and Aesthetics of Annotation | 221

graduate students and literature specialists would identify only the surname, when the text quotes from Milton ("'In dubious battle': Milton, *Paradise Lost*, i: 104")."[3] The annotator of a text intended for specialists in the English Renaissance or for Miltonists might cite the work only ("*Paradise Lost*, i: 104") and not its author. In practice, the editor of a specialist journal might demand a fuller citation; "audience" includes, after all, one's expected editor-publisher. The demand for citation by a journal specializing in the texts being cited can seem pedantic, but professional protocol may require it; hence the annotator has one further audience to satisfy, an institutional one. In sum, whether to annotate and what information to give depends in the first place on the annotator's idea of who the audience is and what it needs to know.

Of course, in practice complications occur, and annotators must negotiate tricky rhetorical spaces. Specialists in one region of literature may be ignorant of others: thus, can the editor of Barbauld's essays in the *Monthly Magazine* (1796–1803) be confident that an allusion to Edmund Burke's *Reflections on the Late Revolution in France* (1790) will be understood by a literary historian who, though interested in Barbauld as a woman writer, may, in order to "get the point" of a passage, need more information about Burke than the bare name and a brief quotation? Or, to go further afield, I recently chatted with the editor of a splendid edition of Elizabeth Bishop's correspondence who had never heard of Barbauld. As a specialist in twentieth-century American poetry he might have needed fuller information even to identify Edmund Burke, let alone catch an allusion to *Reflections*. It is a commonplace that one of the losses resulting from specialization is loss of mutual intelligibility. Annotators must often thread a path between offending some readers by telling them what they already know and depriving others of information they need.

The present volume deals only intermittently with textual editing, yet textual editors face the same questions when they decide whether a word needs glossing, or whether the word even belongs to the text. In these cases, the ignorance that needs to be addressed may be their own as well as their readers'. Recently I came across a word in a Barbauld text, "profusedly," that looked to me like an obvious typo for "profusely." I was about to "correct" it in my transcript but instead decided to consult the *OED*, which records it as a variant of "profusely."[4] In another Barbauld text appears the phrase "going a journey." A coeditor took this to be an error for "going *on* a journey"—but no, the *OED* quotes an instance in which the preposition is absent, and Barbauld herself wrote "go your journey" in a letter.[5] Any textual editor can match these examples, in which an "obvious error" from our perspective turns out to be yesterday's idiom.

And that is the point. Phenomena such as differences in idioms between 1790 and the present day remind us of the truism that "the past is another country." Its pastness—its difference from us—brings me to the ethical aspect of annotation, the dimension in which the annotator mediates between that difference and the knowledge or beliefs of present-day readers. The most basic question to ask of an annotator is, How faithful is your mediation? Can I trust you to tell me what I need to know at this point in the text, and, conversely, *not* to tell me what will be of no use to me, or may even lead me astray? Annotators can fail in faithfulness for many perfectly human reasons: haste, vanity, honest ignorance, inability to find the required source. And yet, as an experience I am about to recount demonstrates, what at first seems an obstacle to faithful annotation can lead to a change of mind about what counts as "faithfulness."

The experience concerns choice of edition to cite in identifying a quotation. Should one cite the most current scholarly edition, such as the Twickenham Pope (in process of being superseded, but still the "standard")? I used to assume—indeed, I still do, with part of my mind—that one should, and in volume 1 of the Oxford Barbauld I cited John Butt's "reduced version" of the Twickenham edition.[6] But because I also had to cite Pope's *Iliad* and that text is not included in Butt, and because in Key West I cannot consult the complete Twickenham edition but do have access to HathiTrust, an online research library of editions out of copyright, I cited Barbauld's allusions to Pope's *Iliad* from a 1760 London edition. Obviously, this edition was not overseen by Pope, nor is it a standard scholarly edition. It was, however, an edition available to Barbauld, published in her country during her lifetime. Whether she owned a set is not known, but she could have had access to it.[7] Indeed, I have now begun to believe that her allusions and quotations should be identified from editions she could have used, even if they do not meet current standards of scholarship.

However, I am still "in transition" on this issue. My changed view does not exclude identifying Barbauld's quotations from modern editions so long as modern editions are agreed to represent accurately the texts she could have known. It would, however, forbid citing *The New Oxford Shakespeare*, which aims to represent the plays as nearly as possible as they were first published— and which is the reference edition in volume 1 of the Collected Barbauld, *The Poems, Revised*. Barbauld surely did not have access to an early quarto; most likely she would have known Shakespeare in Johnson's or Malone's editions, the pages and texts of which differ considerably from those of the *NOS*.[8] The principle of citing contemporary texts will exclude citing reprint editions she could not have known, such as American reprints or reprints issued after her death. Such a reprint might happen to represent accurately the text Barbauld knew, yet I assume no serious annotator would choose to cite one, for two reasons: annotators wish to be perceived as credible (a rhetorical reason), and annotators wish to represent faithfully the author they are annotating (an ethical reason). When annotation consists of citing the source of an author's quotation, it aims to represent a piece of the author's mental universe: the people, the texts, the very copies if possible, the author lived among. One Barbauld book that does survive today is her 1733 copy of Fontenelle's *Entretiens sur le Pluralité des Mondes*, given to her when she was seven years old.[9] Because it was her copy and she came to know the work at such an early age, in my biography of Barbauld I quoted from it in preference to the 1686 first edition. Choice of the edition to cite can be one of the ethical—or less than ethical— ways in which annotation mediates between dead authors and live readers.

There are also sociocultural assumptions inherent in a text that mesh badly, or not at all, with the assumptions of readers now, and therefore require explanation. Not to annotate such passages can give the impression that they can be judged according to the current reader's views. That would be another ethical failing: allowing people to bring all their current views to bear on the author being annotated. Can it be an ethical failing even when we agree that the current views are morally superior to those entertained by others in the past? I think it can, and I will illustrate by means of a particularly difficult case.

In an essay, "The Manufacture of Paper" (published in 1793 in her brother's collection *Evenings at Home*), Barbauld opens her description of how paper was made in her day in these words: "This delicate and beautiful substance is made from the meanest and most disgusting materials, from old rags, which have passed from one poor person to another, and at length have perhaps dropped in tatters from the child of the beggar. These are carefully picked up from dunghills, or bought from servants by Jews, who make it their business to go about and collect them."[10] Her casual use of the word "Jews" in this context—a context including the words "meanest," "disgusting," and "dunghills"—is likely to shock the moral sensibility of anyone today who would be reading a two-hundred-year-old text. Since Barbauld is on record as befriending Jewish women in Stoke Newington, where she lived after 1802, she can probably be acquitted of the charge of being personally anti-Semitic.[11] What should an annotator do? What are the implications of different choices?

Unlike more customary reasons for annotation, the passage presents no unfamiliar word that needs to be explained. So, if an annotator undertook to explain only unfamiliar words, the passage could be left unannotated. That would leave room for readers to wonder why Barbauld wrote "Jews" when, presumably, she meant simply "rag dealers." Did she intend an ethnic slur? Although the passage uses no unfamiliar words, one word in it bears a meaning today that it did not necessarily bear in 1793: "dunghill" in 1793, we learn from the *OED*, could mean simply "trash heap."[12] Beyond that, however, the passage by its very casualness presents something that does need explaining: Barbauld evidently assumed her readers would take for granted that rag dealers would be Jews—or that Jews would be rag dealers. In 1793 London that phenomenon did not need explaining; along with her readers Barbauld knew that the rag trade was plied principally by Jews, and that is what today's annotator needs to explain. So repulsive is any suggestion of anti-Semitism among educated people today, however, that annotators may wish to disassociate themselves as well as Barbauld from it. Hence an annotation to this passage in a draft text of the Collected Barbauld reads: "'Jews... collect them': As an effect of cultural anti-Semitism, rag-collecting was one of the few trades open to poor London Jews in Barbauld's lifetime, and was staffed largely by them: see Joshua van Oven, *Letters on the Present State of the Jewish Poor in the Metropolis* (1802), quoted in George, 135. In her later years in Stoke Newington Barbauld befriended Jewish women among her neighbors." The information in this note that may be new to today's reader begins with the words "rag-collecting." That there existed "cultural anti-Semitism" is not a concept or social behavior that anyone likely to read a literary text today would need to be informed of; the phrase is more like a disclaimer by the annotator, an ethical appeal. Although this note may be adequate to address the passage it annotates, the historical situation and Barbauld's attitude were more complicated than the note suggests. The poorest London Jews, those most likely to work in the rag trade, were from eastern Europe: the Ashkenazim.[13] On the contrary, Sephardic and Dutch Jews, the descendants of those expelled from Spain and Portugal, sometimes did very well economically and could wield considerable economic power: Barbauld's Stoke Newington neighbor Esther Baruch Lousada (1775–1844), whom she invited to join her women's book society, belonged to a wealthy family with interests in the West Indies.[14] Anti-Semitism there certainly was, even against well-to-do Jews, but the difference in class between the poor and rich was probably as great as the anti-Semitism to which both were exposed. Thus, Barbauld's identifying rag collectors as Jews and her befriending Esther

Lousada would have been based as much on economic class as on (in the latter case) resistance to bigotry; Barbauld felt concern for the poor, whether Jewish or gentile, but she sought her friends among the middle and upper classes.

This annotation to Barbauld's description of paper-making has several things to do. It has to provide information about a social situation familiar to Barbauld and her readers, whatever her attitude toward it was, in order to explain her use of a word in a context that might offend today's reader, and just because today's reader may be offended by it, annotators may feel a need to exonerate Barbauld—and even to some extent the annotators themselves—from moral taint. Whether they should give all the information I have just given here is a question of proportion: does a casual mention in a text that has nothing otherwise to do with the subject require this much detail, even though the detail provides a more nuanced explanation of Barbauld's attitude than a reader today might imagine?

The ethical wrong—if "wrong" is not too severe a word—of allowing readers to project their current views onto a text by a dead author is the wrong of depriving them of new information, even when that information may be morally repugnant to their current views. If the past is another country, part of its otherness consists in things that repel people now. To be sure, the difference between then and now is just as likely to arouse pity as disgust: to the modern reader, the past often seems benighted. Ethically responsible annotators have an obligation to curb what historian E. P. Thompson memorably called "the enormous condescension of posterity,"[15] the tendency of people today to feel superior to people of the past. That tendency must be curbed not for the sake of the dead but for the sake of the living. It is well to remember, too, that many social or political phenomena we live with more or less passively would have appalled people who lived two hundred years ago: nuclear weapons, for instance. Try to imagine what an annotator would have to do to explain to someone from Barbauld's time John Hersey's *Hiroshima*.

Annotators have a duty to make texts intelligible to readers, but "making intelligible" is a cloudy concept, a concept (to adopt a favorite Wittgenstein phrase) with blurred edges, and consequently with ethical ambiguities. A leading method of making texts intelligible begins with *drawing analogies*—not between "now" and "then," but between two streams of "then." Annotators inform readers not only of the sources of an author's direct quotations from texts the author knew, but texts or intellectual networks the author drew on without attribution, or even unconsciously. Because this method rests on the breadth of the annotator's knowledge, it has ethical implications. A sketch annotation to a passage in the second of Barbauld's two *Civic Sermons* (1792) draws an analogy between it and a concept by a writer to whose work Barbauld referred elsewhere. This is the passage: "This first society is called a Family. It is the root of every other society. It is the beginning of order, and kind affections, and mutual helpfulness and provident regulations."[16] The annotator cites moral philosopher Francis Hutcheson, with "specific reference to the family extending to the neighborhood and beyond to the whole world in a benevolent ring of mutual care." Barbauld is not quoting Hutcheson and does not name him in this passage. This analogy between her text and an idea by Hutcheson might be simply the annotator's remark, an *aperçu* showing the annotator's reading but telling nothing specifically about Barbauld. It would remain only an analogy were the annotator not to cite Barbauld's own mentions of or quotations from Hutcheson by name elsewhere.[17] Making analogies of this sort when an author can be shown to have been aware of the analogue text helps to make intelligible the author's intellectual environment. The ethical failing of not documenting an analogy—of letting it remain the annotator's *aperçu*—would be self-display by the annotator. Drawing such analogies is ethically ambiguous because it may be a form of vanity—pride in one's knowledge—that prompts the annotator to draw the analogy in the first place. If the analogy can be justified by demonstrating that the author was aware of the purported analogue text, the knowledge will have been productive, and the annotator can be justified in feeling proud of the insight.

But when does "making intelligible" become cover for an annotator's act of self-assertion at the author's expense? Annotations that correct authorial errors or call attention to discrepancies in the text can range from the innocuous to the high-handed. The most elementary correction is of a fact that the author could have known. Barbauld was a good student of geography and an admirer of the new United States, so I was surprised to find her miscalling the Hudson River the Ohio when, in a letter to a friend, she mentions the newly invented steamboat.[18] I treated the error as insignificant, perhaps a memory slip, and corrected it in a note; not to correct it would have seemed inattentive, or might have implied ignorance in me. More problematic is the discovery of discrepancies in an author's text. In a review of a new book, Barbauld presents several translations from its French original as single passages; however, examining the French original, I found that on several occasions Barbauld's "single" passages are drawn from different pages of the whole.[19] The discrepancy thus disclosed could indicate Barbauld's attitude toward the book under review or

The Rhetoric, Ethics, and Aesthetics of Annotation | 227

tell something about reviewing practices in her time. It could be useful information; although its importance is uncertain, it might prompt an inquiry.

What is the value, however, of correcting an error that the author probably shared with her contemporaries? In *Hymns in Prose for Children* (1781), Barbauld writes, "The hen sits upon her nest of straw, she watches patiently the full time, then she carefully breaks the shell, and the young chickens come out."[20] In ornithological fact that is not how chicks are born; they make the first move, to which the hen responds.[21] Barbauld's school at Palgrave kept chickens in its yard; apparently she did not observe them with close attention. Would this correct information improve understanding of the passage from *Hymns in Prose*, or would it only tell us that Barbauld shared a common error about the ways of hens and that the annotator knows better? To generalize, is it helpful for an annotator to notice the author's errors when they may be errors common to her time, or is the annotator using the author's error as an opportunity to show off? Errors common to a time are, after all, part of history; but an annotator of Chaucer's line "Up rose the sun, and up rose Emily" would not convey useful information by remarking that Chaucer's phrase "up rose the sun" was mistaken because it is the earth, not the sun, that moves.

A different kind of self-assertion, one that affects a reader's freedom to interpret, is an annotator's characterization of the text: as, say, "comic," "rhapsodic," "severely critical," or any such interpretive description. Probably no annotator has been entirely innocent of characterizing a text and thus nudging the reader to think about it in a particular way. Indeed, since one of the important purposes of annotation is to affect a reader's perception of a text, such characterizations are not necessarily guilty: of a Barbauld satire, "The Domiphobia, or Dread of Home," in the *Monthly Magazine* (1796), for instance, an annotator might say that it is written "in the guise of a medical professional," a characterization based on, and summarizing, its use of medical terminology. The line between this "summary characterization" and "interpretation," however, is as blurred as any Wittgensteinian could wish: overstepping it or not seems to be a matter of "tact," an unhelpful word. Yet the overstepping is real, and an annotation can preempt a reader's understanding—or simply interfere annoyingly with a reader's experience of the text.

Overstepping can also arouse suspicion that the annotator means to insinuate a view of the author or the subject of the edited text. In *Eighteen Hundred and Eleven* Barbauld herself annotates her reference to agricultural innovations by her friend and political ally William Roscoe: "The Historian of the age of

Leo has brought into cultivation the extensive tract of Chatmoss." Her note is respectful, even elevated, in tone, and it infuriated a political opponent, John Wilson Croker, who answered it scornfully in his review of the poem: Barbauld, he wrote, makes Roscoe's "barns and piggeries . . . objects not only of curiosity but even of reverence and enthusiasm."[22] What one thought of Roscoe—and of *Eighteen Hundred and Eleven* itself—in 1812 depended on one's political loyalties. A century later, when Barbauld was mostly forgotten, her poem could still be used to sponsor a political attitude: in 1911, Warrington town alderman Arthur Bennett published a reprint of it for the purpose of warning England to reform at home lest she lose her world empire.[23] Would Barbauld herself have defended empire? In some ways her poem seems to do so: "Wide spreads thy race from Ganges to the pole, / O'er half the western world thy accents roll." Material here for Bennett's imperialism? Or a statement of the bare fact of British emigration in the early nineteenth century? My annotation opts for the latter, partly I admit to soften the imperialist appearance of the lines, but also, more neutrally and historically, to emphasize the fact itself: "the line as a whole, together with line 82 ('thy accents') records the demographic fact of worldwide Anglophone emigration."[24] Readers who interpret the lines as pro-imperialist despite the annotation will do so on their own initiative, a political choice for which each reader will be responsible.[25]

The annotator's business is to facilitate. However keen annotators may be to offer "readings" of the text, or to show appreciation or disapproval of what the author wrote, they should submit to the same ethical imperative that translators are held to when they work for heads of state in negotiations: do not embellish; do not judge; keep your own views to yourself. To be sure, "facilitate" must sometimes mean "introduce": if an author is not known to readers, neutral annotation may not do enough to explain why the reader should take an interest. Introducing readers to writers whose works have been forgotten requires explaining who the writer is and why she matters. Annotation good for the familiar name must differ from annotation for the unfamiliar. Thus, we close the circle we opened at the start: annotation is a form of rhetoric dependent on one's idea of audience and deployed for a purpose, and according to standards, that must be considered ethical.

Annotations are usually cued by superscript numbers in the text, a practice that can present a different problem. Those numbers were not part of the text as its author (or original printer) left it, and they can distort the appearance of the page—especially if the author considered the original printed appearance of the page integral to the effect of the text. Barbauld's *Lessons for Children* (4 vols., 1778–79) presents a perfect instance. Barbauld emphasized to her printer that she wanted large print on the small pages that were usual in books for children: she regarded the large print as her principal innovation in children's books, and it was noticed and appreciated by her contemporaries. Following her directions resulted in pages containing perhaps ten lines of print. The Oxford edition will respect Barbauld's stated intention; it will present the pages of *Lessons* as she wished them to appear to their young readers.[26] Hence annotations could not be cued by the usual method. In their draft text the editors settled on marginal note numbers, a compromise of course, since there were no note numbers at all on the original pages. An alternative method of cuing might have been to use line numbers, as in the right margins of printed verse. Either way, however, the need to cue affects the appearance of the page.[27]

Here, cuing is an ethical issue because it affects presentation to readers of the author's intention. If the annotator believes the text calls for many annotations, the result may be a crowd of superscript numbers on the page, and insofar as that alters the look of the page for the worse, it is an *aesthetic* issue. Choosing a method of cuing annotations can, indeed, be more an aesthetic than an ethical decision. In the Carl H. Pforzheimer Collection at the New York Public Library, among the letters Barbauld wrote to a pupil there is one, not in her hand but a contemporary copy, in which she recommends French-language books to be read by girls and young women.[28] The letter is filled with names and titles little-known today and requires extensive annotation to identify them. Annotating each name and title in the customary way would produce a page filled with superscript numbers—"speckled," I was going to write, an adjective indicating that the result would be ugly (and even hard to read, for the reader would be continually drawn away from the text by annotation cues). Since the letter is brief, my preference is for identifying the names and titles it mentions in one long "essay" note following its text. This annotation preference is chiefly aesthetic. Whether Barbauld would have agreed with it does not matter. Her wishes are not at issue here, for the letter was not meant for publication, and of course she would not have thought it needed annotation at all. Whether my preference will survive in the finished volume I do not know.

The wish expressed by Simon Leys in *The Hall of Uselessness*—what scholar "would not dream" of being remembered for having written "a few good footnotes"[29]—sounds like a plea for aesthetic as well as scholarly appreciation. Annotations are judged by aesthetic as well as other standards. An annotation that took a hundred words to say something equally sayable in fifty would be blamed for blundering around its subject instead of going directly to the point:

it would be annoying because ungainly. No doubt annotators may work by different aesthetics, but if annotations are expected to be no longer than they need be to communicate the requisite information, conciseness and stylistic economy will be considered virtues—even aesthetic virtues. An example of conciseness, a draft annotation that packs much information into the smallest box the passage arguably requires, pertains to a Barbauld satire in the *Monthly Magazine*, "The Domiphobia, or Dread of Home," about the new fashion of taking holidays at seaside resorts.[30] The *Monthly* was edited by Barbauld's brother, John Aikin, who practiced as a doctor. This is the passage that needs annotation: "I am somewhat at a loss to describe this disorder, because being of very recent appearance in this country, it has escaped the attention of Sauvages, Vogel, Cullen, and all our late Nosologists. It has some symptoms peculiar to the class of fevers, and some to that of inflammations, but it is a disease . . . so original, so much *per se*, that we must be content to let it be the root of a peculiar class, which may hereafter be divided into species." And this is the draft annotation: "'Nosologists': Nosology is a branch of medicine concerned with the classification of diseases, in the manner of Carl Linnaeus; hence the essay's references to 'class' and 'species.' The authors referenced are François Boissier de Sauvages, *Nosologia Methodica* (1763), Rudolph Augustin Vogel, *Historia Materiae Medicae* (1760), and William Cullen, *Synopsis Nosologiae Methodicae* (1769). John Aikin was Cullen's pupil at Edinburgh, 1764–66. Aikin's *General Biography* (1814) contains a biography of Sauvages, and Lucy Aikin mentions Sauvages among additions to Aikin's medical library in 1786 (*MJA*, 1:113)." The annotation identifies the authors named in the text and provides information relevant to readers of an edition that includes Barbauld's essays in her brother's magazine, relevant because her brother was a doctor and she is writing humorously in a medical style that he would have appreciated. The information is factual and presented concisely. The annotation does not impose on its reader an interpretation or characterization of the text. It can be described in terms that are both ethical and aesthetic: it is self-effacing, impersonal, economical. A reader of a draft of the present chapter saw an analogy between this aesthetic of economy and the "Calvinist aesthetic" described many years ago by Donald Davie: an aesthetic of "*simplicity, sobriety, and measure*." An English Dissenter put it this way in describing a new chapel: "commodious and neat, but plain."[31] Certainly annotations can be longer and more detailed than this example, but one assumes that they would be so from necessity (having a lot of ground to cover), not from a taste for rhetorical splendor. The annotations of Edward Gibbon, to be sure, are appreciated for their

The Rhetoric, Ethics, and Aesthetics of Annotation | 231

irony and innuendo, but they are notes to his own text, not games played with someone else's.

A "self-effacing" annotator does not have to be a Uriah Heep: as Leys says, one can be proud of having written a "good note." I am proud, for example, of having discovered in an 1819 Baltimore newspaper a notice of the arrival from London of one "J. Martineau," whose travel to the United States could explain the debut publication of Barbauld's poem "On the Death of Mrs Martineau" in an 1820 Boston reprint of her *Poems* instead of where it might have been expected, in London, and I am proud of having reported this find concisely.[32]

What, then, is a "good note"? An annotator could do worse than observe the advice political consultant Louis Howe gave Eleanor Roosevelt at the start of her career of public speaking, when she was nervous and fluttery. The advice is rhetorical, ethical, and aesthetic all at once: "Have something to say. Say it. And sit down."[33] Give readers the information they need. Give it as concisely as possible. And when you have given it, stop.

NOTES

I thank Elizabeth Kraft, coeditor for other Barbauld editions and editor for the Oxford Barbauld, Andrea Immel, Scott Krawczyk, and Melvyn New for reading drafts of this essay and making valuable suggestions.

　1. Richard McKeon, ed., *Introduction to Aristotle* (New York: Modern Library, 1947), 620.

　2. *The Norton Anthology of English Literature*, 4th ed., ed. M. H. Abrams et al. (New York: W. W. Norton, 1979), 1:1377–79.

　3. *The Collected Works of Anna Letitia Barbauld*, vol. 1, *The Poems, Revised*, ed. William McCarthy (Oxford: Oxford University Press, 2019), 327.

　4. [Barbauld], "Review of Sir John Froissart's Chronicles of England, France, Spain, and the adjoining Countries. By Thomas Johnes," *Annual Review* 5 (1807): 226; *OED*'s examples include usage by John Norris of Bemerton (1698), Richard Steele in *Christian Hero* (1725), and Walter Scott, "Sermon on Bankruptcy" (1799).

　5. Barbauld, "The Misses (addressed to a careless girl.) By the late Mrs. Barbauld," in *The Juvenile Forget Me Not . . . for the Year 1830*, ed. Mrs. S. C. Hall (London: Hailes [1829], 1–8. See *OED*, s.v. "go" I.2.b, "*transitive*: With the action of travelling as object"; examples given are "to go an errand" and "to go a circuit." Barbauld wrote "go your journey" in a letter to Lydia Rickards, July 22, 1799 (Misc. MS 4339, Pforzheimer Collection, New York Public Library).

　6. John Butt, ed., *The Poems of Alexander Pope* (New Haven: Yale University Press, 1963). A new edition in progress was described by Michael F. Suarez at a symposium, "Scholarly Editing of Literary Texts," at Yale University in 2019; see above, Marcus Walsh, "Annotating Pope."

232 | Notes on Footnotes

7. Few of the contents of Barbauld's personal library are known today; for an exception, see n. 9 below. The only library to which she is known to have had access is that of Warrington Academy between 1758 and 1774; its *Catalogue* (1775) lists "Pope's Homer's Iliad and Odyssey, 11 Vols." (p. 6). Those are likely to have been the 1760 *Iliad* (6 vols.) and the 1760 *Odyssey* (5 vols.), taken together.

8. My colleagues in the Oxford Barbauld are not convinced that we should cite from Johnson or Malone in preference to *NOS*; we may end up citing from *NOS* despite my reservation.

9. This copy passed down through her descendants and is now held by the Library of Harris Manchester College, Oxford. I quote from it in *Anna Letitia Barbauld, Voice of the Enlightenment* (Baltimore: Johns Hopkins University Press, 2008).

10. [Barbauld], "The Manufacture of Paper," in *Evenings at Home* (London: Johnson, 1793), 2:140.

11. See McCarthy, *Anna Letitia Barbauld*, 506. Barbauld invited her Jewish neighbor Esther Baruch Lousada to join the women's book club she and her niece founded in the village of Stoke Newington. To be sure, befriending a Jewish person is not, of itself, proof that one is not anti-Semitic.

12. "Trash heap" was evidently its meaning for Joseph Addison, who in *Spectator* 367 remarked that "a beau may peruse his cravat after it is worn out, with greater pleasure and advantage than ever he did in a glass. In a word, a piece of cloth ... may by this means be raised from a dunghill, and become the most valuable piece of furniture in a prince's cabinet" (*Selections from the Spectator, Tatler, Guardian, and Freeholder*, ed. Barbauld [London: Johnson, 1805], 2:120). In Barbauld's reprint, this essay is titled "The Manufacture of Paper." I thank Scott Krawczyk for providing this example.

13. M. Dorothy George, *London Life in the Eighteenth Century* (1925; reprint, Harper and Row, 1964), 125–32.

14. Communication to the author from Miriam Rodrigues-Pereira, Honorary Archivist of the Spanish and Portuguese Jews' Congregation, London, December 18, 2000.

15. E. P. Thompson, *The Making of the English Working Class* (1963; reprint, New York: Vintage Books, 1966), 12.

16. [Barbauld], *Civic Sermons to the People. Number II. From mutual Wants springs mutual Happiness* (London: Johnson, 1792), 6.

17. That is easy to do. Barbauld names Hutcheson approvingly in *Remarks on Mr. Gilbert Wakefield's Enquiry into the Expediency and Propriety of Public or Social Worship* (London: Johnson, 1792), 70. Her father included Hutcheson in his course on Moral Philosophy at Warrington Academy (lecture notes by Benjamin Vaughan, American Philosophical Society MS BV46P.m/no. 6). She refers, as the note will make clear, to Hutcheson's outline of "Our Duties toward Mankind" in his *Introduction to Moral Philosophy* (1747). The idea of the family as the origin of society appeared earlier in Locke's *Second Treatise Concerning Civil Government*. Barbauld names Locke among other influential English writers in *Eighteen Hundred and Eleven*, but Hutcheson was closer to home for her.

18. Barbauld to Lydia Rickards, February 17, 1810 (MS Misc. 4371, Pforzheimer Collection, New York Public Library).

19. This occurs in Barbauld's review of Chateaubriand's *Génie du Christianisme, ou Beautés de la Religion Chrétienne* (*Annual Review*, 1 [1803]: 247–55.

20. [Barbauld,] *Hymns in Prose for Children* (London: Johnson, 1781), hymn II.

21. A description of how chickens are born appears *s.v. Chicken* in Wikipedia.

The Rhetoric, Ethics, and Aesthetics of Annotation | 233

22. Barbauld's note to line 147 of her poem, and Croker's riposte (*Poems, Revised*, 367). She calls Roscoe "the Historian of the Age of Leo" in recognition of his multivolume *History of the Life and Pontificate of Leo the Tenth* (1805). On the political animus of the abuse heaped on her poem, see E. J. Clery, *Eighteen Hundred and Eleven: Poetry, Protest, and Economic Crisis* (Cambridge: Cambridge University Press, 2017).

23. Barbauld, *Poems, Revised*, 255.

24. Ibid., 365 (note to lines 81–82). As the note further says, Barbauld's old Palgrave pupil Thomas Douglas organized large-scale emigration to Canada of rural people displaced by enclosure of common land.

25. That choice will be made in the face of other Barbauld texts, such as *Sins of Government Sins of the Nation* (1793), which militate against imperialism.

26. In arguing to our Oxford editor the need to print *Lessons* that way, I cited Beatrix Potter as an analogy: reprinting *Peter Rabbit* or *Benjamin Bunny* without her illustrations would be unthinkable.

27. It might be argued that because readers of this scholarly edition will not be children, annotations can be cued as they usually are in scholarly texts. However, if the aim of a scholarly edition is to reproduce the text as its author wished it to appear, the text of *Lessons for Children* must be as free as possible of annotation cues. Wherever placed, they unavoidably subvert that aim.

28. MS Misc. 4379.

29. See Melvyn New's introduction to this collection.

30. The piece is A2 in William McCarthy, "Uncollected Periodical Prose by Anna Letitia Barbauld," *Studies in Bibliography* 59 (2015): 225–48.

31. For both quotations, see McCarthy, *Anna Letitia Barbauld*, 47.

32. Barbauld, *Poems, Revised*, 226.

33. Jean Edward Smith, *FDR* (New York: Random House, 2008), 200.

CONTRIBUTORS

Kate Bennett teaches English at Magdalen College, Oxford. She has held research fellowships at Christ Church, Oxford, the British Academy, and Warwick University, and was a fellow at Pembroke College, Cambridge. Her edition of John Aubrey's *Brief Lives with an Apparatus for the Lives of Our English Mathematical Writers* won the British Academy's Rose Mary Crawshay Prize in 2017 and was a *Times Literary Supplement* Book of the Year. She is now editing Aubrey's *Life of Thomas Hobbes*, writing a new scholarly biography of Aubrey, and working on a history of the early modern anecdote.

Robert DeMaria Jr. is the Henry Noble MacCracken Professor of English Literature at Vassar College, where he has taught for forty-seven years. As general editor of the Yale Edition of the Works of Samuel Johnson, he brought that project to conclusion in 2018 with the publication of the twenty-third and final volume. Currently, he is preparing an edition of the *Tatler* for Cambridge University Press and working on an edition of Johnson's poetry in the Longman's Annotated English Poets series.

Michael Edson is Associate Professor of English at the University of Wyoming and Associate Editor for *Eighteenth-Century Life*. His articles have appeared in *Journal for Eighteenth-Century Studies*, *The Eighteenth Century*, *Textual Cultures, 1650–1850*, and *Studies in Eighteenth-Century Culture*. His edited book *Annotation in Eighteenth-Century Poetry* appeared in 2017.

Robert D. Hume is Evan Pugh University Professor at Penn State University. He is the author of sixteen books, including *Dryden's Criticism*, *The Development of English Drama in the Late Seventeenth Century*, and *The Publication of Plays in London, 1660–1800: Playwrights, Publishers, and the Market* (with Judith Milhous). With Harold Love, he is coeditor of *Plays, Poems, and Miscellaneous Writings of George Villiers, Second Duke of Buckingham*. He is coeditor of two "lost" plays discovered in manuscript: *The Country Gentleman*, by Sir Robert Howard and the Duke of Buckingham (with A. H. Scouten), and

236 | Contributors

Elizabeth Polwhele's *The Frolicks, or The Lawyer Cheated* (with Judith Milhous). He is currently at work on two books, a study of historicist methodologies for literary study, 1926–2017, dealing with a dozen scholars from R. S. Crane to Margaret Ezell, and, with Claire Bowditch, an account of Aphra Behn's finances: *forc'd to write for Bread and not ashamed to own it.*

Stephen Karian is Professor and Catherine Paine Middlebush Chair of English at the University of Missouri. His publications include *Jonathan Swift in Print and Manuscript* and articles in *The Age of Johnson, Huntington Library Quarterly, Irish Historical Studies, SEL Studies in English Literature, 1500–1900, Studies in Bibliography, Swift Studies,* and elsewhere. With James Woolley, he has coedited Swift's complete poems in four volumes for the Cambridge Edition of the Works of Jonathan Swift. His next editorial project is Pope's *Miscellany Poems* for the Oxford Edition of the Writings of Alexander Pope.

Elizabeth Kraft is Professor Emerita of English at the University of Georgia. She is the coeditor of *The Poems of Anna Letitia Barbauld, The Selected Poetry and Prose of Anna Letitia Barbauld,* and Samuel Richardson's *Sir Charles Grandison.* She is sole editor of Charlotte Smith's *The Young Philosopher* and of Barbauld's literary criticism, volume 3 of *The Collected Works of Anna Letitia Barbauld* (forthcoming). Her recent monographs include *Restoration Courtship Comedies and Hollywood Remarriage Films: In Conversation with Stanley Cavell.* She is also the editor of *The Bloomsbury Cultural History of Comedy in the Age of Enlightenment,* and the guest editor of a special issue of *European Romantic Review* on "Women and Protest."

Anthony W. Lee has published numerous books and essays on Samuel Johnson and eighteenth-century literature and culture. He most recent volume, *A "Clubbable Man": Essays on Eighteenth-Century Literature in Honor of Greg Clingham,* appeared in 2022. He has taught at several colleges and universities, including the University of Arkansas, Arkansas Tech University, Kentucky Wesleyan College, the University of the District of Columbia, Arkansas Governor's School, and the University of Maryland University College, where he served as Director of the English and Humanities Program for three years.

Thomas Lockwood is Professor Emeritus and former chair of the Department of English at the University of Washington. He has edited the drama volumes of the Oxford Wesleyan edition of the works of Henry Fielding.

His most recent work is *The Life of Jonathan Swift*, forthcoming from Wiley-Blackwell.

William McCarthy is the author of *Anna Letitia Barbauld, Voice of the Enlightenment*, General Editor of *The Collected Works of Anna Letitia Barbauld* (in progress), editor of volume 1 in that edition, *The Poems, Revised* (based on *The Poems of Anna Letitia Barbauld*, coedited with Elizabeth Kraft), coeditor of *Selected Poetry and Prose of Anna Letitia Barbauld* (with Elizabeth Kraft), and author of *Hester Thrale Piozzi: Portrait of a Literary Woman*.

Melvyn New, Professor Emeritus, University of Florida, was General Editor of the Florida Edition of the Works of Laurence Sterne, the ninth and final volume of which was published in 2014. He is a coeditor of the Cambridge Edition of Samuel Richardson's *Sir Charles Grandison*, published in four volumes in 2022. Among his most recent publications are "Single and Double: *Memoirs of Martinus Scriblerus* and *Tristram Shandy*" (*Swift Studies* 36); "Boswell and Sterne in 1768" (in *Laurence Sterne's A Sentimental Journey: A Legacy to the World*, ed. W. B. Gerard and M.-C. Newbould); and "'The Life of a Wit Is a Warfare upon Earth': Sterne, Joyce, and Their Portraits of the Artist" (the *Shandean* [forthcoming]).

Maximillian E. Novak is Distinguished Research Professor of English at the University of California, Los Angeles. He has published widely on seventeenth- and eighteenth-century literature, has annotated a number of volumes in the "California Dryden," Thomas Southerne's *Oroonoko*, and five volumes in the Stoke Newington Edition of the Writings of Daniel Defoe, including Defoe's *Farther Adventures and Serious Reflections*.

Shef Rogers is Associate Professor of English at the University of Otago in Dunedin, New Zealand, where he teaches and researches eighteenth-century literature and book history as well as New Zealand colonial literature and publishing. He is the president of SHARP (Society for the History of Authorship, Reading and Publishing) and editor of the Bibliographical Society of Australia and New Zealand's journal, *Script & Print*.

Robert G. Walker is Senior Research Fellow, Washington and Jefferson College. He is the author of *Eighteenth-Century Arguments for Immortality and Johnson's "Rasselas"* and the coeditor of *Swiftly Sterneward: Studies on*

Laurence Sterne and His Times. His writings on eighteenth-century writers (Boswell, Johnson, Richardson, Sterne, Swift) and modern writers (Borneman, Ford, Hemingway, Koestler, Malaparte, Wain, Waugh, Welty) have appeared in several collections and more than twenty-five different journals and annuals, including *Age of Johnson*, *English Studies*, *Huntington Library Quarterly*, *Modern Philology*, *Philological Quarterly*, *Scottish Literary Review*, *Sewanee Review*, *Shandean*, *Studies in Scottish Literature*, *Times Literary Supplement*, and *1650–1850*. He is currently a contributing editor of the *Scriblerian*, and has essays forthcoming in *Studies in Philology* and *The Library*.

Marcus Walsh is Emeritus Professor of English Literature, Liverpool University. He edited two volumes of the *Poetical Works of Christopher Smart*, and *A Tale of a Tub and other Works* for the Cambridge Edition of the Works of Jonathan Swift. He is the author of *Shakespeare, Milton and Eighteenth-Century Literary Editing: The Beginnings of Interpretative Scholarship*. He is a General Editor of the new Oxford Edition of the *Writings of Alexander Pope* and is currently editing (with Dr. Hazel Wilkinson) the volume containing Pope's *Ethic Epistles*. He has published many essays on the history, practice, and theory of literary editing, including "Hypotheses, Evidence, Editing, and Explication," "Edmond Malone" (in *Dryden, Pope, Johnson, Malone*, ed. Claude Rawson), and, most recently, "Mimesis and Understanding in Samuel Johnson's Notes to Shakespeare (1765)" (*Age of Johnson*) and "Edmond Malone in the Margins: Annotated Books in Bodley" (*Bodleian Library Record*).

INDEX

Adams, William, 114–15, 122, 124
adaptation, literary, 30–32, 44
  See also drama, editing of; Dryden, John
Addison, Joseph, 96, 98, 108, 116, 156n4
  and the Kit-Cats, 179
  works of: *Cato*, 145, 153; *Dialogue upon
    the Usefulness of Ancient Medals*, 149
    (see also *Spectator, The*)
advertising, eighteenth-century, 74, 92n5
Aikin, John, 203, 230
  Evenings at Home, 223
  General Biography, 230
  Monthly Magazine, The, 230
  See also Barbauld, Anna Letitia
Ancients and Moderns controversy, the, 102
anecdotes, 203
  See also biography
Anne (queen), 63, 65–66
annotation, scholarly
  advantages of: expansion of knowledge,
    x, 39, 144–45; explication, xi, 5–6;
    interpretation, 6–7, 155–56, 174–75;
    pleasure in devising, 5–6, 38, 155, 210
  and biographical information, 12, 16–17,
    35, 59n34, 192
  and literary criticism, 5–7, 12–14, 27,
    112–13, 131–34, 147–48, 159n37,
    185–86
  and translation, 21–22, 29, 33, 130, 139,
    164, 166, 172, 181, 208, 226, 229
  as rhetorical art, 25, 25n14, 219
  difficulties of: choice of version to
    annotate, 10–11, 75–76, 117–18,
    222–23; complex allusions, 15–16,
    35–36, 68–69, 98–99, 109n2, 114–15,
    136–37, 177–78, 180–81, 195–96;
    complex publication histories, 13–15,
    44, 64–65, 102–3; diverse reader-
    ships, xi, 4, 19–20, 62–63, 101–2,

112–15, 117–18, 127, 219–20, 223–24;
    ethical considerations, 212–13, 221–
    25; inevitable outdatedness, 1, 9n8,
    9n9, 71, 146, 158n20, 192; interpre-
    tive complexity, 36–38, 149–50,
    225–26; laboriousness, 19, 34, 35–36,
    168, 189; necessary selectiveness,
    4–5, 10–11, 13–14, 33–34, 125–27,
    157n17, 165–66, 193–94, 215–16,
    220–21, 230–31; obscure sources,
    35–36, 95–96, 130–31; overelabora-
    tion, 2–3, 5 ; role of authorial
    intention, 12, 62, 96–98, 102–3,
    109–10n5, 113–14, 117–19, 121, 135,
    229; unidentifiable sources, 141–42;
    verbal obscurity, 31–32, 96, 100–101,
    103–4, 150; volume of material,
    11–13, 27–28, 31–33, 36–37, 48–49
  drawbacks of: ix; copiousness, 172, 180,
    186–87, 189–90, 193–94, 215–16,
    230–31; errors, 5, 189–90, 191–92,
    194; inadequacy, 146, 166–67, 180–
    81; subjective interpretation, 6–7,
    24–25, 205
  formats of, xii, 14–15, 47, 49–50, 74–75,
    228–30
  history of, ix–x, xiiin8, 9n10, 10, 193–94
  methodologies for creation of: collabo-
    ration, 26, 34–35, 51–52, 95–96,
    133–35, 168, 205–6, 214; data collec-
    tion, 3–4, 9n8, 9n9, 9n13, 28, 208–9;
    online resources, 9n8, 9n9, 9n13,
    208–9; relation to previous editions,
    4, 11, 26–27, 47–48, 60n35, 63–64,
    67–68, 77–78, 126–27, 131–33, 148,
    152, 188–89, 204–5; "social editing,"
    112, 117–19; use of original texts,
    11–12, 16, 153–54
  of drama. (*see* drama, editing of)

240 | Index

annotation, scholarly *(continued)*
  of satire *(see* satire, seventeenth- and
    eighteenth-century)
  purposes of: as bibliographical record, 5,
    11, 16; correction of errors, 21–22,
    149, 186, 188–89, 190–91, 226–27;
    description of material text, 14, 22;
    enhancing readerly engagement,
    75–76; explanation of context,
    12–14, 17–18, 34–37, 42–46, 51–53,
    64–65, 106–7, 113–14, 198–200, 210–
    11, 224–25; explication of factual
    content, 1–2, 5–6, 11–12, 17–20,
    24–25, 41–43, 62–63, 115–16, 134–35,
    144–45, 173–74 ; explication of ver-
    bal obscurity, 22, 31–32, 35, 95,
    100–106, 109, 172–73, 223–24; iden-
    tification of sources, 6, 10–11, 15–16,
    32–33, 98–99, 117–18, 144–45, 148–
    49, 208–9; interpretation, 6–7,
    12–13, 130–31, 133–35, 211–13, 227–28;
    recovery, xi, 33–34, 41–42, 62, 113–
    14, 131, 149, 205, 207, 211
  seventeenth- and eighteenth-century,
    xiii n7, 9n10, 10, 12, 52, 62, 182n8
  theory of, xi–xii, 73–74, 76, 93n13, 117,
    119–20, 131–32, 135, 220
  See also edition, scholarly
anti-Semitism, eighteenth-century, 224
  See also Smith, Charlotte
apothecaries, seventeenth-century, 119–20,
    123–24
  See also Garth, Samuel
Aristarchus of Samothrace, ix, 13, 19
Armstrong, John, 200, 203
Ashmolean Museum, 12
  See also Aubrey, John
Astell, Mary, 147, 157n12
  influence on Daniel Defoe of, 35
  Letters Concerning the Love of God (with
    John Norris of Bemerton), 147
  Serious Proposal to the Ladies, 35
  See also Norris, John, of Bemerton
Atterbury, Francis, Bishop of Rochester, 97
Aubrey, John, 10–16, 18–19, 22
  as annotator, 13, 16, 18
  as collaborative writer, 11–13, 14

as polymath, 18–19
Ashmolean Museum, gifts to, 12
Brief Lives: and memoranda, 16; and
  seventeenth-century biography, 10,
  12; composition of, 11, 14; eclecticism
  of, 12, 14–15, 16, 19–20, 22–23, 24;
  editions of, 10–11, 13–16, 25; factual
  richness of, 12, 17–18, 19–20, 23–24;
  manuscript of, 10–12, 14–15, 21, 23;
  non-English text in, 21–22; questionable reliability of, 17; unresolved
  issues relating to, 15, 18, 24; written
  style of, 19, 22, 23–24; *(see also*
  Malone, Edmond)
personal collections of, 12, 16, 19
personal connections of, 17–18
reputation of (negative), 11–12
topographical works of, 11, 23
works of: "Account of the Conversion
  of William Twisse, An," xi, 10;
  *Apparatus to the Lives of our English
  Mathematical Writers, An*, 10; *Essay
  Towards the Description of the North
  Division of Wiltshire, An*, 13; *Life of
  Thomas Hobbes of Malmesbury, The*,
  11, 20; *Miscellanies*, 11, 24; *Natural
  History and Antiquities of the
  County of Surrey, The*, 13; *Perambu-
  lation of Surrey, A*, 13
Austen, Jane, 139–40
  Mansfield Park, 139–40
authorial intention, theories of, 113–14, 118–
  19 135
  See also annotation, difficulties of

backnotes. *See* edition, scholarly
Barbauld, Anna Letitia, 203, 204–5
  allusions in the work of, 204, 206, 208,
    222
  and nosology, 230
  and Shakespeare, 222–23
  as contemporary authority, 216
  as editor of Samuel Richardson, 216
  books owned by, 223
  discrepancies in, 226–27
  editions of, 204, 216; Broadview Press,
    208; Oxford University Press, 204,

Index | 241

216; University of Georgia Press, 204, 208; extensive learning of, 206–7, 216 interest in hot-air balloons of, 204–5 literary criticism of, 204, 216 literary influences on, 232n17 *Poems Revised, The*, 204 works of: "An Inventory of the Furniture in Dr. Priestley's Study," 206–7; *Civic Sermons*, 226; "Domiphobia, or Dread of Home, The," 227, 230; *Eighteen Hundred and Eleven*, 227–28, 232n17; "First Fire, The," 206; *Hymns in Prose for Children*, 227; "Ice House, The," 206; *Lessons for Children*, 228–29, 233n27; "Manufacture of Paper, The," 223–24; "On the Death of Mrs. Martineau," 231; "To a Little Invisible Being Who Is Expected Soon to Become Visible," 205; "To Mrs. P[riestley]," 207; "Washing-Day," 204–5
Barry, Elizabeth, 53
Bate, W. J., 171, 177–78, 180
Battestin, Martin C., 6, 41–42, 113–14, 116, 132
Battle of the Boyne, the, 69, 123
Bayle, Pierre, 9n10, 193
    Dictionnaire historique et critique, 9n10, 193
Beeston, William, 15
Behn, Aphra, 8, 30, 56
    as playwright, 44, 48–49, 50
    Cambridge edition of, 50
    Oroonoko, 30 (*see also* Southerne, Thomas)
Bentinck, Henry, Earl of Portland, 69
Bentley, Richard, 96, 100–102
    Paradise Lost, edition of, ix, 101
    See also Pope, Alexander; Swift, Jonathan
Bettterton, Thomas, 46, 59n34
Bible, the, eighteenth-century familiarity with, 9n10, 154, 214
biography
    in notes, 162, 220
    seventeenth-century approaches toward, 10, 12

Bliss, Philip, 14
Bodleian Library, the, 12, 15, 165
book design, eighteenth-century, 74, 94–94n14
    See also digital editions
bookselling, eighteenth-century, 19, 216
    See also publishing, eighteenth-century
Boswell, James, 162, 181, 184n38, 186, 188, 194–95, 197
    as annotator, 194–96, 199, 200
    borrowings of, 188–89, 198–99
    Boswell: The Great Biographer (journals of, trade edition), 195
    Hypochondriack, The, 185, 189, 195, 196–97
    Life of Samuel Johnson, The, 169, 181, 182–83n10, 183n15, 185, 186–88, 195
    misogyny of (alleged), 189
    works of: *Boswell in Search of a Wife*, 189; *Boswell Laird of Auchinleck, 1778–1782*, 188–89, 190; *Journey to the Western Isles of Scotland, A* (with Samuel Johnson), 167, 210; *London Journal, The*, 189
    Yale edition of, 171, 188–89
    See also Johnson, Samuel
Boyle, Richard, 15
    See also *Brief Lives*
Boyle, Henry, 68
Brack, O M, 146, 169
Bree, Linda, 113
British Library, the, 65, 157n17
British Critic, The, 203
Brontë, Emily, 116
Browne, Thomas, 132, 172–75, 176, 183n14
    Christian Morals, 172, 173, 175 (*see also* Johnson, Samuel)
Buckingham, George, 51, 52
    Rehearsal, The, 42, 50–51, 52; uncertain role in composition of, 51; (*see also* Dryden, John)
    works of (including uncertain attributions): *Chances, The*, 44, 49; *Miscellaneous Works*, 51; *Restauration, The* (?), 49
Bullock, William, 46
    See also Farquhar, George

242 | Index

Burke, Edmund, 211, 221
  Reflections on the Revolution in France,
    221
  See also Barbauld, Anna Letitia
Burnet, Gilbert, Bishop of Salisbury, 97–98
  See also Pope, Alexander
Burney, Frances, 137, 211
  Cecilia, 213
Butler, Joseph, 150
Butler, Samuel, ix, 114
  Hudibras, ix, 198

Calves-Head Club, 67, 70
  See also Swift, Jonathan
Cambridge, Richard Owen, 168
  Scribleriad, The, 168
card games, seventeenth-century, 19, 20.
Castlemaine, Barbara, Countess of, 18
  See also Aubrey, John
Carter, Elizabeth, 175
  See also Johnson, Samuel
Cave, Edward, 3
  See also Richardson, Samuel
Chambers, Ephraim, 148
  Cyclopædia, 148
Chambers, Sir Robert, 171
Charles I (king), 23
  execution of, 67, 69
Charles II (king), 29, 53
  and Exclusion Crisis, 31
  licentious reign of, 29
  See also Dryden, John
Charlett, Arthur, 122, 124
  See also Garth, Samuel
Charron, Pierre, 152–53
  Of Wisdome, 152
  See also Sterne, Laurence
Chaucer, Geoffrey, ix, 32, 227
Churchill, Charles, 114, 115
  See also satire, eighteenth-century
Cibber, Colley, 142, 86
  See also adaptation, literary
citation. *See* edition, scholarly
classroom texts. *See* edition, scholarly
Clinton, Henry, 7th Earl of Lincoln, 69
coinage, seventeenth- and eighteenth-
    century, 56n7
  See also money, historic values of

Coley, Henry, 17
collaboration, authorial, 13, 16, 51, 171
Collier, Jane, 211
Collier, Jeremy, 43
Collins, William, 200
Complete Peerage, The, 68
  See also politics, seventeenth- and
    eighteenth-century
Coke, Roger, 98
Cooke, Thomas, 98
  Battle of the Poets, The, 98
  Scandalous Chronicle, The, 98
Cooper, Anthony Ashley. *See* Shaftesbury,
    3rd Earl of
Congreve, William, 43, 46–47, 48, 97
  compared with William Wycherley,
    47–48
  editions of, 55–56; University of Chicago
    Press, 47, 54; Oxford University
    Press, 47–48, 50, 56n2
  intellectual richness of, 48, 54
  Love for Love, 43, 46
copyright legislation, eighteenth-century, 74
Cowley, Abraham, 140
  Chronicle: A Ballad, The, 140
Cowper, Sarah, Lady, 69
Cowper, Spencer, 105–6
Cumming, Thomas, 190, 192, 210n14
  See also Johnson, Samuel
Crowne, John, 30
Curley, Thomas M., 171
Curll, Edmund, 13, 126
Curran, Stuart, 206, 217n10
Curtis, Lewis Perry, 159n29
Cuzzoni, Francesca, 135

Daniel, Samuel, 31
Davenant, William, 27, 40n2
  collaboration with John Dryden, 27, 28,
    40n2
  Enchanted Island, The, 27–29
  See also Dryden, John
Davis, Herbert, 43, 47–48, 54
  See also Congreve, William
Defoe, Daniel, 27, 33–34, 38, 40n15
  bankruptcy of, 34–35
  complex allusions in the work of, 35,
    38–39

deep knowledge of, 33–37, 39
editions of: Pickering & Chatto, 38–39;
  Stoke Newington, 33–34
historical contexts of the works of, 35,
  38–39
puzzling allusions in the work of, 35–36
religious position of, 39
varied career of, 38
works of: *Atlas Maritimus*, 38; *Caledonia*, 33; *Christianity Not as Old as the
  Creation*, 39; *Colonel Jack*, 38; *Consolidator, The*, 33, 34, 35–36, 37; *Essay
  upon Projects, An*, 34–35; *Farther
  Adventures of Robinson Crusoe*, 36,
  37; *History of the Union*, 33; *Jure
  Divino*, 33; *Moll Flanders*, 38; *New
  Family Instructor*, 38; *Robinson Crusoe*, 27, 36; *Roxana*, 38; *Review, the*,
  36; *Serious Reflections ... of Robinson
  Crusoe*, 38–39
Dennis, John, 26, 96, 101
dictionaries, historical emergence of, 74,
  162, 168, 205
  See also Johnson, Samuel
digital editions, 93n8, 163
  advantages of, 73–75
  affordability of, 77
  and accessibility, 150
  production of, 74–75
  See also facsimiles
Dodsley, Robert, 137
drama, editing of
  and adaptation, 44, 48–50
  and eighteenth-century money, 43–44
  as distinct from other genres, 41, 48, 54
  significance of performance history to,
    42, 44–47, 54
  significance of contextual information
    to, 43, 50–53
  textual issues pertaining to, 42–43, 46,
    49
Drury Lane Theatre, 86, 142
  See also Fielding, Henry
Dryden, John, ix, 48, 80, 97, 125, 157n14, 190
  accusations of borrowing by, 48
  allusion in, 29, 31, 48, 125, 181
  and adaptation of Shakespeare, 27–29,
    31–32, 33, 39

and heroic drama, 29–30, 31, 33, 51–52
approach to comedy of, 29
borrowings from, 191
collaborations with others by, 27–28, 30,
  40n2, 40n12
considerable learning of, 32–33, 48
editions of: California (University Press
  of), 26–28, 30–31, 33–34, 48, 56, 138,
  171; *Critical and Miscellaneous Prose
  Works*, ix, 113, 126, 129n33 (*see also*
  Malone, Edmond Longman)
influence of Thomas Rymer on, 32
literary criticism of, 30, 32–33, 98
political interests of, 31
satires of, 115
satire on, 30, 42, 51–52, 67 (*see also*
  Buckingham, George)
works of: *All for Love*, x, 27, 31–32;
  Absalom and Achitophel, 125, 126;
  Conquest of Granada, The, 29, 33, 52,
  57n13; "Containing the Grounds of
  Criticism in Tragedy," 32; *Enchanted
  Island, The*, 27, 28–29, 32; *Evening's
  Love, An*, 27, 29; "Hind and the
  Panther, The," 190–91; *Essay of
  Dramatick Poesie*, 30, 32, 98; *Limber-
  ham*; *Notes and Observations on the
  Empress of Morocco*, 30; *Tempest, The*;
  Troilus and Cressida, 31–32; *Tyrannic
  Love*, 27, 29

Edgeworth, Maria, 136–37, 146–47
  Absentee, The, 136
  Belinda, 137, 146, 157n11, 217n14
  Castle Rackrent, 213
  Leonora, 137
editions, scholarly
  and facsimiles, 22, 73–77, 92n2, 92n7,
    93n8, 93n10, 208
  and glossing, xiiin5, 15, 64–65, 137, 139,
    165, 172–74, 180, 207, 212
  and pagination, 15
  and publishers, 4, 34, 76, 93n12
  as critical enterprise, 7, 36, 146, 152–53,
    154, 216
  availability of, 8, 9n13
  components of: backnotes, 5, 126, 135;
    citation, ix, 2; critical apparatus, 14;

244 | Index

editions, scholarly *(continued)*
  endnotes, 44, 50, 130, 180, 193–94; footnotes, 5, 44, 49–50, 53, 67, 118, 126, 130–32, 161, 164, 168, 193–94; glossaries, 22, 106; headnotes, 14, 16–17, 206; index, 12, 14, 15, 17, 19, 163
  design of, 75, 94n14
  facing-page format in, xii; advantages of, 73–77, 92n1, 94n14; drawbacks of, 74, 77, 92n7; layout of, 75–76, 93n8
  financial considerations pertaining to, 3, 5, 8
  limitations of, 4, 46, 62, 113, 117, 125, 146, 222
  online access to, 8, 9 n13
  precedents of, ix, 113, 125, 132, 148, 152, 166, 200, 222
  readership of, 4, 125–27, 153–54, 233n27
  supersedable nature of, 4, 147, 150
  theories of, 76
  value of, 4, 7–8, 9n13, 34, 62, 182n1, 214, 216
  versus classroom or textbook editions, 9n13, 146–47, 156, 159n29, 171, 182n4, 208, 214, 220
  wider public appeal of, 4, 8, 117
  See also annotation, scholarly
Egan, Gabriel, 75
Ehrenpreis, Anne Henry, 207
Ellis, Frank H., 67–69, 118, 120–21, 123–27
endnotes. *See under* editions, scholarly
Erasmus, Desiderius, 10, 165
  Epistolæ, 10
  See also Aubrey, John
Estcourt, Richard, 46
  See also Farquhar, George
Etherege, George, 47
Exclusion Crisis, the, 31, 53
  See also Charles II (king)
Expedition of Humphry Clinker, The, 46

facing-page format. *See under* edition, scholarly
facsimiles. *See under* edition, scholarly
Farquhar, George, 43–46, 49, 138
  actors in first performances of, 46
  and divorce, 45–46 (*see also* Milton, John)

  Beaux Stratagem, The, 43, 45–46
  Inconstant, The, 44, 49, 138
Fielding, Henry, 7–8, 131–32, 136, 214
  approach to comedy of, 134, 138, 140, 141
  as novelist, 113
  as playwright, 54, 132, 141–42
  eclectic allusions in, 138
  editions of, 131–32; Wesleyan-Oxford, 131, 134
  misleading allusions of, 116, 134–35, 137–39
  works of: *Covent-Garden Journal, The*, 134; *Historical Register for the Year 1736, The*, 141–42; *Joseph Andrews*, 6; *Love in Several Masks*, 133; *Modern Husband, The*, 135; *Tom Jones*, 3, 7, 132, 136; *Tragedy of Tragedies*, 137; *Vernoniad, The*, 116
Finch, Daniel, Earl of Nottingham, 67
Fitzroy, Charles, 2nd Duke of Cleveland, 69
Fleeman, J. D., 161, 171
Fletcher, John, 29, 44, 46, 49
  Wild Goose Chase, The, 44, 49
  See also Buckingham, George; Dryden, John
Fletcher, Loraine, 208, 212
Folger Library, the, 93n8
Fontenelle, Bernard de
  Discours sur la nature de l'églogue, 179 (*see also* pastoral poetry)
  Entretiens sur le Pluralité des Mondes, 223 (*see also* Barbauld, Anna Letitia)
footnotes. *See under* edition, scholarly
Franklin, Benjamin, 162, 164–65, 192
French Revolution, the, 208, 211, 213
  See also Smith, Charlotte
Friedman, Arthur, 41–42, 47–48, 56n3, 57n15, 132

Garrick, David, 44, 51
Garth, Samuel, 97, 114, 119
  The Dispensary, 113–18; Alexander Pope's copy of, 127; and mock-heroic, 118, 120; and the medical profession, 119–20, 123–24; contemporary readership of, 121–25; keys to, 121–23; obscure allusions in, 121–25, 127; satiric targets of, 118–20, 125

Gay, John, 183n13
    Trivia, 84
genius
    eighteenth-century concepts of, 33, 169,
        196, 197
    of Shakespeare, 28–29, 32–33
Gentleman's Magazine, The, 200
Gerard, Alexander, 169
    Essay on Genius, An, 169
Gibbon, Edward, 169, 186–87
    as annotator, 193, 230
    Decline and Fall of the Roman Empire,
        The, 187
Godwin, William, 208, 210
    Enquiry Concerning Political Justice, 210
glossaries. *See under* edition, scholarly
Goldsmith, Oliver, 145, 156n5, 199–200
    Hermit, The, 199
    Vicar of Wakefield, The, 199
Graffigny, Françoise de, 210
Gray, Thomas, x, 200
    Elegy in a Country Churchyard, An, 200
    Ode on a Distant Prospect of Eton Col-
        lege, 137
Grayson, Nancy, 206, 207
Grierson, Herbert, 39
Green, Matthew, 198
Greenberg, Robert A., 76
Grey, Zachary, ix
Grundy, Isobel, 206
Guatimozin, Aztec emperor, 204
    See also Barbauld, Anna Letitia
Gwyn, Nell, 45

Hall, Bishop Joseph, 151
Hamilton, Albert, 132
Hammond, Lansing Van der Heyden, 148,
    152, 157–58n19
Hammond, Paul, 113, 190
Handel, George Frederick, 135
Hanoverian succession, the, 70
Harley, Robert, Earl of Oxford, 63, 65
Harris, Jocelyn, 214
Hart, Charles, 45, 57n13
    See also Wycherley, William
Hays, Mary, 211
Haywood, Eliza, 143n23, 146
    Invisible Spy, The, 146

headnotes. *See under* edition, scholarly
Hearne, Thomas, 114–15
Hill, G. B., xi, 162–65, 169, 187–88
Hobbes, Thomas, 11, 13, 20, 37, 181
    See also Aubrey, John
Homer, ix, 32, 78, 80
    Iliad, The, 32
Hooke, Robert, 15
    See also Aubrey, John
Hooker, E. N., 26
Hopton, Arthur, 10
    Concordance of Years, A, 10 (*see also*
        Aubrey, John)
Horace, 70, 183n19
    See also Boswell, James; Pope, Alexander
hot-air balloons, 204–5
    See also Montgolfier
Houghton House, 107
Hume, Patrick, ix
Hume, Robert D., 45, 46, 50, 54, 115, 191
Huntington Library, the, 127
Hurd, Richard, 197
Hutcheson, Francis, 226, 232n17
    See also Barbauld, Anna Letitia

index. *See under* editions, scholarly
internet, the
    advantages to annotation of, 3, 9n8, 9n9,
        208
    drawbacks of, 9n8, 215
    online research tools of: C18-L, 208;
        ECCO, 9n8, 146, 214; EEBO, 214;
        Google, 74, 191, 214; Google Books,
        214 ; JSTOR, 214; LION, 146, 208;
        Oxford Scholarly Editions Online, 8
    See also annotation, scholarly; World
        Wide Web
Irish Rebellion, the, 208
    See also Smith, Charlotte

Jackson, John, Canon, 13
    See also Aubrey, John
Jacobean drama, 31
Jacobitism, 38, 97
James II (king), 31
Jenyns, Soame, 199
Johnson, Benjamin, 46
    See also Farquhar, George

246 | Index

Johnson, Samuel, 3, 167, 171
  allusions of, 165–66, 167–68, 169, 177,
    178, 180–81
  and *Christian Morals* (Thomas Browne),
    183n13, 172–74, 175
  and quotation, 195–96
  and the "common reader," 116, 183n16
  Annotated Rambler, The (scholarly edi-
    tion), 170n9; annotation in, 180–81;
    compared with the Yale edition,
    179–80; rationale of, 172, 179, 181
  as annotator, ix-x, 172–74, 176–77,
    183n13, 194
  as editor, 28, 173–75, 180, 222–23
  as literary critic, 49, 52, 134, 159n35, 167,
    169, 172, 174, 178–79, 183n20
  collaboration with others by, 171
  Diaries, Prayers, and Annals (Yale edi-
    tion), 161, 164
  diction of, 171–72, 176–77, 182–83n10
  Dictionary of the English Language, A,
    74, 101, 110n12, 168, 169, 172–73,
    175–76; and quotation, 183n14, 195;
    fourth edition of, 177; and *Johnson
    on the English Language* (Yale edi-
    tion), 168 ; *Plan* of, 162; publication
    of, 74, 173; *Preface* to, 162
  editions of, 171, 180, 182n4; Yale, x, xii, 8,
    160–61, 163–64, 168, 170n3, 183n41
  Lives of the Poets, The, xi, 169–70; edi-
    tions of, 164, 169–71; Oxford
    University Press edition of, 180, 200;
    Johnson's annotation of, 172, 194
  on annotation, ix-x, 167, 172
  photographic memory of, 181
  politics of, 167
  Rambler, The, 3, 8–9n6, 169, 178; com-
    plex allusions of, 166, 171, 177–78,
    180–81 ; diction of, 175–76; editions
    of, xii, 182n4, 184n31; Elizabeth Car-
    ter's contributions to, 175;
    inadequate Yale edition of, 165–67,
    171; literary criticism in, 3, 161, 178–
    79; meanings of "nature" in, 176–77
  Rasselas, Prince of Abyssinia, 167–69,
    191; allusions in, 168 ; Yale edition of,
    167–69
  religious practice of, 192

  style of, 175–76, 180–81
  vast erudition of, 173–74, 180, 181–82
  works of: *Adventurer, The*, 161; *Annals*,
    161, 162, 164; *Idler, The*, 161, 169;
    *Journey to the Western Islands of
    Scotland, A* (with James Boswell),
    167, 210; *London*; *Sermons*, 167;
    "Vision of Theodore, The," 166-67;
    Voyage to Abyssinia, A, 176
  See also Boswell, James
Jonson, Ben, xiiin7, 15, 18–20, 23, 29, 168
  Christmas, His Masque, 20
  Epicene, 23
  "Execration upon Vulcan, An," 18
  Gypsies Metamorphos'd, The, 20
  Works, xiiin7, 20
  See also Aubrey, John
journals, scholarly, 5, 145, 186, 188, 193, 194

Kettell, Ralph, 22, 24
  See also Aubrey, John
Keymer, Thomas, 6, 158n21, 213
Kolb, Gwin J., 161, 167–69

Latin, and eighteenth-century readers, 123–
  25, 164, 176, 181, 212
Le Bossu, René, 33
Lee, Nathaniel, 40n12
  Rival Queens, The, 46, 57n13
Leigh, Francis, 46
  See also Farquhar, George
Letters of Oliver Goldsmith, The (Cam-
  bridge edition), 145–46
Leys, Simon, 1–2, 3, 4–5, 8n1, 8n3, 229, 231
Lhuyd, Edward, 12
  See also Ashmolean Museum, the
libraries, significance to research of, 8, 9n13,
  28, 205, 208
Lincoln's Inn Fields (theater), 47
linguistic shifts, eighteenth-century, 74
literacy, eighteenth-century, 74
Locke, John, 37, 147–49, 158n22, 158n23,
  232n17
  *Essay Concerning Human Understand-
    ing, An*, 148–49, 158n22
  *Second Treatise Concerning Civil Gov-
    ernment*, 232n17
  See also Sterne, Laurence

Index | 247

Longinus, and the sublime, 33
Lonsdale, Roger, 169, 171, 180, 199–200, 205
Love, Harold, 44, 49, 50–51, 54
Lumley, Richard, Earl of Scarborough, 69
Lyttleton, George, 137

Mack, Maynard, 74–75
Malebranche, Nicolas, 148–49
Malone, Edmond, ix, 11, 14, 15, 222
Mandeville, Bernard, 37
Manley, Delarivier, 69, 114–15
    New Atalantis, The, 69, 114–15
Markley, A. A., 210
Marlborough, John Churchill, first Duke
    of, 65, 215
Marvell, Andrew, 16, 37
May, James E., 191
McCleod, Randall, 73–74, 76, 93n14
McGann, Jerome, 76, 92n3, 117
McKenzie, D. F., 43, 47–48, 50, 54, 62, 76,
    92n3, 113
McLaverty, James, 113
Merton, Robert K., 4
Milhous, Judith, 45–46, 59n34
Milton, John, 18, 19, 37, 45, 80, 101, 13, 160,
    181, 220–21
    Doctrine and Discipline of Divorce, The,
    45 (*see also* Farquhar, George)
    Paradise Lost, 101–2, 220–21
    See also Aubrey, John
Miner, Earl, 30
money, historic values of, xii, 43–44, 56n7
Monk, Samuel, 30
Montagu, Charles, 1st Earl of Halifax, 68
Montagu, Elizabeth, 4, 211
Montagu, Sir James, 68
Montagu, John, 2nd Duke of, 68
Montaigne, Michel de, 152–53
    See also Sterne, Laurence
Montgolfier, Joseph-Michel and Jacque-
    Étienne, 204
    See also Barbauld, Anna Letitia
Monthly Magazine, The, 221, 227, 230
    See also Aikin, John
Monthly Review, The, 197
Motteux, Peter, 179
Nalson, Valentine, 150–52, 159n7
    See also Sterne, Laurence

New, Melvyn, 95, 190, 192, 213–14, 217n14
New York Public Library, 229
    See also Barbauld, Anna Letitia
newspapers, eighteenth-century, 74, 92n5
Norris, John, of Bemerton, 147–49, 152,
    158n21, 158n23
    Letters Concerning the Love of God (with
    Mary Astell), 147
    See also Astell, Mary; Sterne, Laurence
nosology, 230
notes, scholarly. *See* annotation, scholarly

Observator, The, 66, 70
    See also Swift, Jonathan
Oldmixon, John, 97–98
    See also Pope, Alexander
online research tools. *See under* internet,
    the
Osborne, Francis, 198
    Advice to a Son, 198
Otway, Thomas, 53, 59n32, 138, 139
    Caius Marius, 138
    Venice Preserv'd, 53
Oxford, in the seventeenth century, 17, 20,
    22, 24
    See also Aubrey, John
Oxford English Dictionary, The (*OED*), as
    annotative tool, 22, 42, 100, 101,
    103–4, 105, 159n37, 214, 221, 224
Oxford Prophecy, The, 64–66
    See also Swift, Jonathan

Palladian architecture, 107
Parliament, English, 35, 68
pastoral poetry, eighteenth-century, 177–79,
    184n28
Penn, William, 16
    See also Aubrey, John
Pennant, Thomas, 210
    Tour of Scotland, A, 210
Pepys, Samuel, 18
Percy, Thomas, 199
Peter the Great, 35
Philips, Ambrose, 178, 200
Pittis, William, 66–67
    Aesop at Oxford, 66
    Windsor Prophecy, The, 66–67 (*see also*
    Swift, Jonathan)

248 | Index

plagiarism, as related to allusion, 195–97, 200, 201n18, 201n20
Poems on Affairs of State, 67, 115
politics, seventeenth- and eighteenth-century,
and society, 108, 125, 141, 225
and the press, 142
annotation of, 35, 37
as integral to literary contexts, 18, 31–33, 49, 51–53, 70, 96, 108, 125, 210–11, 227–28
factionalism of, 97, 125
Tory, 53, 70, 125
Whig, 53, 67–70, 96–98, 125
Pope, Alexander, 2, 172, 177, 200, 214
allusions in, 6, 92n6, 95, 96–97, 102–3, 181
and Jonathan Swift, 97, 102–3, 114–15
and pastoral poetry, 178–79, 184n28
as annotator, ix–x, 96, 98, 127
as literary critic, 67, 98
as satirist, 101–4, 114–16, 118, 125
complex lexical range of, 100–101, 103–4, 109
contemporary contexts of, 96
editions of, ix, 8, 95, 114; Oxford University Press, 8, 95–96, 99; Twickenham, 8, 50, 92n1, 92n6, 98, 116, 126, 160, 222
Epistles (collective): allusions in, 96; composition of, 96; contemporary contexts of, 96–97
Epistle to Arbuthnot, 96–103: allusions in, 98, 101; and "Sporus," 99, 116; lexical complexity of, 99–100; literary satire in, 101–2; rhyme scheme of, 101–2
Epistle to Burlington, 103–9: approach to architecture in, 107, 111n23; contemporary literary contexts of, 108; influence of Shaftesbury on, 108, 111n25; meanings of "sense" and "taste" in, 104–8 ; publication of, 103
manuscripts of the works of, 99
printing history of the works of, 96–97, 99, 102
revision practices of, 102–3, 109, 110n9
topical allusions in, 96–97, 98, 101–2, 114–15, 116

works of: *Dunciad, The* (composite sense of), 96, 125, 126, 206; *Dunciad, The* (1728), 115, 116; *Dunciad Variorum, The*, 92n6; "Ethic Epistles," 95; *First Epistle of the Second Book of Horace Imitated, The*, 67; *Iliad, The*, 222, 232n7; *Imitations of Horace*, 116; *Miscellanies* (with Jonathan Swift), 102; *Works*, 95–96
Popish Plot, the, 14, 18, 53
Post-Boy, The, 70
Powlett, Charles, 2nd Duke of Bolton, 69
Preston, Thomas R., 146
Priestley, Joseph, 205, 206
See also Barbauld, Anna Letitia
printing practices, eighteenth-century, 74, 76, 95–95n14
Protestantism, seventeenth- and eighteenth-century, 9n10, 192
pseudonymity. *See under* satire, eighteenth-century
publishing, eighteenth-century, 74

Quakerism, eighteenth-century, 190, 192
See also Cumming, Thomas

Radcliffe, Ann, 216
Mysteries of Udolpho, The, 216
Rapin, René, 33, 179
Dissertatio de carmine pastorali, 179
Redford, Bruce, 171
religion, in eighteenth-century life, 36, 37, 39, 108, 150, 177, 182n2, 192
See also Defoe, Daniel
Restoration drama, 27, 29, 30, 32, 33, 47
See also editing: of drama
Review of English Studies, The, 187
Reynolds, Joshua, 169, 177
Discourses on Art, 177
Richardson, Jonathan, 110n9, 169
Richardson, Samuel, 3, 214
as printer, 8–9n6
correspondence of, 3, 214, 216
editions of: Cambridge University Press, 3, 6, 157n17, 213, 216; Oxford University Press, 214
literary circle of, 216

Sir Charles Grandison, Cambridge University Press edition of, 213–16: biblical resonances in, 214; compared with Oxford University Press edition, 214
works of: *Clarissa*, 126, 216; *Pamela*, 216
See also Barbauld, Anna Letitia; Johnson, Samuel
Roberts, Sir Sidney, 171
Robertson, William, 204
History of America, The, 204
Rochester, John Wilmot, 2nd Earl of, 46
Valentinian, 46
Rogers, Katherine, 206
Rogers, Pat, 64, 68, 69, 76, 88, 143n23
Rogers, Samuel, 186
Roland, Madame, 210
Memoirs, 210
Rousseau, Jean-Jacques, 36, 210
Rowe, Elizabeth Singer, 156n3
Rowe, Nicholas, ix, 46, 154, 178
Fair Penitent, The, 154
Tamerlane, 46, 178
See also Johnson, Samuel
Royal College of Physicians, the, 119
See also Garth, Samuel
Royal Society, the, 24, 28, 35
See also Defoe, Daniel
Rymer, Thomas, 32–33
Tragedies of the Last Age, 32 (*see also* Dryden, John)

Sabor, Peter, 6, 213
Sacheverell, Henry, 66, 69, 143n23
satire, seventeenth- and eighteenth-century
and pseudonymity, 112, 120, 121, 124, 125, 126
annotation of, xii, 110n7, 114, 118–19, 125, 126–27, 227
contemporary contexts of, 61–62
devices of, 113–14, 118, 124
explanatory keys for, 121–22
forms of, 88
literary, 51–52
political, 33, 51–53, 59n31, 65, 70, 96–97, 125, 141, 142

positive purposes of, 119
problem of exclusivity in, 112–15, 118, 120, 125 (*see also* Garth, Samuel)
readership of, 112–15, 118, 127
social, 45, 51, 141, 230
targets of, 51, 114
topical: contemporary contexts of, 61–62, 63; devices of, 112–13, 116; difficulty of annotating, 61–63, 64, 110n7; falsehoods belonging to, 61, 62, 68; obscurity of, 61, 63, 70–71, 113, 115–16; (*see also* Swift, Jonathan)
Scott, Walter, 138–39
as editor, 138–39
Heart of Midlothian, The, 139
Waverley, 139
Scriblerians, the, 149
Memoirs of Martinus Scriblerus, 6
Selden, John, 10, 18
See also Aubrey, John
Settle, Elkanah, 30
See also Dryden, John
Seymour, Charles, 6th Duke of Somerset, 65
Seymour, Elizabeth, Duchess of Somerset, 63
See also Swift, Jonathan
Sewell, George, 102
Shadwell, Thomas, 27, 30, 55
See also Dryden, John
Shaftesbury, 3rd Earl of (Anthony Ashley Cooper), 37, 53, 100, 107–8, 111n25
Characteristicks, 108
Moralists, The, 100
See also Defoe, Daniel; Pope, Alexander
Shakespeare, William, 19, 167
adaptations of, ix, x, 27–29, 31–32, 36, 39, 40n2, 49–50, 142 (*see also* Dryden, John)
allusions to, 15, 31, 32, 42, 137–38, 139, 152, 209, 214, 222–23
annotation of, 28, 101, 172–75, 180, 183n13
criticisms of, 29, 32, 33
editions of, 28, 32, 93, 101–2, 172, 174, 187, 194
performance history of, 27–29

250 | Index

Shakespeare, William *(continued)*
  works of: *Antony and Cleopatra*, x, 31;
    Hamlet, 33, 101, 161, 196; *King John*,
    142; *Tempest, The*, 27–29, 32; *Troilus
    and Cressida*, 31–32
  See also Aubrey, John
Sheridan, Richard Brinsley, 186–87, 213
  School for Scandal, The, 213
Siddons, Sarah, 53
Smith, Adam, 154, 181
  Theory of Moral Sentiments, A, 154
Smith, Charlotte, 137, 207
  and America, 207
  and botany, 212–13
  and the bible, 214
  and the French Revolution, 208, 211, 213
  editions of: University Press of Ken-
    tucky novels, 207–8; Oxford English
    Novels, 207; Oxford World's Classic,
    208; Pickering and Chatto, 210
  literary circle of, 213
  Old Manor House, The, 137, 207–8
  Young Philosopher, The, 207–13; allu-
    sions in, 210, 212–13; and Scotland,
    211–13; annotation of, 208–9, 211;
    anti-Semitism in, 213; contemporary
    contexts of, 210–11; epigraphs in,
    209–10 ; intellectual ambition of,
    211–12 ; political dimensions of, 208,
    211–12, 213; publication process of,
    213–14
Smith, John, 190
Smollett, Tobias, 8
  Expedition of Humphry Clinker, The,
    146
social contexts, seventeenth- and
    eighteenth-century
  significance to literature, 16–17, 35,
    36–37, 43, 76, 96, 101, 125, 225
  significance to annotation, xii
Society of Apothecaries, the, 119
  See also Garth, Samuel
sources. *See under* annotations, scholarly
South Sea Bubble, the, 116
Southerne, Thomas, 30–31, 46, 48
  Maid's Last Prayer, The, 48
  Oroonoko, 30–31, 46
Spectator, The, 3, 37, 92n1, 108, 214, 232n12

See also Addison, Joseph; Steele, Richard
Spence, Joseph, 172
  Anecdotes, 172
Spenser, Edmund, xiiin7, 162, 178, 184n28,
  187
Stanton, Judith Phillips, 208
Starr, G. A., 38–39
St. James's Chronicle, The, 199
Steele, Richard, 37, 231n4
  Tatler, The, 37, 214
  See also *Spectator, The*
Stephen, Leslie, 36, 40n15
  See also Defoe, Daniel
Sterne, Laurence
  and Anglicanism, 150–51, 153, 158n21
  bawdry of, 150, 153
  Biblical allusion in, 154
  borrowings of, 152–53, 154–55
  editions of: Penguin, 146; textbook, 146,
    159n29; University Press of Florida,
    x, 3–4, 6, 9n9, 144, 147, 154, 158n20,
    159n29, 171, 192, 213
  *Life and Opinions of Tristram Shandy,
    Gentleman, The*, 145–49; allusions
    in, 6, 8n2, 147–48, 149, 152, 157n14;
    and the War of the Spanish Succes-
    sion, 215; annotation of, 6, 148, 149;
    influence of John Locke on, 147–49,
    157n16; unreliable citation in, 149
  literary circle of, 4, 8n2
  misattributions to, 145
  *Sentimental Journey through France and
    Italy, A*, 151–55; allusions in, 153–55;
    approach to sensibility in, 153–54;
    composition of, 154; editions of, 148,
    152; relation of Sterne's *Sermons* to,
    148–49, 150; significance of *Sermons*
    to, 148–49, 150, 151
  Sermons, 148–52; allusions in, 151–52;
    annotation of, 9n9, 150; borrowings
    in, 148, 150–54, 157–58n19, 159n27,
    159n36; influence of John Norris on,
    147, 148–49, 152, 158n21, 158n22; rela-
    tion to Sterne's fictional work of,
    148–49, 150–51
Stillingfleet, Edward, 190–91
Stoke Newington, 223–24
  See also Barbauld, Anna Letitia

Index | 251

Stout, Gardner, 148, 152, 154, 158–59n19, 159n35
Strauss, Albrecht B., 171, 180
Summers, Montague, 48, 55–56, 56n3, 57n15
Sutherland, James, 92n6
Swedenberg, H. T., 26, 40n16
Swift, Jonathan, 37, 134, 138, 157n14
  and Alexander Pope, 97, 102–3, 114–15
  allusions in, 37, 67–69, 80, 84, 86, 181
  annotation of, 63, 70–71, 76–91
  as annotator, 77
  as satirist, 6, 63, 70–71, 102, 114–15
  early readership of, 61–62, 115
  editions of, 76–77, 94n15, 114, 134;
    Cambridge University Press, x, 63,
    94n15, 138; Norton Critical, 76–91;
    Oxford Authors, 76–91; Penguin,
    76–91; Yale University Press, 67, 115
  Toland's Invitation to Dismal, 67–70;
    annotation of, 67–68; complex allu-
    sions of, 67; composition of, 69–70;
    in *Poems on Affairs of State* (Yale),
    67; political contexts of, 67–70;
    reception of, 70
  Windsor Prophecy, The, 63–67; and con-
    temporary similar poems, 64–67;
    annotation of, 64, 67; initial circula-
    tion of, 63–64; political contexts of,
    63–65
  works misattributed to, 70–71
  works of: *Battel of the Books, The*, 102;
    Conduct of the Allies, The, 63; *Gar-
    den Plot, The*, 71; *Importance of the
    Guardian Considered, The*, 114;
    Journal to Stella, 63, 65, 69; *Miscella-
    nies* (with Alexander Pope), 102;
    Modest Proposal, A, 84; "Rhapsody,
    A," 77–91; *Tale of a Tub, A*, 8n2, 37,
    115, 157n14

Talbot, Catherine, 175
Tale of a Disbanded Courtier, A, 66
  See also Swift, Jonathan
Tate, Nahum, 49
  King Lear, 49
Tatler, The. *See* Steele, Richard
Taylor, Aline Mackenzie, 53, 58–59n30
Taylor, E. Derek, 147, 213

textbook editions. *See* edition, scholarly
theatergoing, Restoration period, 28, 42, 51,
  54
theatergoing, eighteenth-century, 59n34,
  138, 141
Theobald, Lewis, 101–2
  Shakespeare Restored, 101 (*see also* Bent-
    ley, Richard; Pope, Alexander)
Times Literary Supplement, 187, 193
Toland, John, 67
  See also Swift, Jonathan
Tonge, Israel, 18
  See also Aubrey, John
Tory politics. *See under* politics, seven-
  teenth- and eighteenth-century
Tracy, Clarence, 180
translation. *See under*, annotation, scholarly
Twisse, William, xi, 24
  See also Aubrey, John

United Company (theatrical), 46
  See also Congreve, William

value of money, historical differences of. *See*
  annotation, of drama
Vanbrugh, John, 198
  Provoked Wife, The, 198
Verbruggen, John, 46
  See also Farquhar, George
Vesey, Elizabeth, 4
Virgil, 80, 92n1, 138, 178–79, 196
Vitruvian architecture, 107
Voltaire, 33, 161, 164, 210
  Dialogues, 210

Wallis, John, 168
  Grammatic Lingua Anglicana, 168 (*see
    also* Johnson, Samuel)
Walpole, Horace, 157n17, 160, 162–63
  Yale University Press edition of, 162–63
Walpole, Robert, 86, 116, 142
War of the Spanish Succession, 63, 215
  See also Swift, Jonathan
Warburton, William, ix, 8n2, 110n9, 162
  See also Pope, Alexander; Sterne,
    Laurence
Whig politics. *See under* politics, seven-
  teenth- and eighteenth-century

252 | Index

Whitefield, George, 196
Wilkes, John, 115, 195
William III (king), 35, 97
William Andrews Clark Memorial Library
    (UCLA), 26, 28
    See also Dryden, John
Williams, Aubrey, 193
Williams, Harold, 64, 67–69, 77
"Windsor Prophecy" poems. *See under*
    Swift, Jonathan
Wollstonecraft, Mary, 208, 211
    See also Smith, Charlotte
women's writing, scholarly editing of, 34,
    146–47, 205–6, 207–8, 211, 229
Womersley, David, 171
Wood, Anthony, 11–12, 14, 22
    See also Aubrey, John

Woolley, David, 77
Woolley, James, 63, 71n3
Work, James A., 152, 159n29
World Wide Web, the, 9n9
    See also internet, the
Wren, Sir Christopher, 15
    See also Aubrey, John
Wycherley, William, 43–45, 47–48, 54
    Country-Wife, The, 45, 47, 57n15
    libertine attitudes of, 45, 57n14
    limited intellectual range of, 47–48
    Plain-Dealer, The, 43, 57n14
    relative ease in annotating works of, 54

Young, Edward, 198–200

Zwicker, Steven N., 128, 190–91

THE PENN STATE SERIES IN THE HISTORY OF THE BOOK
James L. W. West III, *General Editor*

Editorial Board
Robert R. Edwards (Pennsylvania State University)
Paul Eggert (Loyola University Chicago)
Simon Eliot (University of London)
Beth Luey (Massachusetts Historical Society)
Willa Z. Silverman (Pennsylvania State University)

PREVIOUSLY PUBLISHED TITLES IN THE PENN STATE SERIES IN THE HISTORY OF THE BOOK

Peter Burke, *The Fortunes of the "Courtier": The European Reception of Castiglione's "Cortegiano"* (1996)

Roger Burlingame, *Of Making Many Books: A Hundred Years of Reading, Writing, and Publishing* (1996)

James M. Hutchisson, *The Rise of Sinclair Lewis, 1920–1930* (1996)

Julie Bates Dock, ed., *Charlotte Perkins Gilman's "The Yellow Wall-paper" and the History of Its Publication and Reception: A Critical Edition and Documentary Casebook* (1998)

John Williams, ed., *Imaging the Early Medieval Bible* (1998)

Ezra Greenspan, *George Palmer Putnam: Representative American Publisher* (2000)

James G. Nelson, *Publisher to the Decadents: Leonard Smithers in the Careers of Beardsley, Wilde, Dowson* (2000)

Pamela E. Selwyn, *Everyday Life in the German Book Trade: Friedrich Nicolai as Bookseller and Publisher in the Age of Enlightenment* (2000)

David R. Johnson, *Conrad Richter: A Writer's Life* (2001)

David Finkelstein, *The House of Blackwood: Author-Publisher Relations in the Victorian Era* (2002)

Rodger L. Tarr, ed., *As Ever Yours: The Letters of Max Perkins and Elizabeth Lemmon* (2003)

Randy Robertson, *Censorship and Conflict in Seventeenth-Century England: The Subtle Art of Division* (2009)

Catherine M. Parisian, ed., *The First White House Library: A History and Annotated Catalogue* (2010)

Jane McLeod, *Licensing Loyalty: Printers, Patrons, and the State in Early Modern France* (2011)

Charles Walton, ed., *Into Print: Limits and Legacies of the Enlightenment; Essays in Honor of Robert Darnton* (2011)

James L. W. West III, *Making the Archives Talk: New and Selected Essays in Bibliography, Editing, and Book History* (2012)

John Hruschka, *How Books Came to America: The Rise of the American Book Trade* (2012)

A. Franklin Parks, *William Parks: The Colonial Printer in the Transatlantic World of the Eighteenth Century* (2012)

Roger E. Stoddard, comp., and David R. Whitesell, ed., *A Bibliographic Description of Books and Pamphlets of American Verse Printed from 1610 Through 1820* (2012)

Nancy Cervetti, *S. Weir Mitchell: Philadelphia's Literary Physician* (2012)

Karen Nipps, *Lydia Bailey: A Checklist of Her Imprints* (2013)

Paul Eggert, *Biography of a Book: Henry Lawson's "While the Billy Boils"* (2013)

Allan Westphall, *Books and Religious Devotion: The Redemptive Reading of an Irishman in Nineteenth-Century New England* (2014)

Scott Donaldson, *The Impossible Craft: Literary Biography* (2015)

John Bidwell, *Graphic Passion: Matisse and the Book Arts* (2015)

Peter L. Shillingsburg, *Textuality and Knowledge: Essays* (2017)

Steven Carl Smith, *An Empire of Print: The New York Publishing Trade in the Early American Republic* (2017)

Colm Tóibín, Marc Simpson, and Declan Kiely, *Henry James and American Painting* (2017)

Filipe Carreira da Silva and Mónica Brito Vieira, *The Politics of the Book: A Study on the Materiality of Ideas* (2019)

Colm Tóibín, *One Hundred Years of James Joyce's "Ulysses"* (2022)

Milton Keynes UK
Ingram Content Group UK Ltd.
UKHW010335060324
438908UK00006B/954